STAR WARS
AGE OF REPUBLIC
VILLAINS

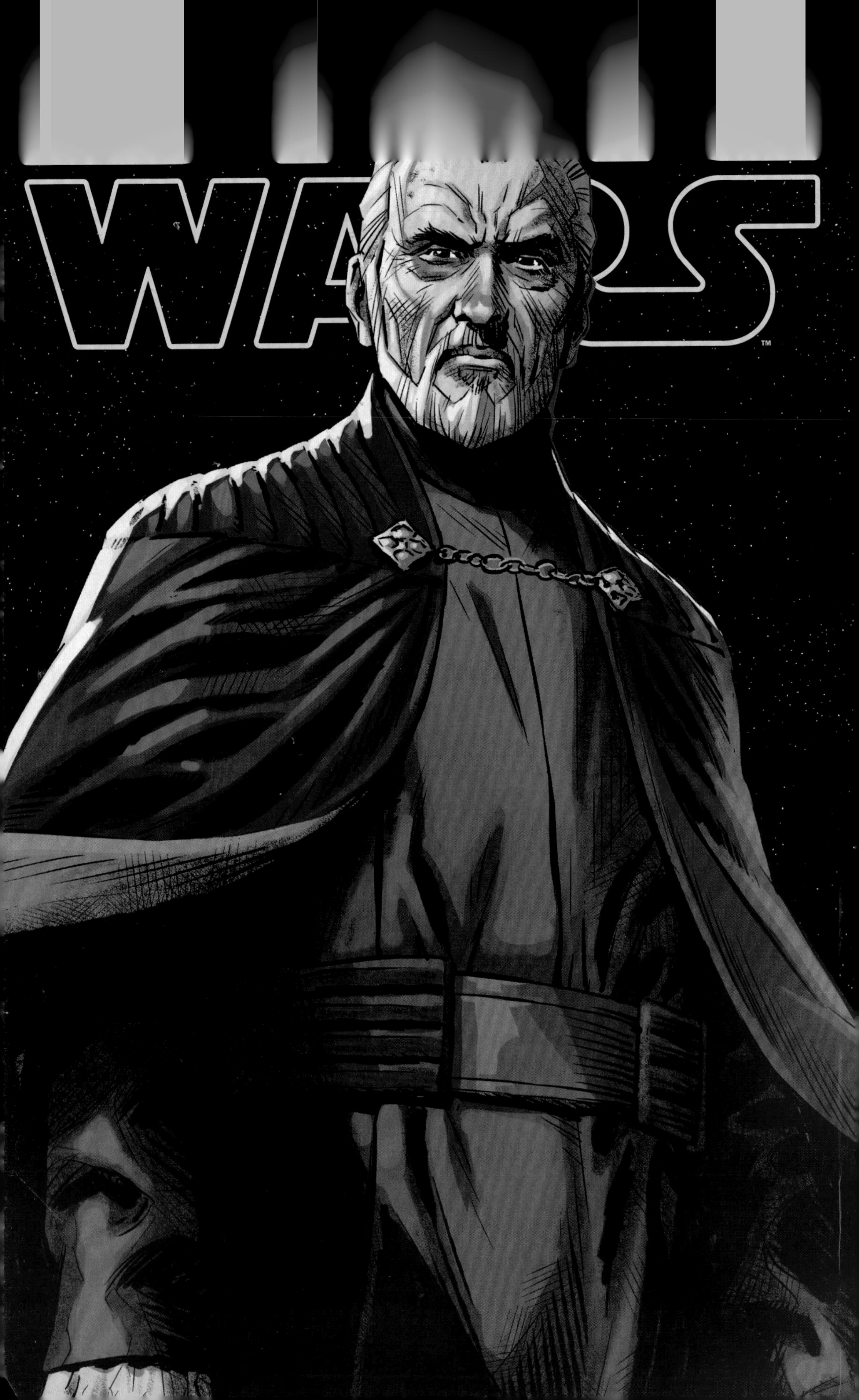
WARS™

AGE OF REPUBLIC

VILLAINS

Writer	**JODY HOUSER**
Artist	**LUKE ROSS**
Color Artist	**JAVA TARTAGLIA**
Cover Art	**PAOLO RIVERA**

STAR WARS: AGE OF REPUBLIC SPECIAL #1
"THE WEAPON"

Writer	**JODY HOUSER**
Artist	**CARLOS GÓMEZ**
Color Artist	**DONO SÁNCHEZ-ALMARA**
Cover Art	**ROD REIS**

Letterer	**VC'S TRAVIS LANHAM**
Assistant Editor	**TOM GRONEMAN**
Editor	**MARK PANICCIA**

Editor in Chief	**C.B. CEBULSKI**
Chief Creative Officer	**JOE QUESADA**
President	**DAN BUCKLEY**

For Lucasfilm:

Senior Editor	**ROBERT SIMPSON**
Executive Editor	**JENNIFER HEDDLE**
Creative Director	**MICHAEL SIGLAIN**
Lucasfilm Story Group	**JAMES WAUGH, LELAND CHEE, MATT MARTIN**

Collection Editor	JENNIFER GRÜNWALD	VP Production & Special Projects	JEFF YOUNGQUIST		
Assistant Editor	CAITLIN O'CONNELL	SVP Print, Sales & Marketing	DAVID GABRIEL		
Associate Managing Editor	KATERI WOODY	Book Designer	ADAM DEL RE		
Editor, Special Projects	MARK D. BEAZLEY				

STAR WARS: AGE OF REPUBLIC — VILLAINS. Contains material originally published in magazine form as STAR WARS: AGE OF REPUBLIC — COUNT DOOKU #1, STAR WARS: AGE OF REPUBLIC — DARTH MAUL #1, STAR WARS: AGE OF REPUBLIC — GENERAL GRIEVOUS #1, STAR WARS: AGE OF REPUBLIC — JANGO FETT #1 and STAR WARS: AGE OF REPUBLIC SPECIAL #1. First printing 2019. ISBN 978-1-302-91729-6. Published by MARVEL WORLDWIDE, INC., a subsidiary of MARVEL ENTERTAINMENT, LLC. OFFICE OF PUBLICATION: 135 West 50th Street, New York, NY 10020. STAR WARS and related text and illustrations are trademarks and/or copyrights, in the United States and other countries, of Lucasfilm Ltd. and/or its affiliates. © & TM Lucasfilm Ltd. No similarity between any of the names, characters, persons, and/or institutions in this magazine with those of any living or dead person or institution is intended, and any such similarity which may exist is purely coincidental. Marvel and its logos are TM Marvel Characters, Inc. **Printed in Canada.** DAN BUCKLEY, President, Marvel Entertainment; JOHN NEE, Publisher; JOE QUESADA, Chief Creative Officer; TOM BREVOORT, SVP of Publishing; DAVID BOGART, Associate Publisher & SVP of Talent Affairs; DAVID GABRIEL, SVP of Sales & Marketing, Publishing; JEFF YOUNGQUIST, VP of Production & Special Projects; DAN CARR, Executive Director of Publishing Technology; ALEX MORALES, Director of Publishing Operations; DAN EDINGTON, Managing Editor; SUSAN CRESPI, Production Manager; STAN LEE, Chairman Emeritus. For information regarding advertising in Marvel Comics or on Marvel.com, please contact Vit DeBellis, Custom Solutions & Integrated Advertising Manager, at vdebellis@marvel.com. For Marvel subscription inquiries, please call 888-511-5480. **Manufactured between 3/15/2019 and 4/16/2019 by SOLISCO PRINTERS, SCOTT, QC, CANADA.**

10 9 8 7 6 5 4 3 2 1

"ASH"

Sith Apprentice Darth Maul has long waited in the shadows under the tutelage of Darth Sidious for the day when they would bring about the destruction of the Jedi Order. But Maul's lust for battle drives him to act. And with the dark side of the Force as his weapon, the Jedi's days are numbered....

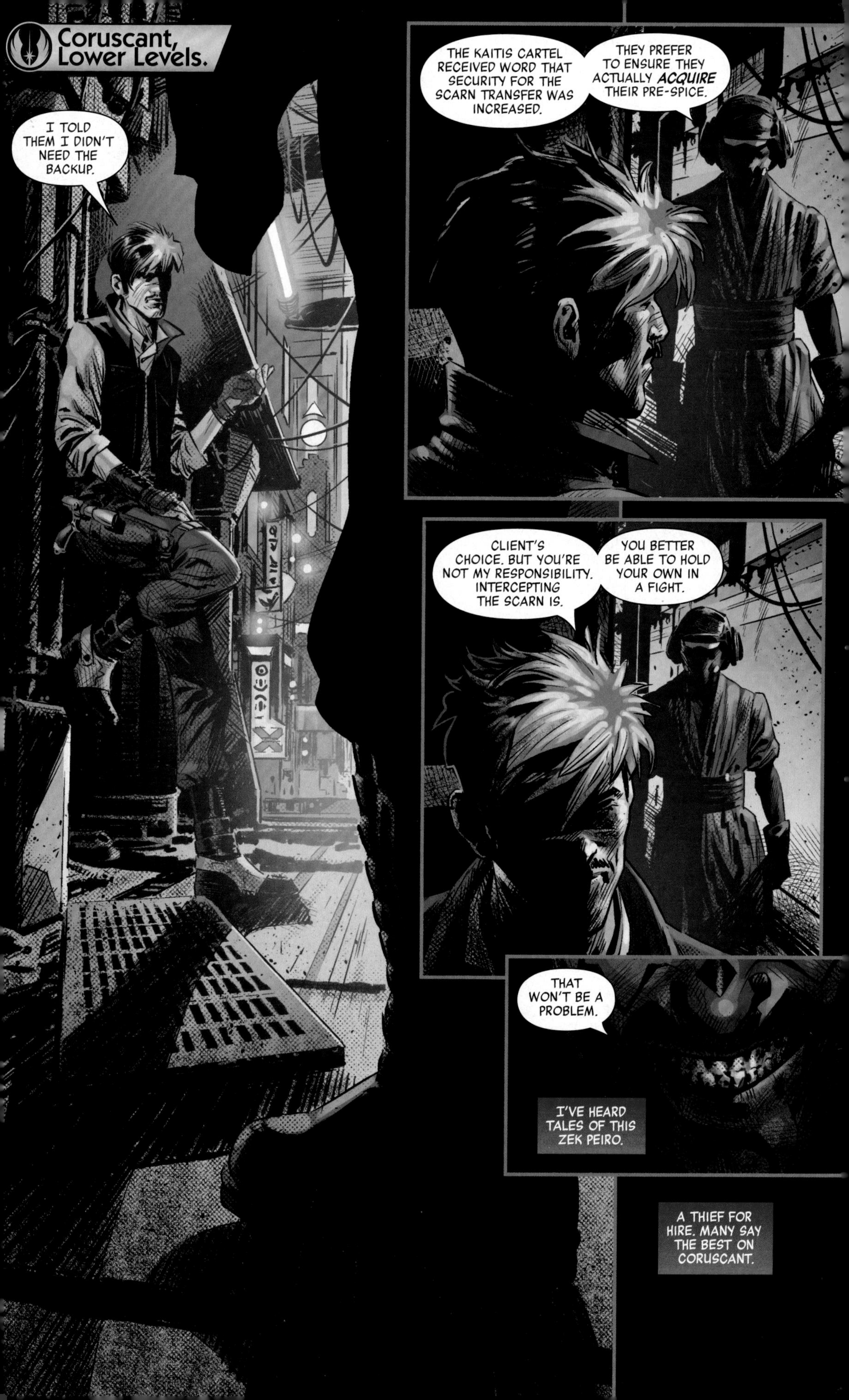
Coruscant, Lower Levels.
I TOLD THEM I DIDN'T NEED THE BACKUP.
THE KAITIS CARTEL RECEIVED WORD THAT SECURITY FOR THE SCARN TRANSFER WAS INCREASED.
THEY PREFER TO ENSURE THEY ACTUALLY ACQUIRE THEIR PRE-SPICE.
CLIENT'S CHOICE. BUT YOU'RE NOT MY RESPONSIBILITY. INTERCEPTING THE SCARN IS.
YOU BETTER BE ABLE TO HOLD YOUR OWN IN A FIGHT.
THAT WON'T BE A PROBLEM.
I'VE HEARD TALES OF THIS ZEK PEIRO.
A THIEF FOR HIRE. MANY SAY THE BEST ON CORUSCANT.

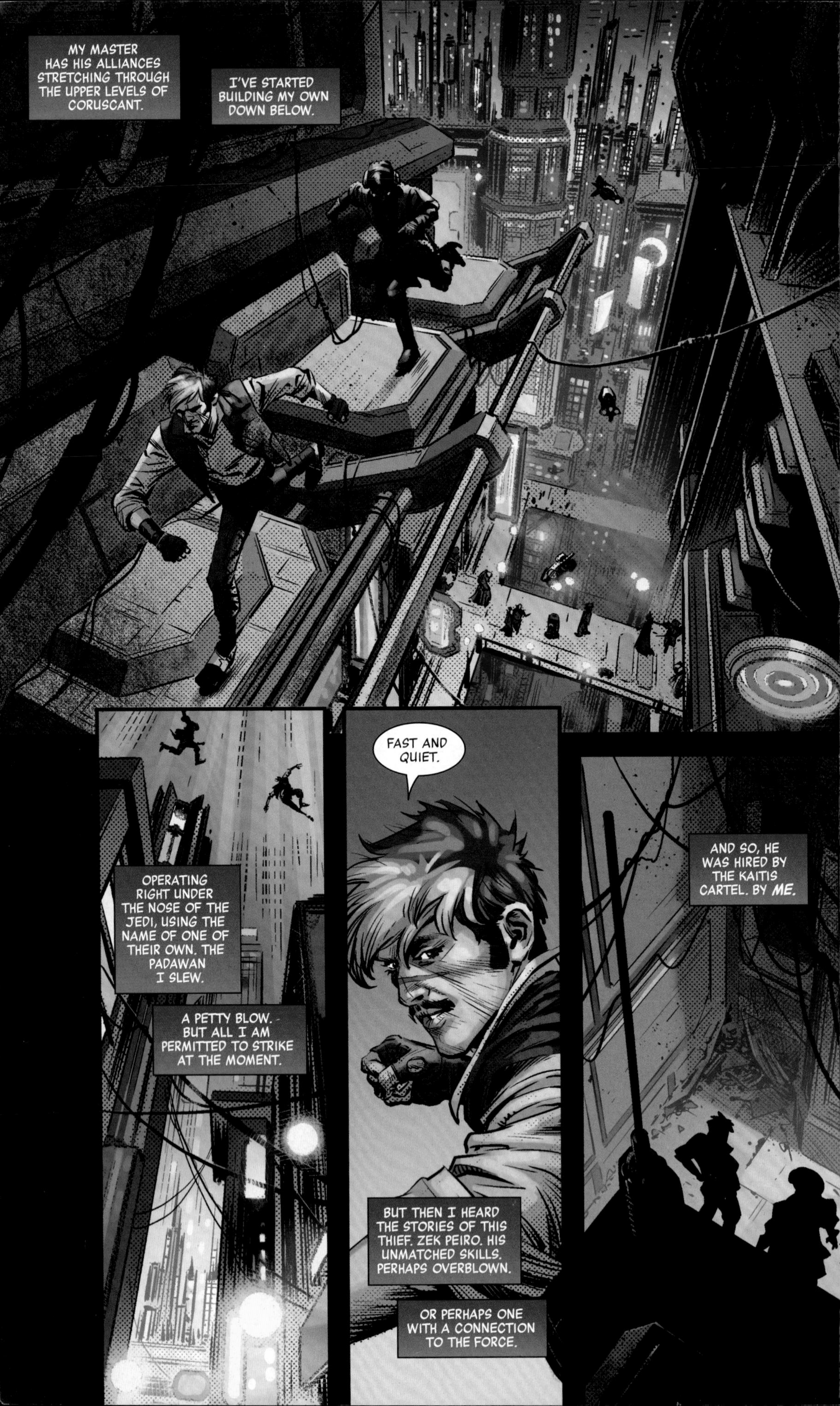
MY MASTER HAS HIS ALLIANCES STRETCHING THROUGH THE UPPER LEVELS OF CORUSCANT.
I'VE STARTED BUILDING MY OWN DOWN BELOW.
OPERATING RIGHT UNDER THE NOSE OF THE JEDI, USING THE NAME OF ONE OF THEIR OWN. THE PADAWAN I SLEW.
A PETTY BLOW. BUT ALL I AM PERMITTED TO STRIKE AT THE MOMENT.
FAST AND QUIET.
BUT THEN I HEARD THE STORIES OF THIS THIEF. ZEK PEIRO. HIS UNMATCHED SKILLS. PERHAPS OVERBLOWN.
OR PERHAPS ONE WITH A CONNECTION TO THE FORCE.
AND SO, HE WAS HIRED BY THE KAITIS CARTEL. BY ***ME.***

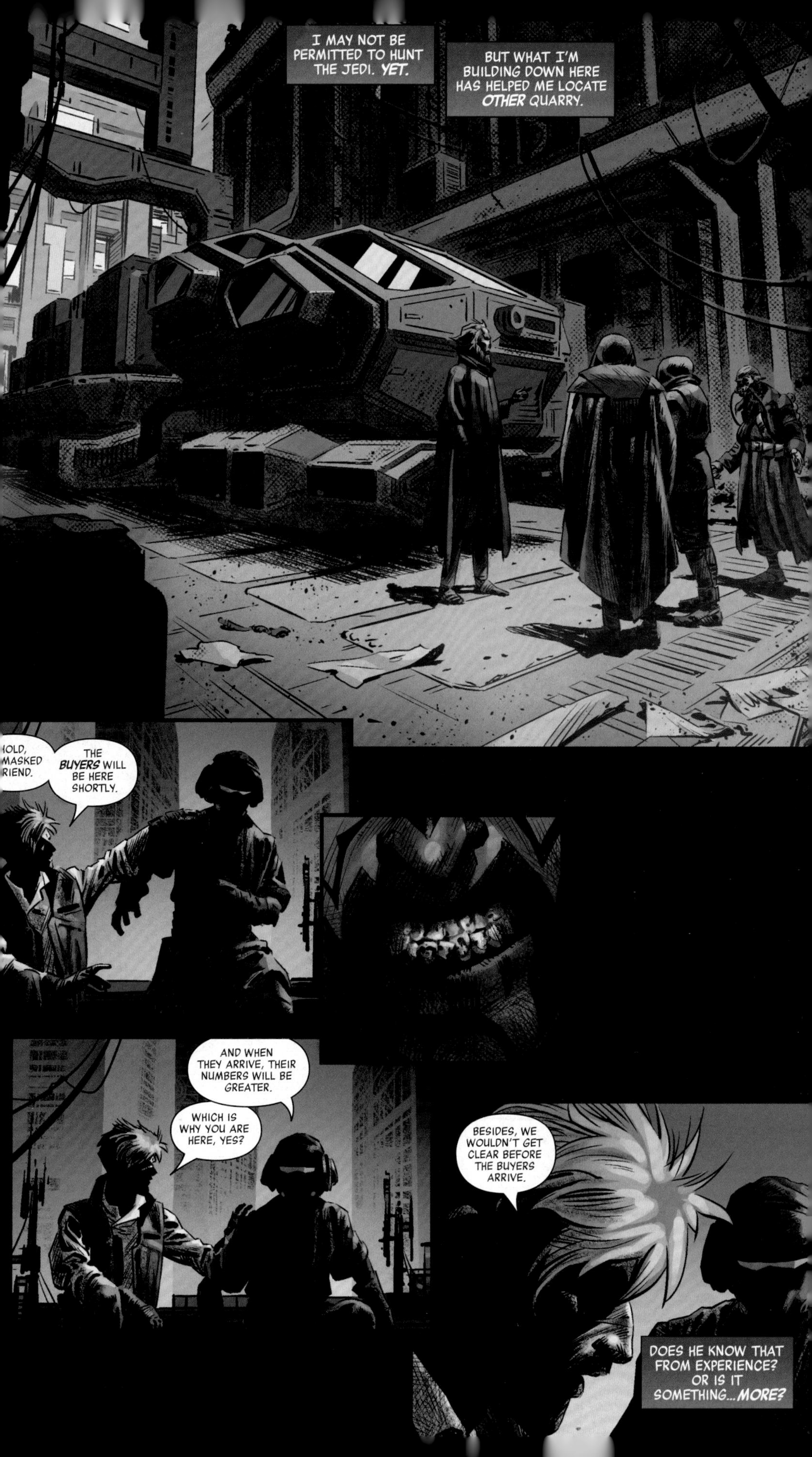
I MAY NOT BE PERMITTED TO HUNT THE JEDI. YET.
BUT WHAT I'M BUILDING DOWN HERE HAS HELPED ME LOCATE OTHER QUARRY.
HOLD, MASKED FRIEND.
THE BUYERS WILL BE HERE SHORTLY.
AND WHEN THEY ARRIVE, THEIR NUMBERS WILL BE GREATER.
WHICH IS WHY YOU ARE HERE, YES?
BESIDES, WE WOULDN'T GET CLEAR BEFORE THE BUYERS ARRIVE.
DOES HE KNOW THAT FROM EXPERIENCE? OR IS IT SOMETHING... MORE?

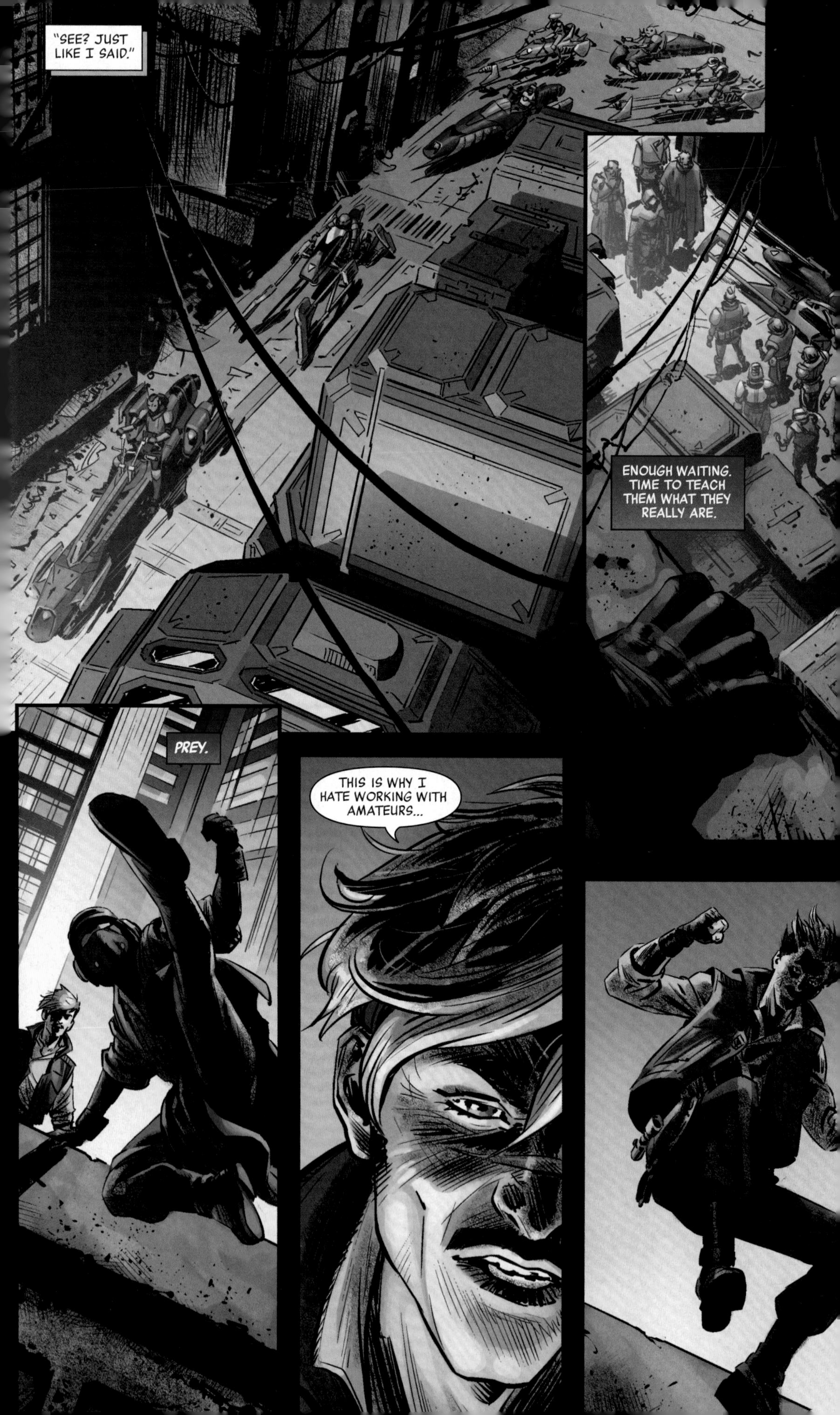
"SEE? JUST LIKE I SAID."
ENOUGH WAITING. TIME TO TEACH THEM WHAT THEY REALLY ARE.
PREY.
THIS IS WHY I HATE WORKING WITH AMATEURS...

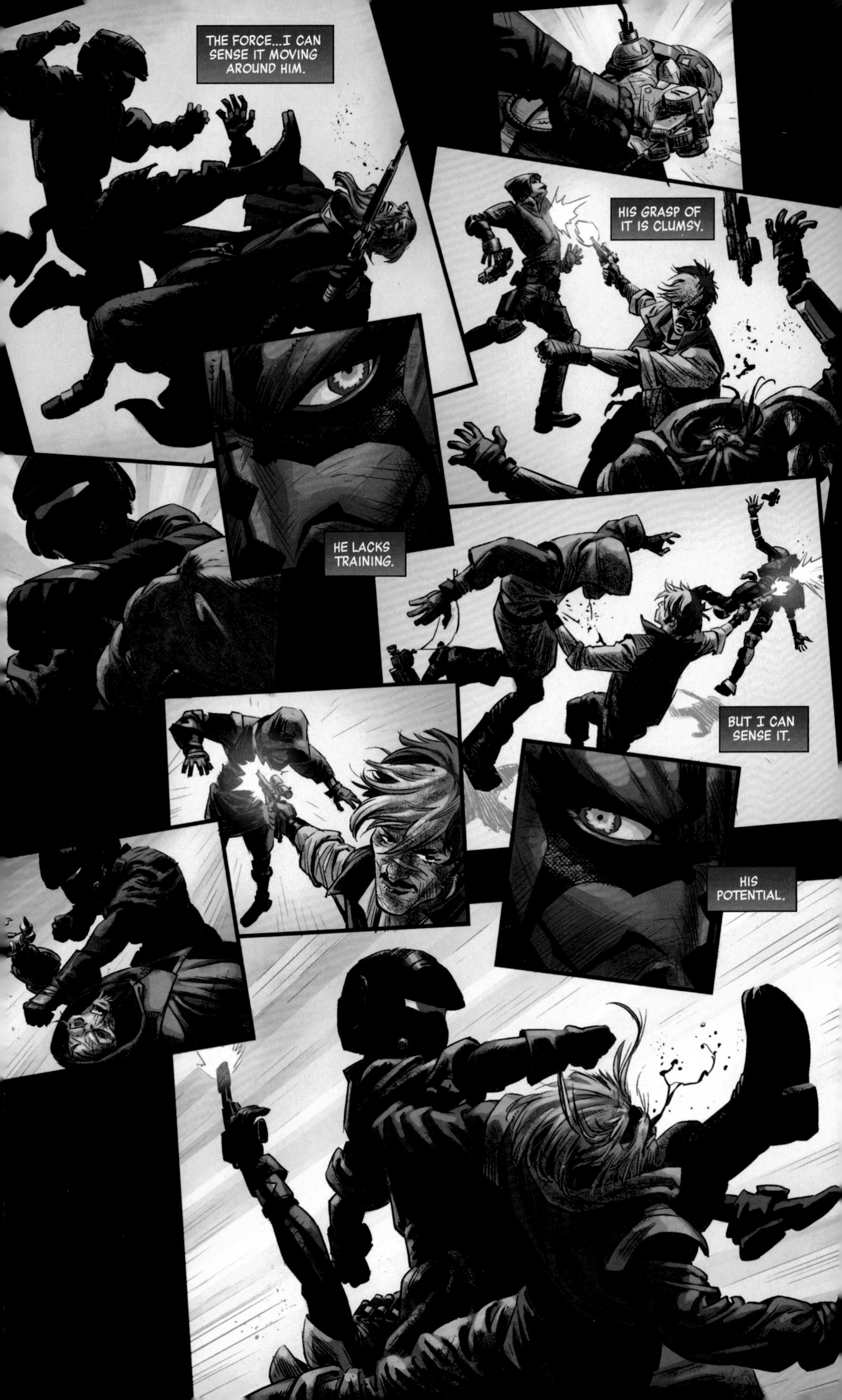
THE FORCE...I CAN SENSE IT MOVING AROUND HIM.
HIS GRASP OF IT IS CLUMSY.
HE LACKS TRAINING.
BUT I CAN SENSE IT.
HIS POTENTIAL.

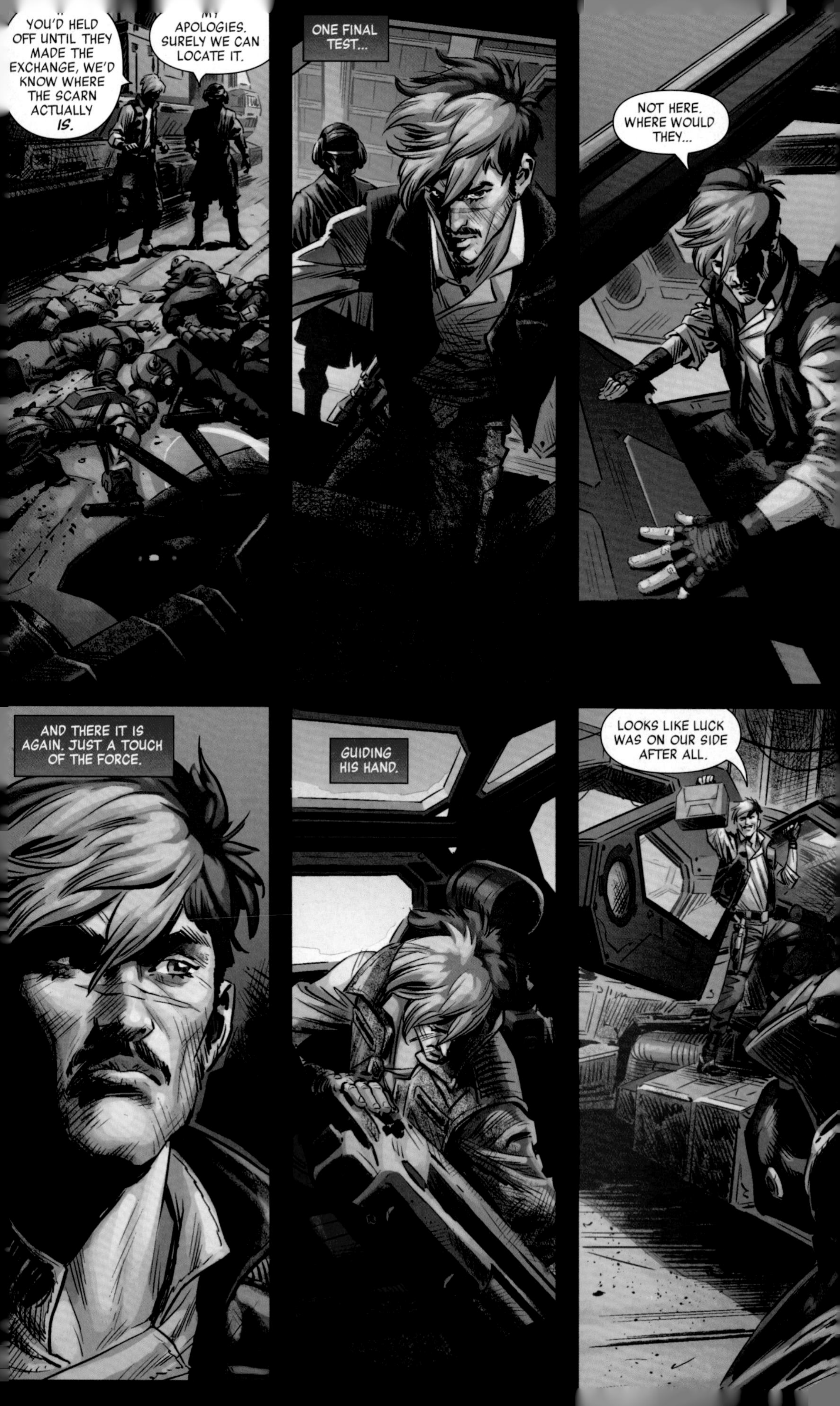
YOU'D HELD OFF UNTIL THEY MADE THE EXCHANGE, WE'D KNOW WHERE THE SCARN ACTUALLY *IS.*
APOLOGIES. SURELY WE CAN LOCATE IT.
ONE FINAL TEST...
NOT HERE. WHERE WOULD THEY...
AND THERE IT IS AGAIN. JUST A TOUCH OF THE FORCE.
GUIDING HIS HAND.
LOOKS LIKE LUCK WAS ON OUR SIDE AFTER ALL.

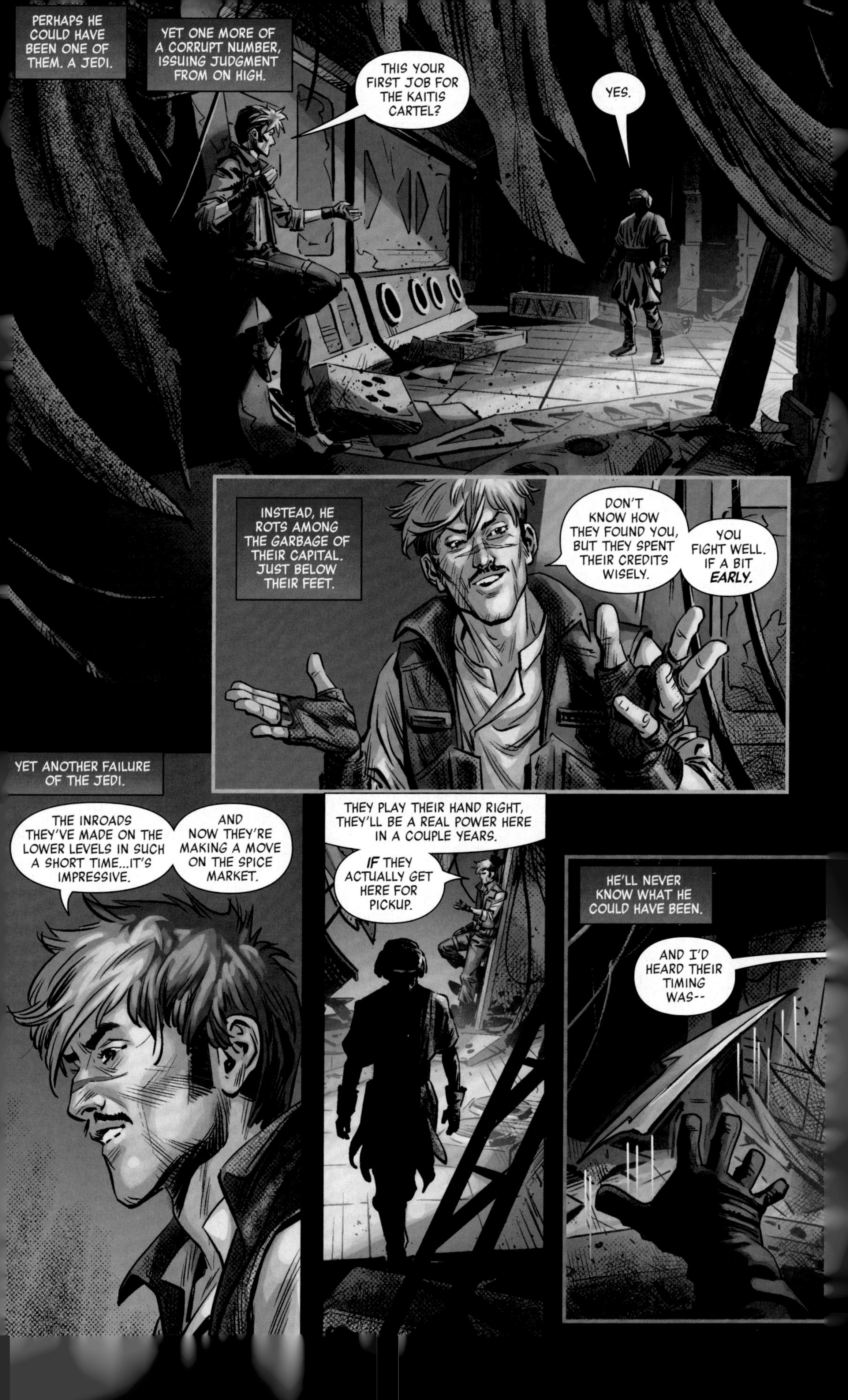
PERHAPS HE COULD HAVE BEEN ONE OF THEM. A JEDI.
YET ONE MORE OF A CORRUPT NUMBER, ISSUING JUDGMENT FROM ON HIGH.
THIS YOUR FIRST JOB FOR THE KAITIS CARTEL?
YES.
INSTEAD, HE ROTS AMONG THE GARBAGE OF THEIR CAPITAL. JUST BELOW THEIR FEET.
DON'T KNOW HOW THEY FOUND YOU, BUT THEY SPENT THEIR CREDITS WISELY.
YOU FIGHT WELL. IF A BIT *EARLY.*
YET ANOTHER FAILURE OF THE JEDI.
THE INROADS THEY'VE MADE ON THE LOWER LEVELS IN SUCH A SHORT TIME...IT'S IMPRESSIVE.
AND NOW THEY'RE MAKING A MOVE ON THE SPICE MARKET.
THEY PLAY THEIR HAND RIGHT, THEY'LL BE A REAL POWER HERE IN A COUPLE YEARS.
IF THEY ACTUALLY GET HERE FOR PICKUP.
HE'LL NEVER KNOW WHAT HE COULD HAVE BEEN.
AND I'D HEARD THEIR TIMING WAS--

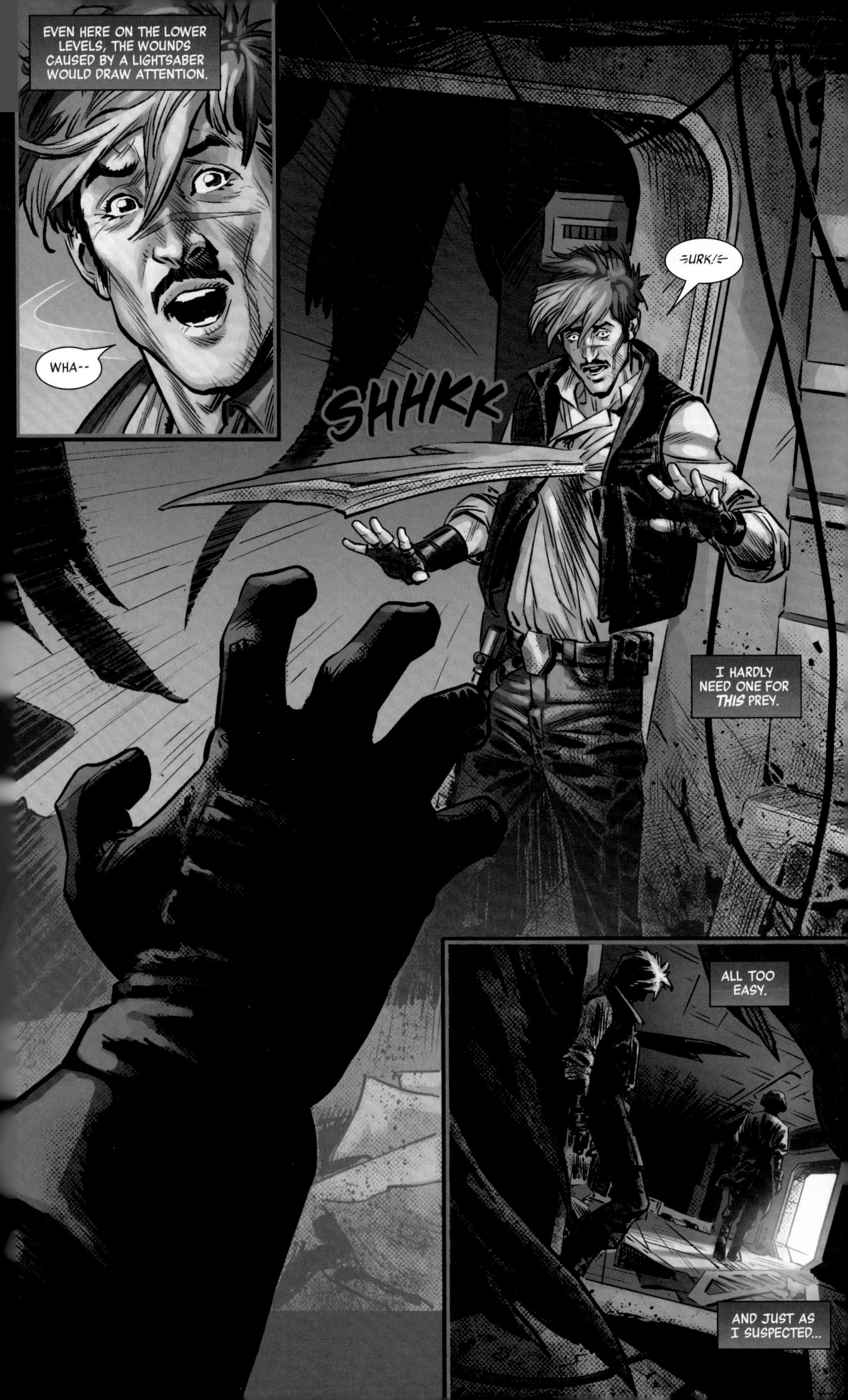
EVEN HERE ON THE LOWER LEVELS, THE WOUNDS CAUSED BY A LIGHTSABER WOULD DRAW ATTENTION.
WHA--
I HARDLY NEED ONE FOR *THIS* PREY.
SHHKK
URK!
ALL TOO EASY.
AND JUST AS I SUSPECTED...

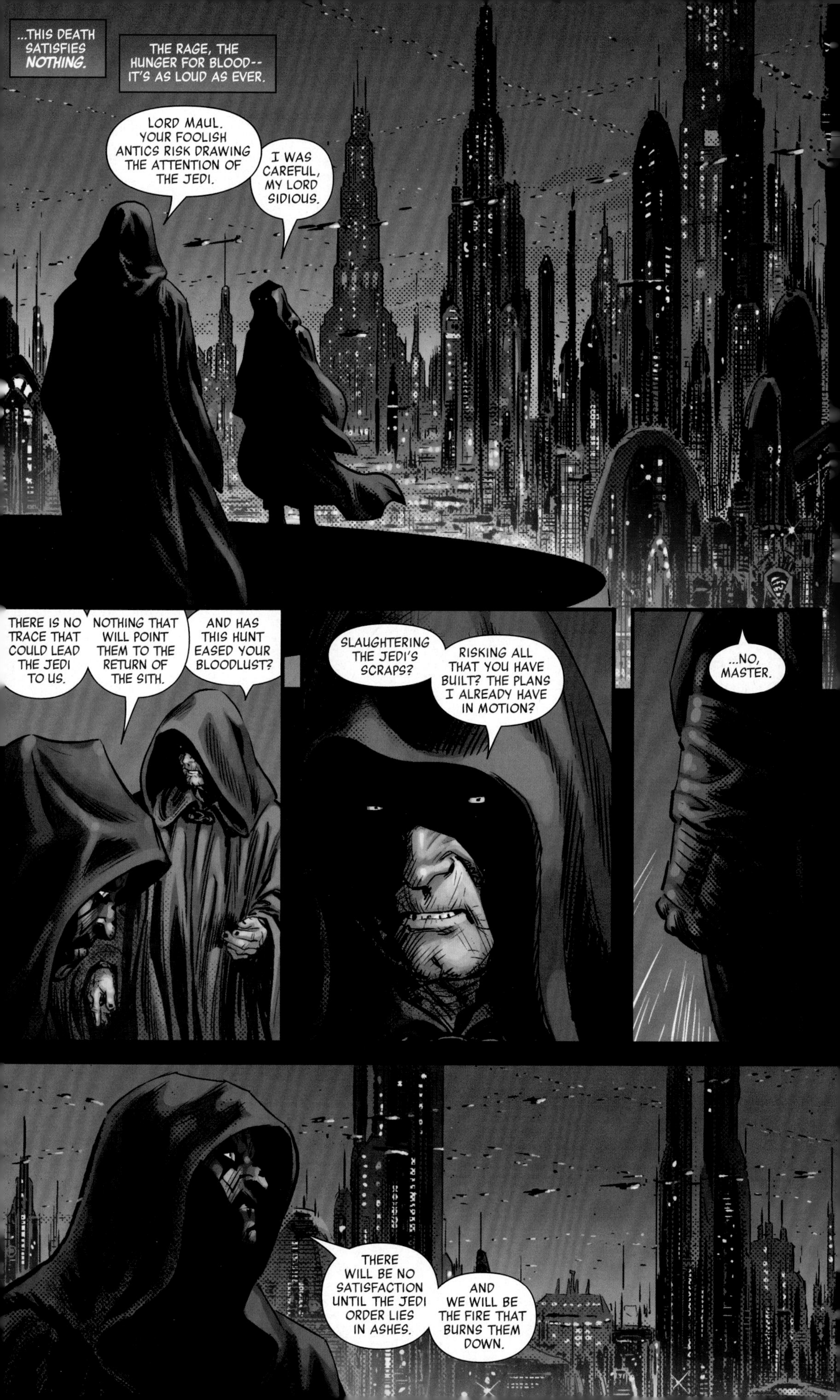
...THIS DEATH SATISFIES *NOTHING.*
THE RAGE, THE HUNGER FOR BLOOD-- IT'S AS LOUD AS EVER.
LORD MAUL. YOUR FOOLISH ANTICS RISK DRAWING THE ATTENTION OF THE JEDI.
I WAS CAREFUL, MY LORD SIDIOUS.
THERE IS NO TRACE THAT COULD LEAD THE JEDI TO US.
NOTHING THAT WILL POINT THEM TO THE RETURN OF THE SITH.
AND HAS THIS HUNT EASED YOUR BLOODLUST?
SLAUGHTERING THE JEDI'S SCRAPS?
RISKING ALL THAT YOU HAVE BUILT? THE PLANS I ALREADY HAVE IN MOTION?
...NO, MASTER.
THERE WILL BE NO SATISFACTION UNTIL THE JEDI ORDER LIES IN ASHES.
AND WE WILL BE THE FIRE THAT BURNS THEM DOWN.

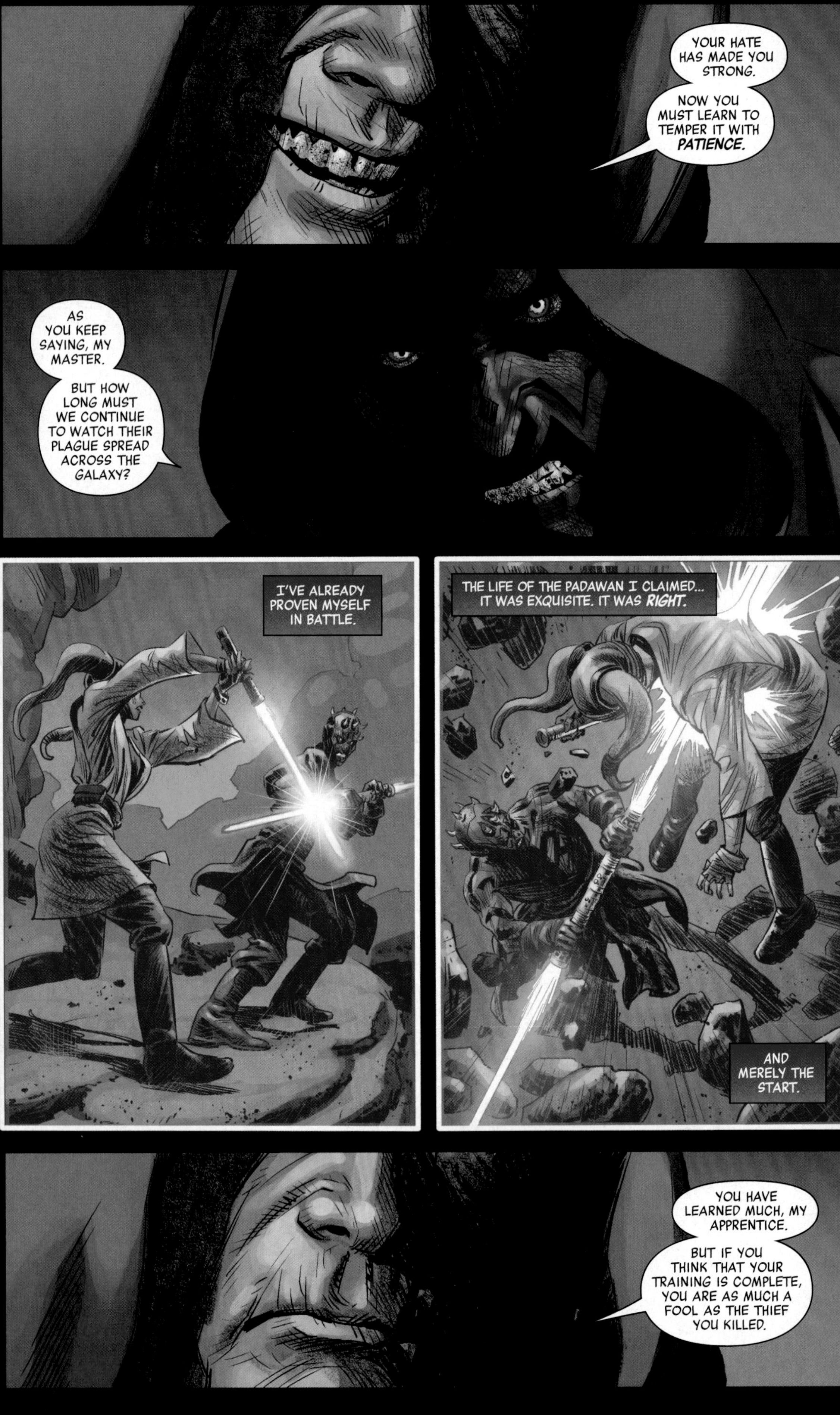

YOUR HATE HAS MADE YOU STRONG.
NOW YOU MUST LEARN TO TEMPER IT WITH *PATIENCE.*
AS YOU KEEP SAYING, MY MASTER.
BUT HOW LONG MUST WE CONTINUE TO WATCH THEIR PLAGUE SPREAD ACROSS THE GALAXY?
I'VE ALREADY PROVEN MYSELF IN BATTLE.
THE LIFE OF THE PADAWAN I CLAIMED... IT WAS EXQUISITE. IT WAS *RIGHT.*
AND MERELY THE START.
YOU HAVE LEARNED MUCH, MY APPRENTICE.
BUT IF YOU THINK THAT YOUR TRAINING IS COMPLETE, YOU ARE AS MUCH A FOOL AS THE THIEF YOU KILLED.

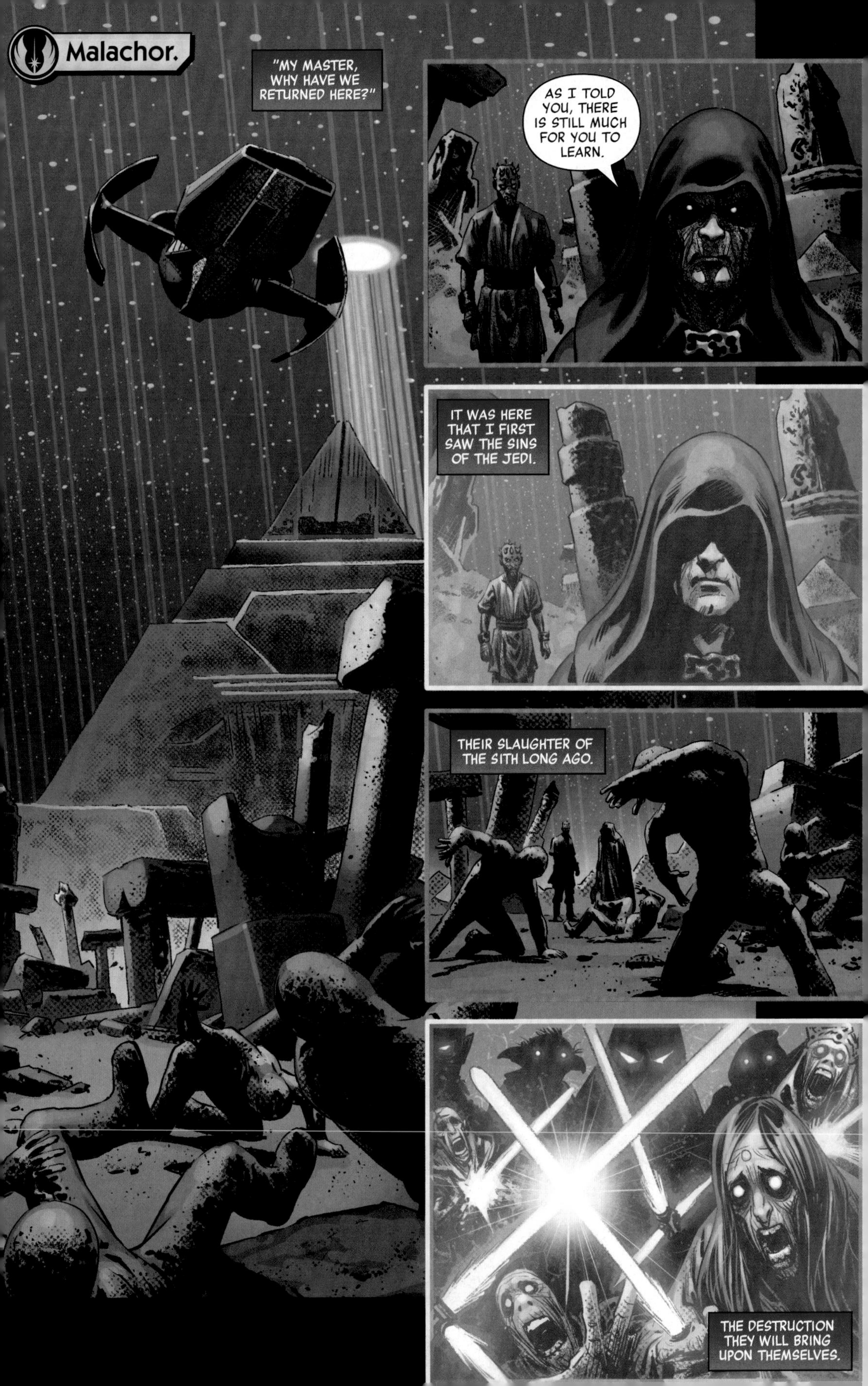
Malachor.
"MY MASTER, WHY HAVE WE RETURNED HERE?"
AS I TOLD YOU, THERE IS STILL MUCH FOR YOU TO LEARN.
IT WAS HERE THAT I FIRST SAW THE SINS OF THE JEDI.
THEIR SLAUGHTER OF THE SITH LONG AGO.
THE DESTRUCTION THEY WILL BRING UPON THEMSELVES.

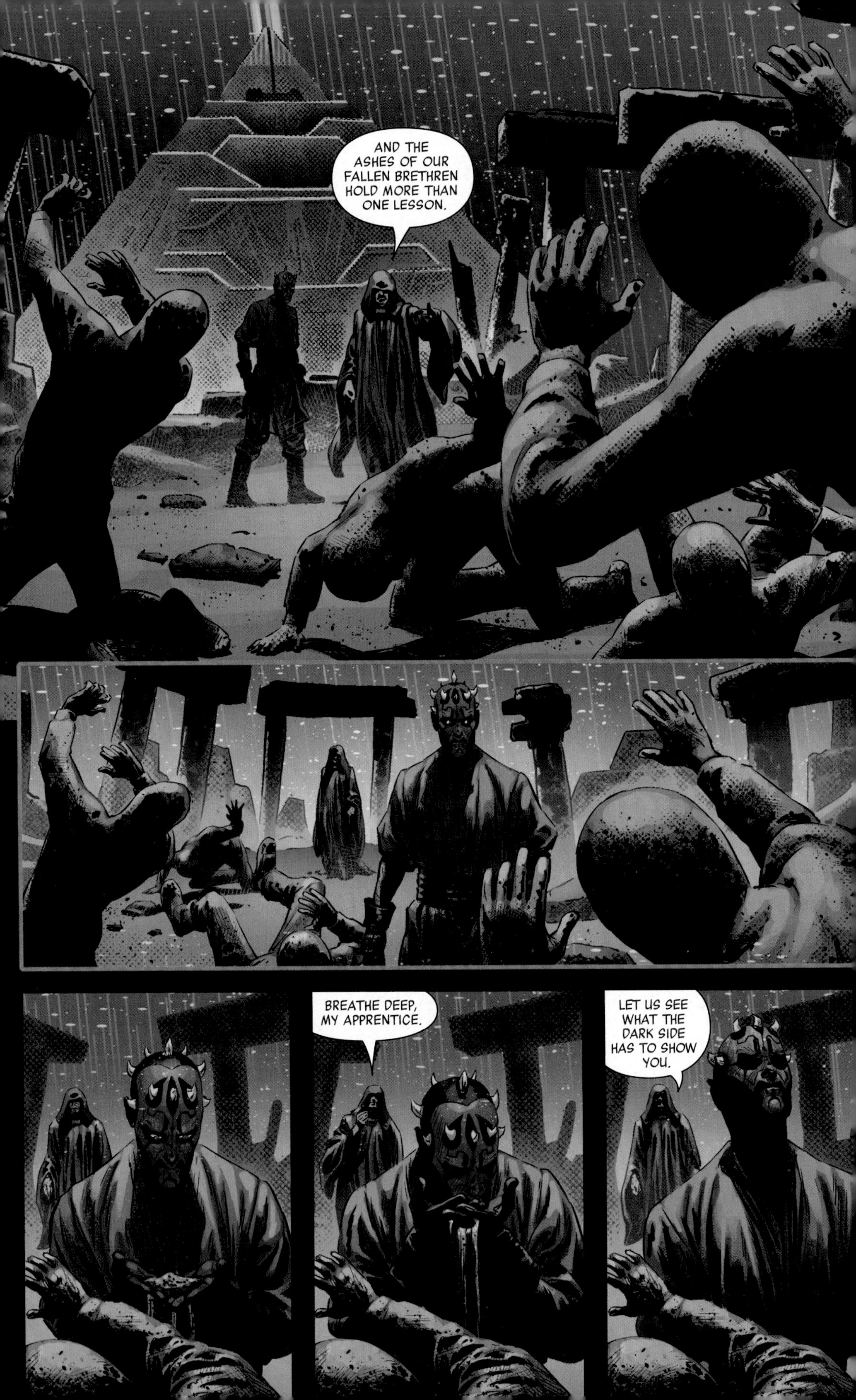
AND THE ASHES OF OUR FALLEN BRETHREN HOLD MORE THAN ONE LESSON.
BREATHE DEEP, MY APPRENTICE.
LET US SEE WHAT THE DARK SIDE HAS TO SHOW YOU.

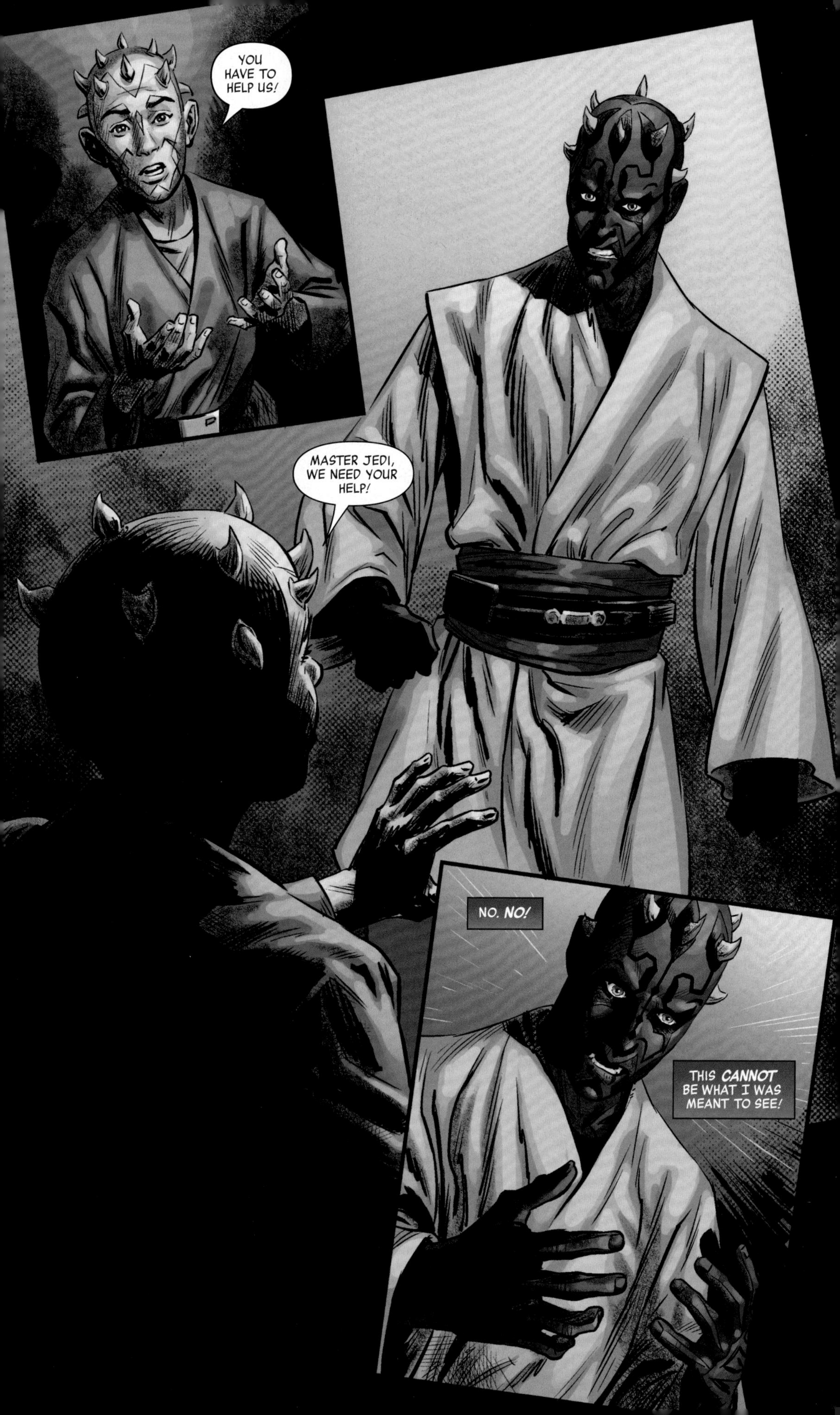
YOU HAVE TO HELP US!
MASTER JEDI, WE NEED YOUR HELP!
NO. NO!
THIS CANNOT BE WHAT I WAS MEANT TO SEE!

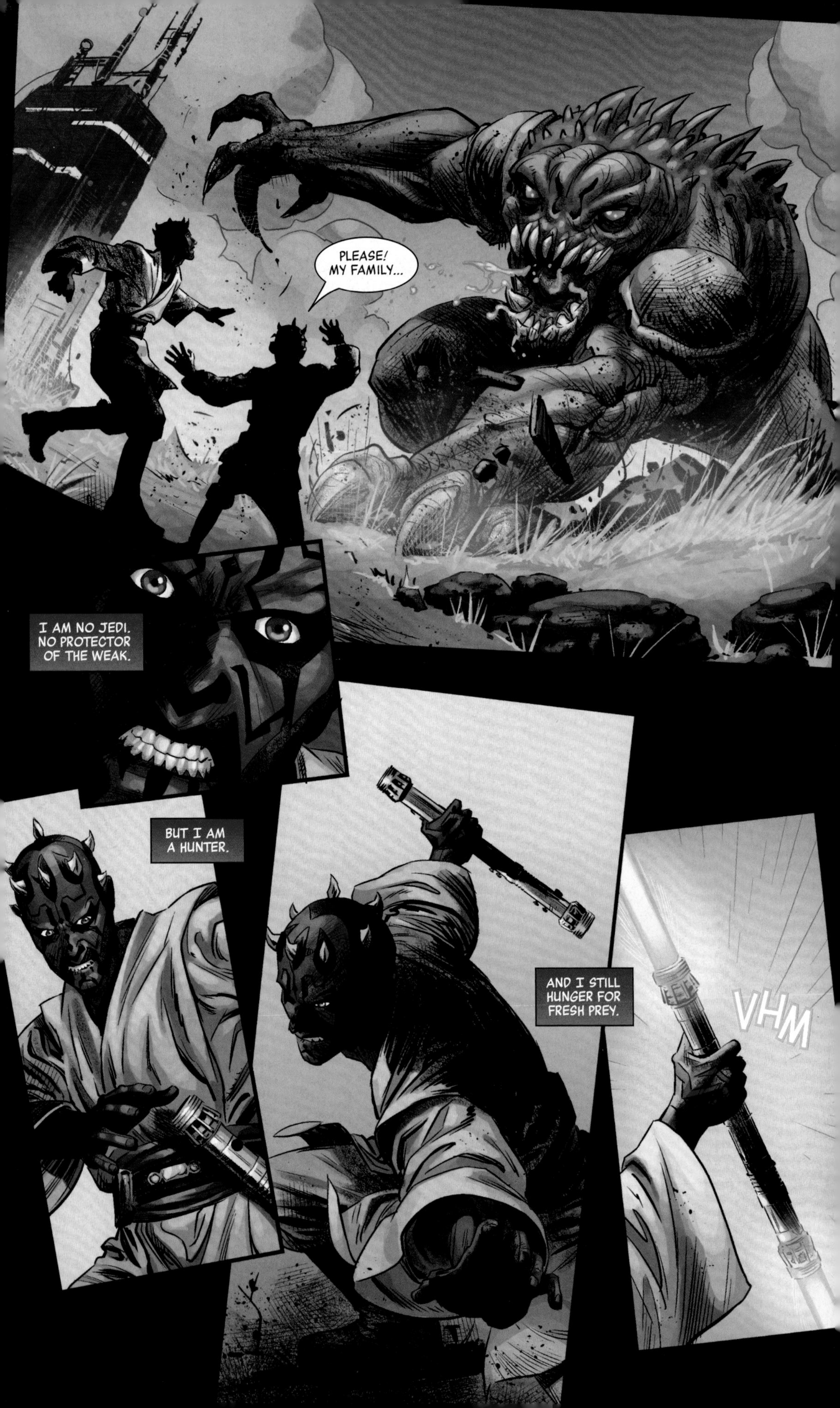
PLEASE! MY FAMILY...
I AM NO JEDI. NO PROTECTOR OF THE WEAK.
BUT I AM A HUNTER.
AND I STILL HUNGER FOR FRESH PREY.
VHM

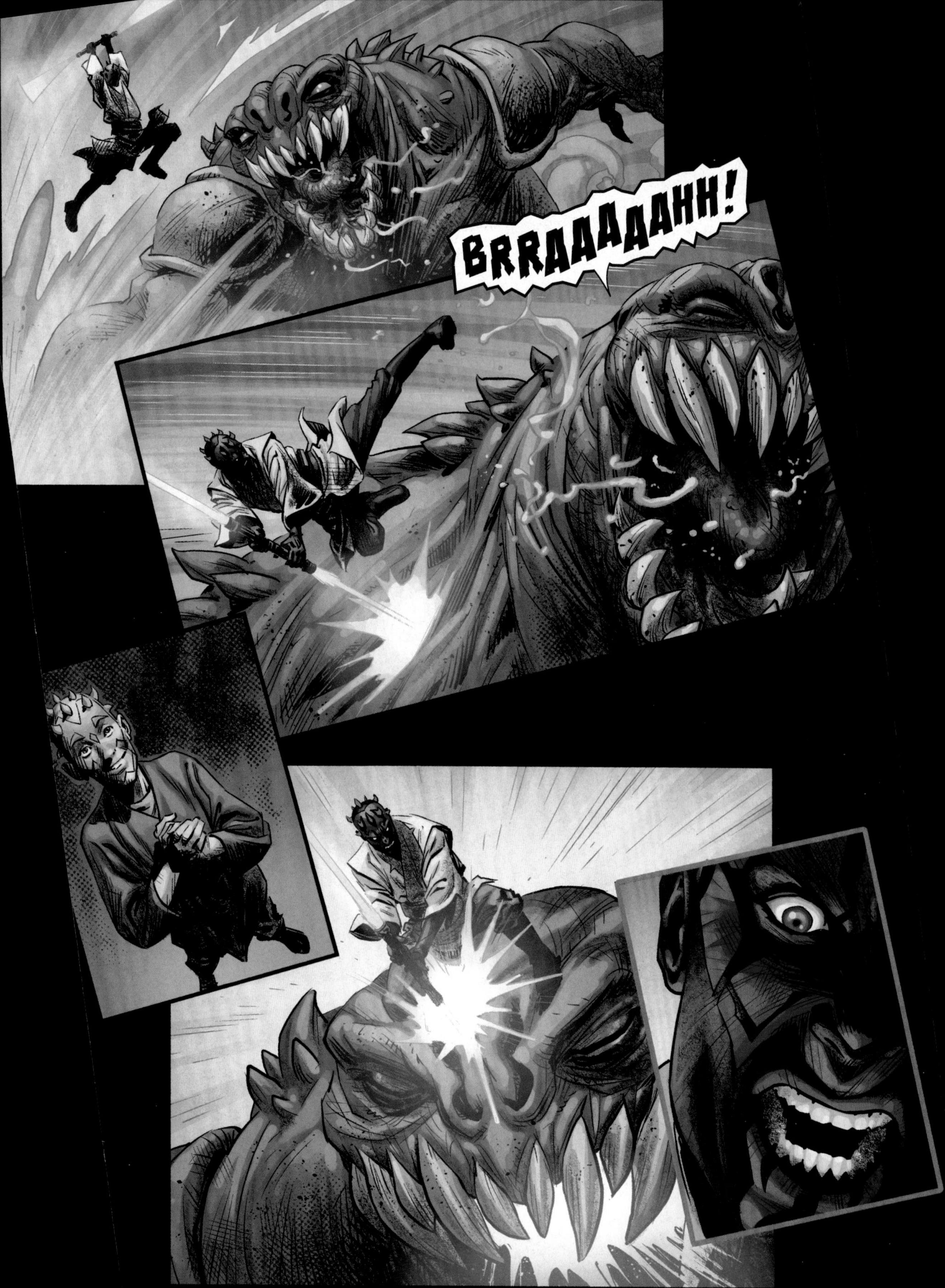
BRRAAAAAHH!

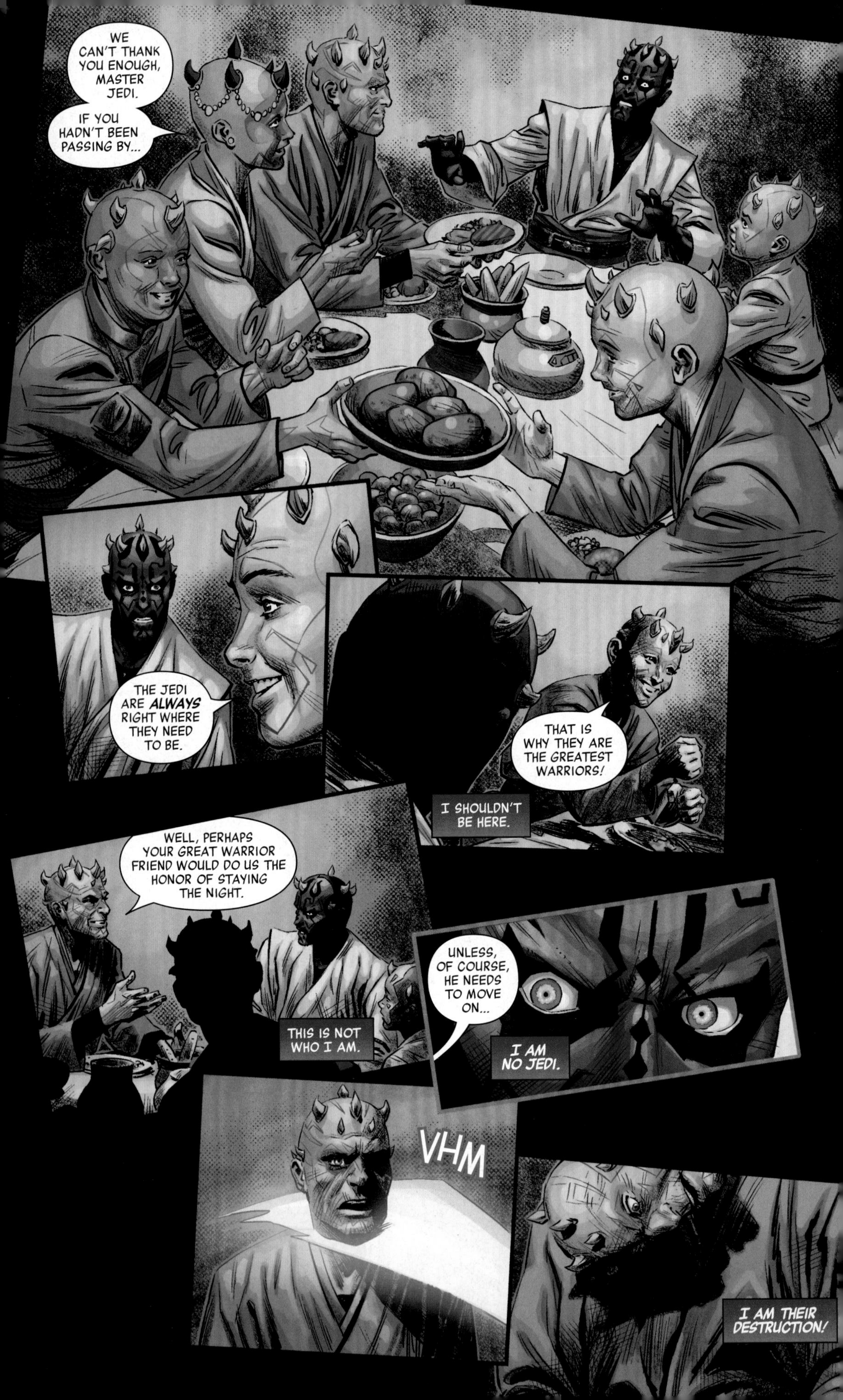

WE CAN'T THANK YOU ENOUGH, MASTER JEDI.
IF YOU HADN'T BEEN PASSING BY...
THE JEDI ARE ALWAYS RIGHT WHERE THEY NEED TO BE.
THAT IS WHY THEY ARE THE GREATEST WARRIORS!
I SHOULDN'T BE HERE.
WELL, PERHAPS YOUR GREAT WARRIOR FRIEND WOULD DO US THE HONOR OF STAYING THE NIGHT.
THIS IS NOT WHO I AM.
UNLESS, OF COURSE, HE NEEDS TO MOVE ON...
I AM NO JEDI.
VHM
I AM THEIR DESTRUCTION!

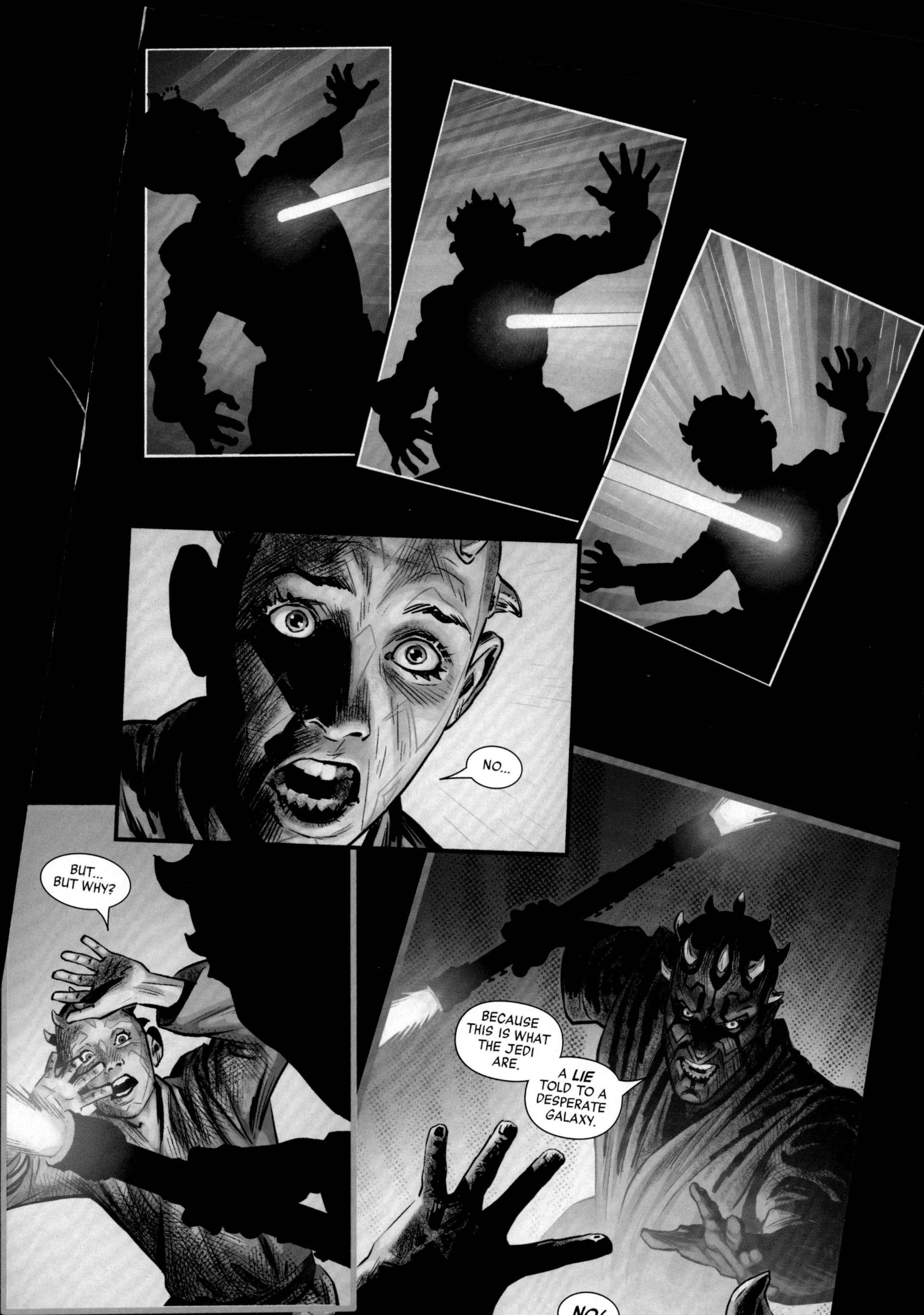
NO...
BUT... BUT WHY?
BECAUSE THIS IS WHAT THE JEDI ARE.
A LIE TOLD TO A DESPERATE GALAXY.

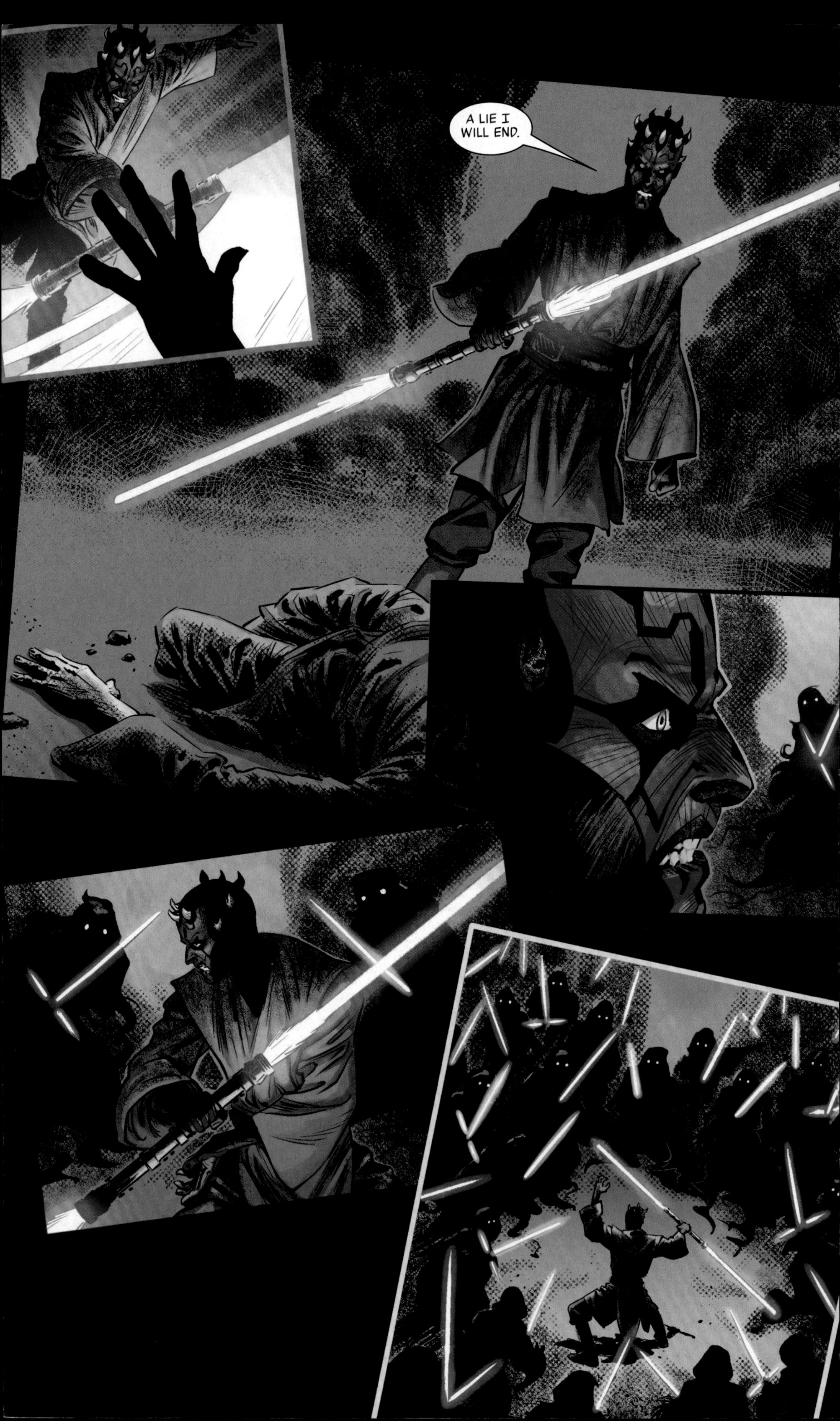
A LIE I WILL END.

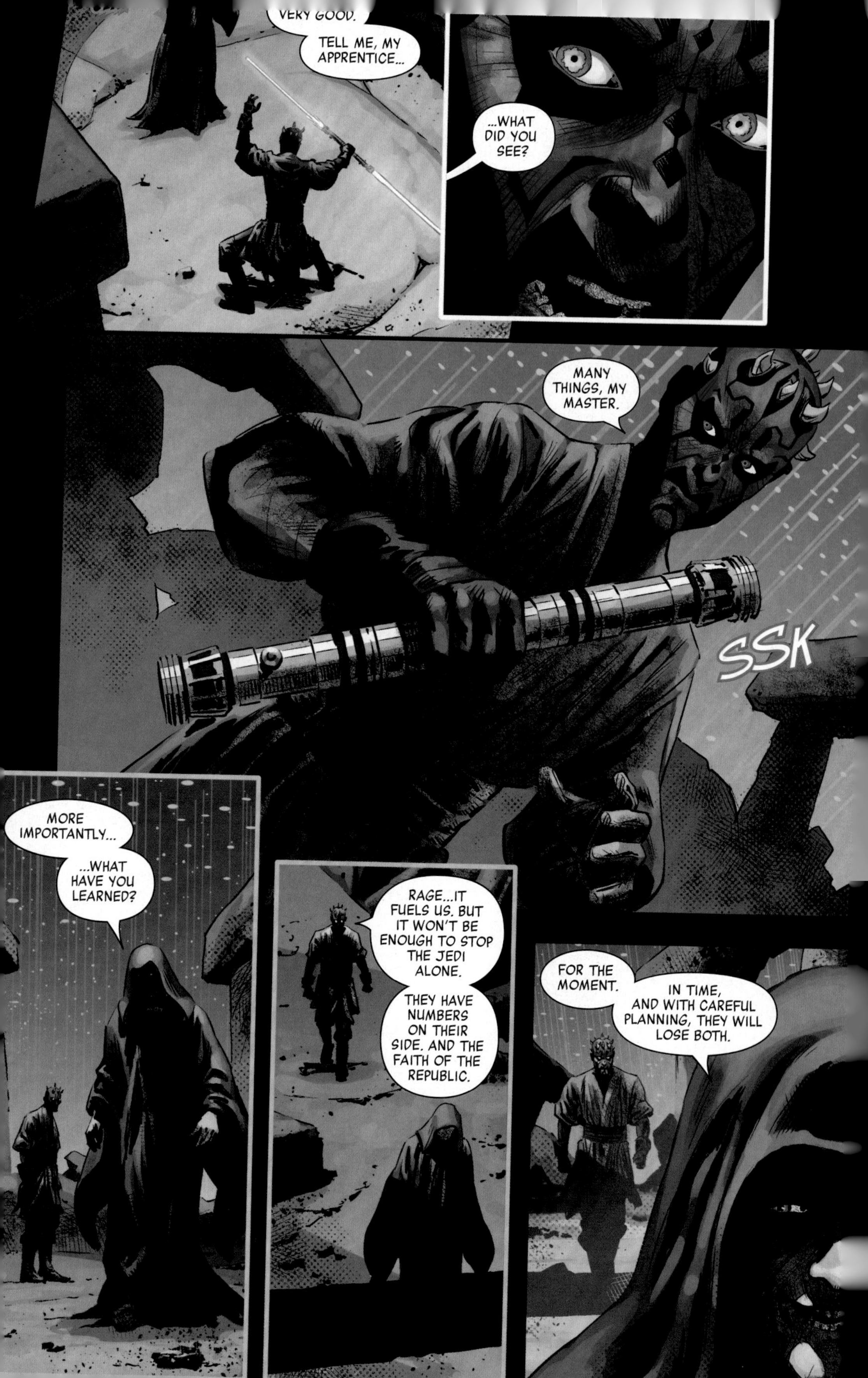
VERY GOOD.
TELL ME, MY APPRENTICE...
...WHAT DID YOU SEE?
MANY THINGS, MY MASTER.
SSK
MORE IMPORTANTLY...
...WHAT HAVE YOU LEARNED?
RAGE...IT FUELS US. BUT IT WON'T BE ENOUGH TO STOP THE JEDI ALONE.
THEY HAVE NUMBERS ON THEIR SIDE. AND THE FAITH OF THE REPUBLIC.
FOR THE MOMENT.
IN TIME, AND WITH CAREFUL PLANNING, THEY WILL LOSE BOTH.

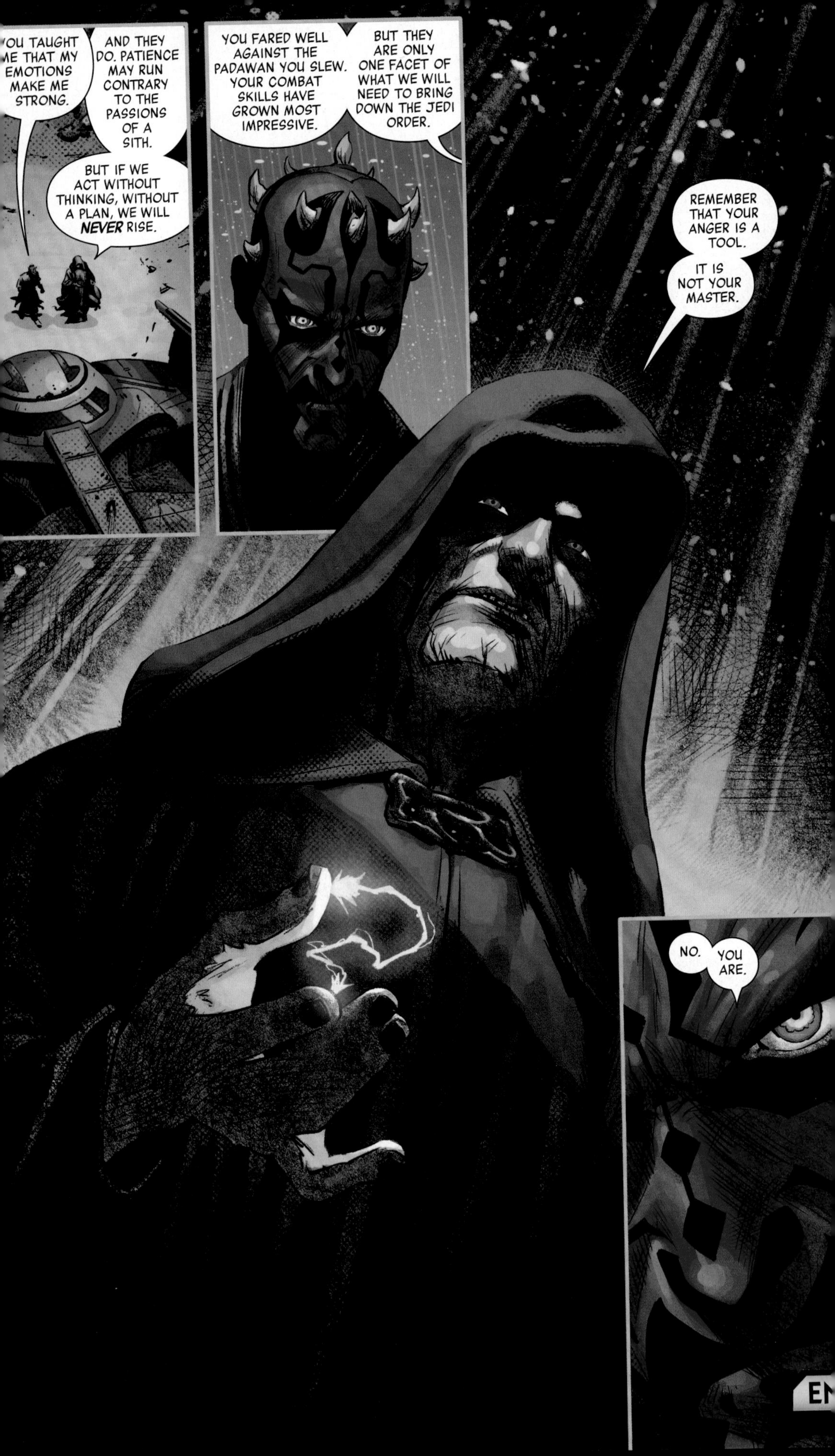
YOU TAUGHT ME THAT MY EMOTIONS MAKE ME STRONG.
AND THEY DO. PATIENCE MAY RUN CONTRARY TO THE PASSIONS OF A SITH.
BUT IF WE ACT WITHOUT THINKING, WITHOUT A PLAN, WE WILL NEVER RISE.
YOU FARED WELL AGAINST THE PADAWAN YOU SLEW. YOUR COMBAT SKILLS HAVE GROWN MOST IMPRESSIVE.
BUT THEY ARE ONLY ONE FACET OF WHAT WE WILL NEED TO BRING DOWN THE JEDI ORDER.
REMEMBER THAT YOUR ANGER IS A TOOL.
IT IS NOT YOUR MASTER.
NO.
YOU ARE.

YOU CAN'T KEEP A GOOD SITH DOWN

Darth Maul was killed—and then got a new lease on life.

By Glenn Greenberg

He had appeared in only one *Star Wars* movie—1999's *The Phantom Menace*, in which he uttered only a few sentences. All we knew about him was that he had a striking look, amazing fighting abilities, a hatred for the Jedi and a cool double-bladed lightsaber. Then he met his end at the hands of Jedi Knight Obi-Wan Kenobi, with his bisected body plummeting down a reactor shaft. But Darth Maul, the Sith who served Darth Sidious and slew Qui-Gon Jinn during a spectacular duel, returned to forge a whole new path.

As many *Star Wars* fans know, Maul's surprising return happened in the *Star Wars: The Clone Wars* animated series. It was revealed that he drew upon his anger and hatred, using the dark side of the Force to keep himself alive despite losing his lower half. Determined to survive, Maul constructed mechanical legs to replace the real ones he had lost.

The Clone Wars also filled in Maul's backstory, revealing his early life as a native of the planet Dathomir and that he had a brother, Savage Opress. Indeed, it was Savage Opress who found the still-alive Maul, his body and mind both shattered, and brought him home. There, Maul was restored by dark magicks. Eventually, he returned to action, with his brother as his apprentice. But instead of continuing as a Sith, Maul embarked on a journey into the galaxy's underworld, where he ultimately became a crime lord. Along the way, he found himself earning—and surviving—the wrath of his former master, Darth Sidious, aka Emperor Palpatine.

Life Force

The idea for Maul's resurrection stemmed from creator George Lucas himself, who suggested the idea to *The Clone Wars* supervising director Dave Filoni.

"I found it funny in *The Phantom Menace* when Darth Maul got cut in half," Filoni told *Entertainment Weekly* in 2011, when Maul's return was announced. "I thought George was definitively saying to the fans, 'There's no way this character is coming back.' ... Fast-forward ten years, and *I'm* the one to bring Maul back."

At *Star Wars* Celebration Orlando 2017, Filoni explained that Lucas had originally approached him by saying, "I've got an idea and you're going to love it." But when Lucas suggested bringing Maul back, Filoni's response was, "It's over. He's cut in half. How does that work?" According to Filoni, Lucas replied, "I don't know. Figure it out."

Filoni has theorized that Lucas made the suggestion, in part, because he had come to feel that Maul was underused in *The Phantom Menace* and that the character still had potential. Did he *ever*! Maul appeared in multiple episodes of both *The Clone Wars* and its successor series, *Star Wars Rebels*, in which he and Obi-Wan Kenobi crossed lightsabers once again in the episode "Twin Suns."

Comeback Kid

If there were any lingering doubts that Maul really survived being sliced in two, they were put to rest in May 2018, when the film *Solo: A Star Wars Story* shocked and delighted audiences by putting the erstwhile Sith Lord back on the big screen after nineteen years. Tying directly into the events of *The Clone Wars*, *Solo* confirmed that Maul was still very much alive and was now running the criminal organization Crimson Dawn.

Not bad at all for a guy who started out with roughly ten minutes of screen time, barely any dialogue, and one of the most memorable death scenes in the entire *Star Wars* saga.

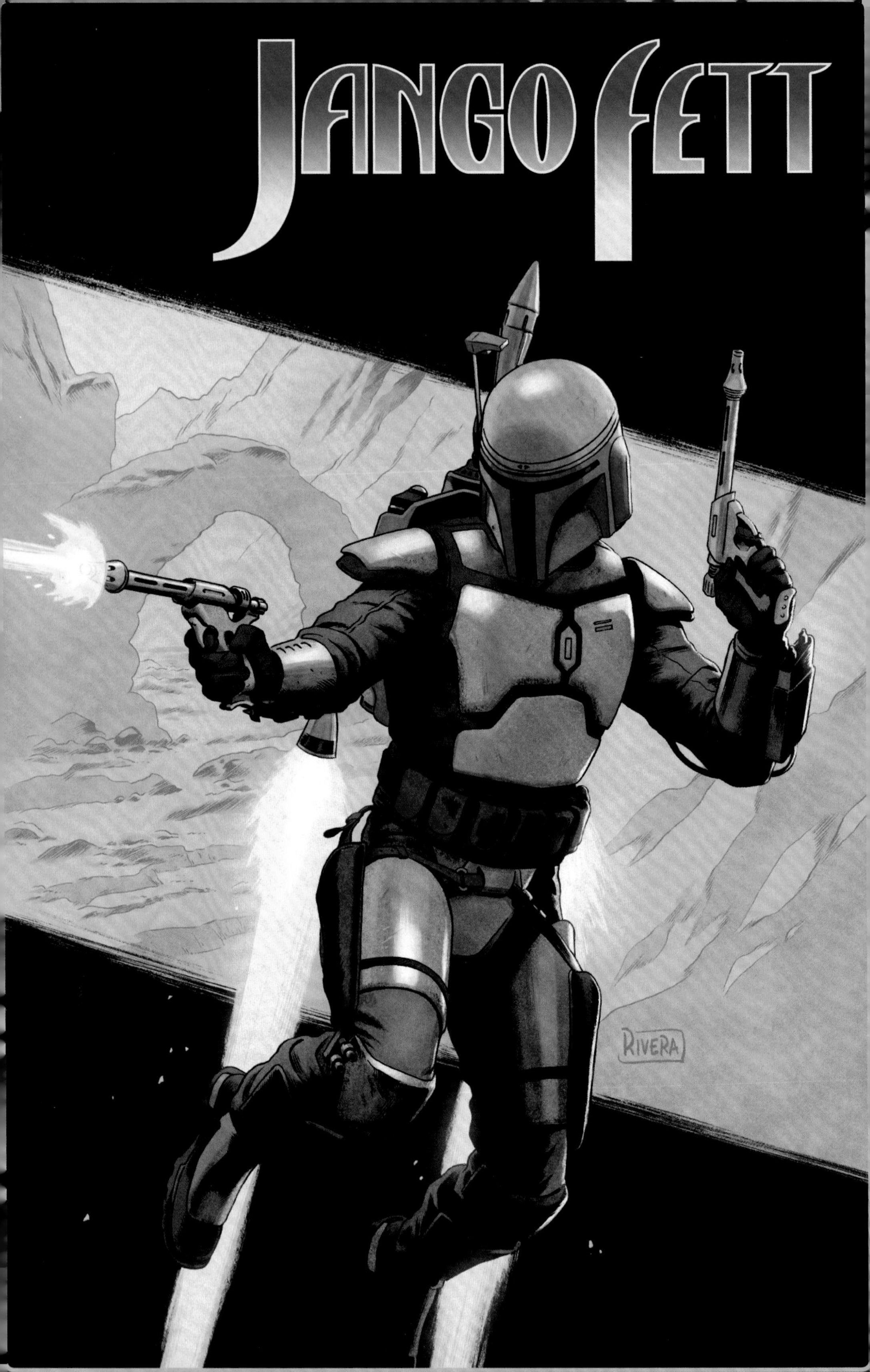
JANGO FETT
RIVERA

“TRAINING”

Jango Fett is one of the most feared bounty hunters in the galaxy, a cold-blooded and ruthless assassin who always gets the job done no matter what it takes. If Jango’s past has been built on violence and destruction , what’s left to build his future?

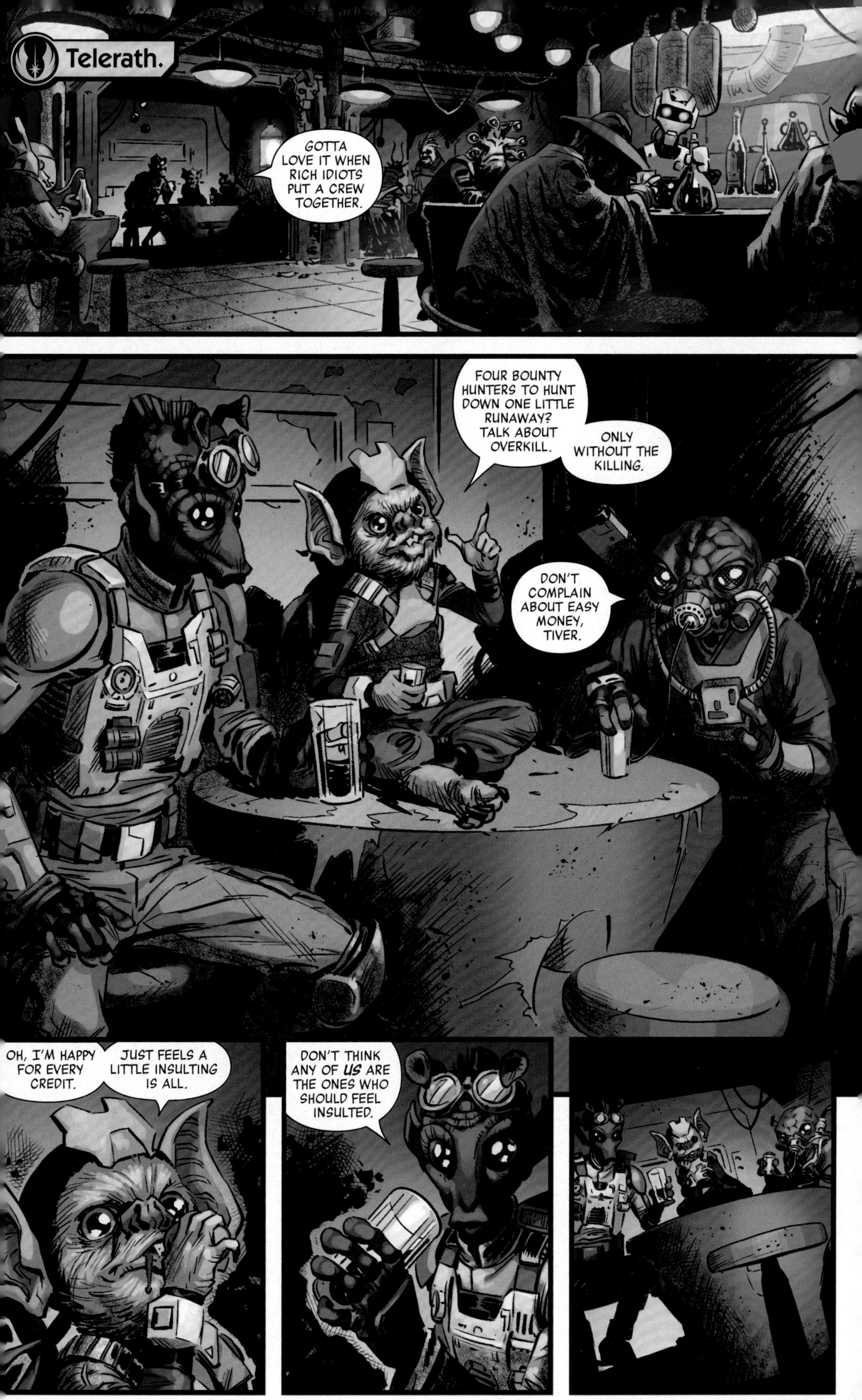

Telerath.
GOTTA LOVE IT WHEN RICH IDIOTS PUT A CREW TOGETHER.
FOUR BOUNTY HUNTERS TO HUNT DOWN ONE LITTLE RUNAWAY? TALK ABOUT OVERKILL.
ONLY WITHOUT THE KILLING.
DON'T COMPLAIN ABOUT EASY MONEY, TIVER.
OH, I'M HAPPY FOR EVERY CREDIT.
JUST FEELS A LITTLE INSULTING IS ALL.
DON'T THINK ANY OF *US* ARE THE ONES WHO SHOULD FEEL INSULTED.

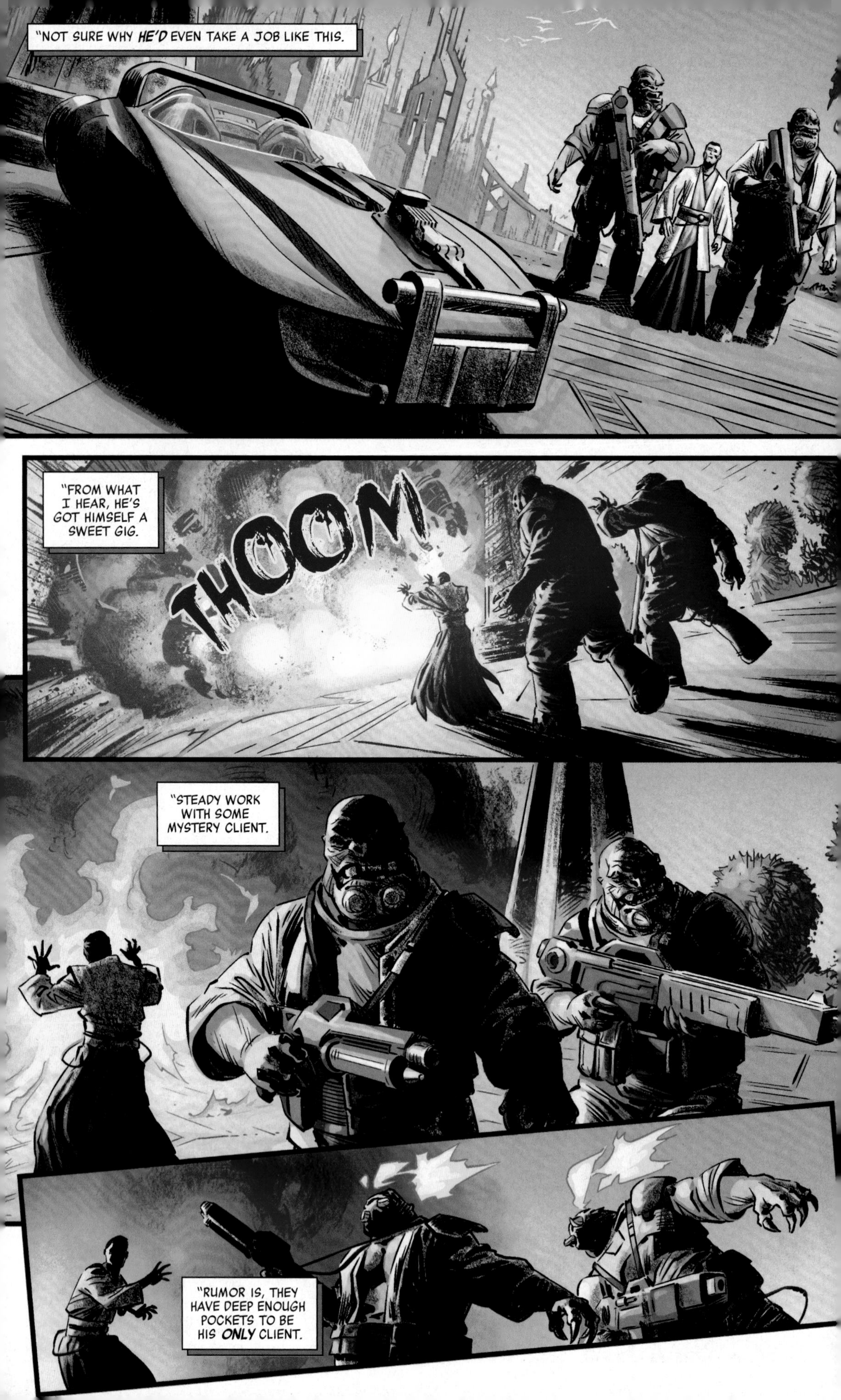
"NOT SURE WHY HE'D EVEN TAKE A JOB LIKE THIS.
"FROM WHAT I HEAR, HE'S GOT HIMSELF A SWEET GIG.
THOOM
"STEADY WORK WITH SOME MYSTERY CLIENT.
"RUMOR IS, THEY HAVE DEEP ENOUGH POCKETS TO BE HIS ONLY CLIENT.

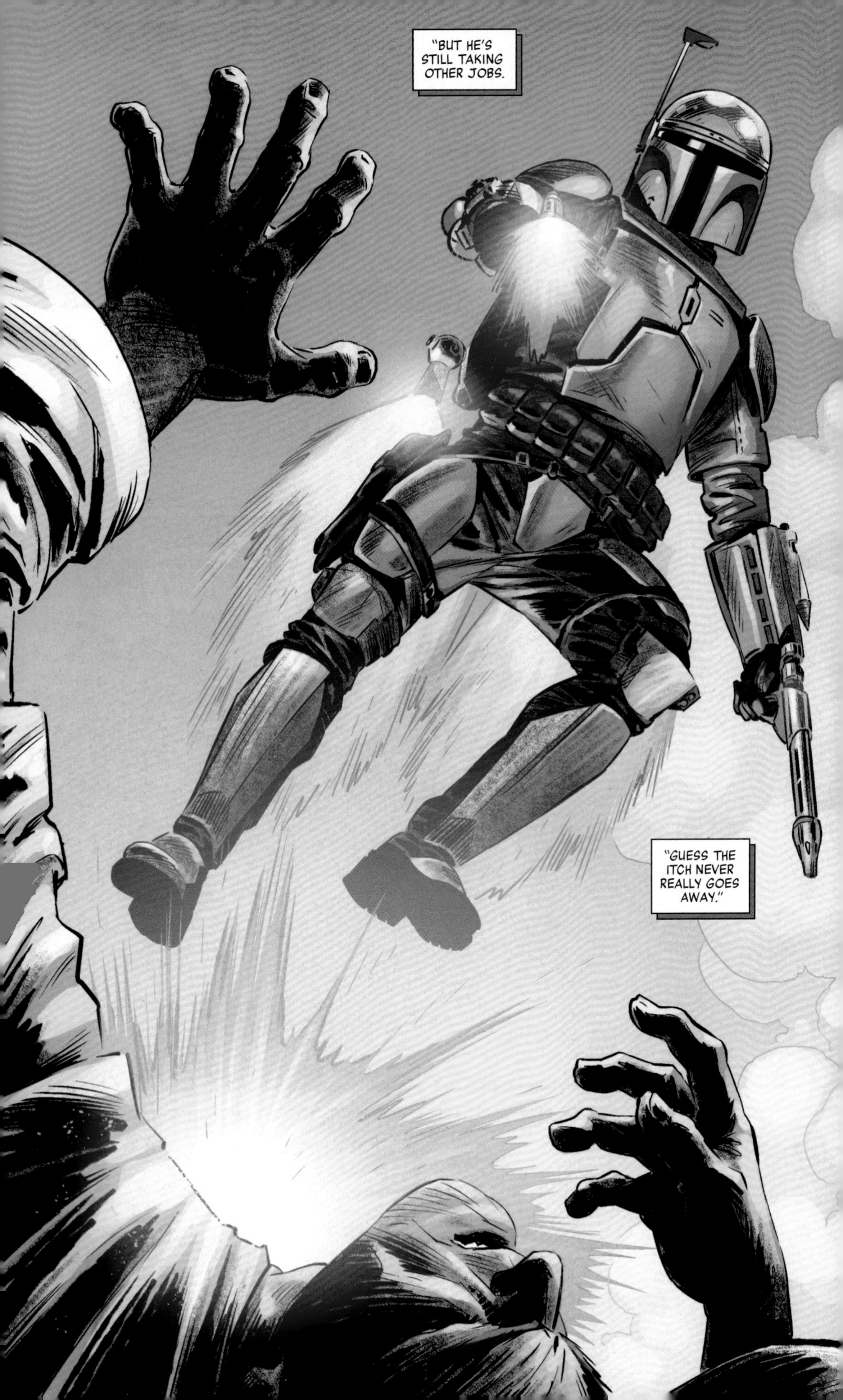
"BUT HE'S STILL TAKING OTHER JOBS.
"GUESS THE ITCH NEVER REALLY GOES AWAY."

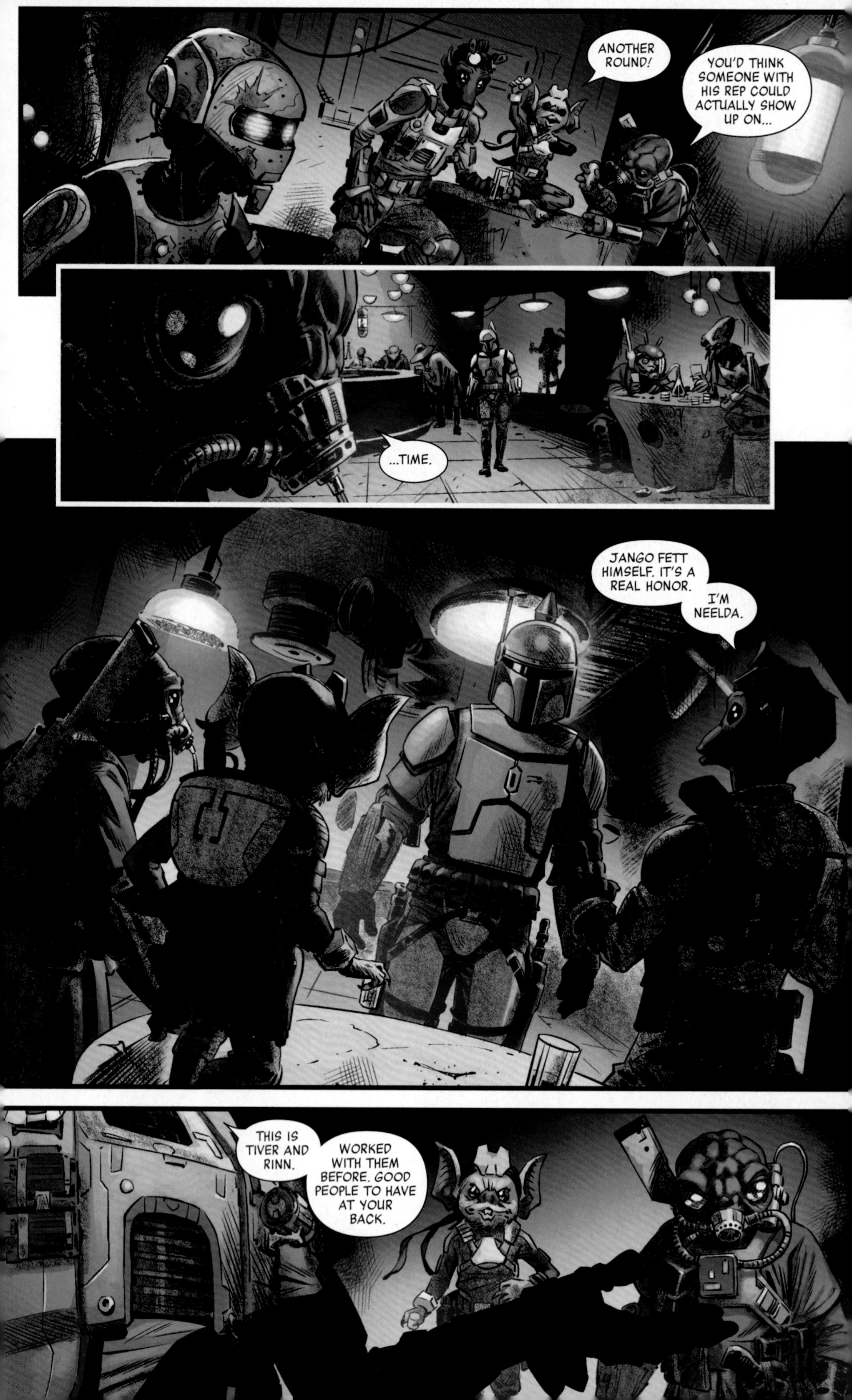
ANOTHER ROUND!
YOU'D THINK SOMEONE WITH HIS REP COULD ACTUALLY SHOW UP ON...
...TIME.
JANGO FETT HIMSELF. IT'S A REAL HONOR.
I'M NEELDA.
THIS IS TIVER AND RINN.
WORKED WITH THEM BEFORE. GOOD PEOPLE TO HAVE AT YOUR BACK.

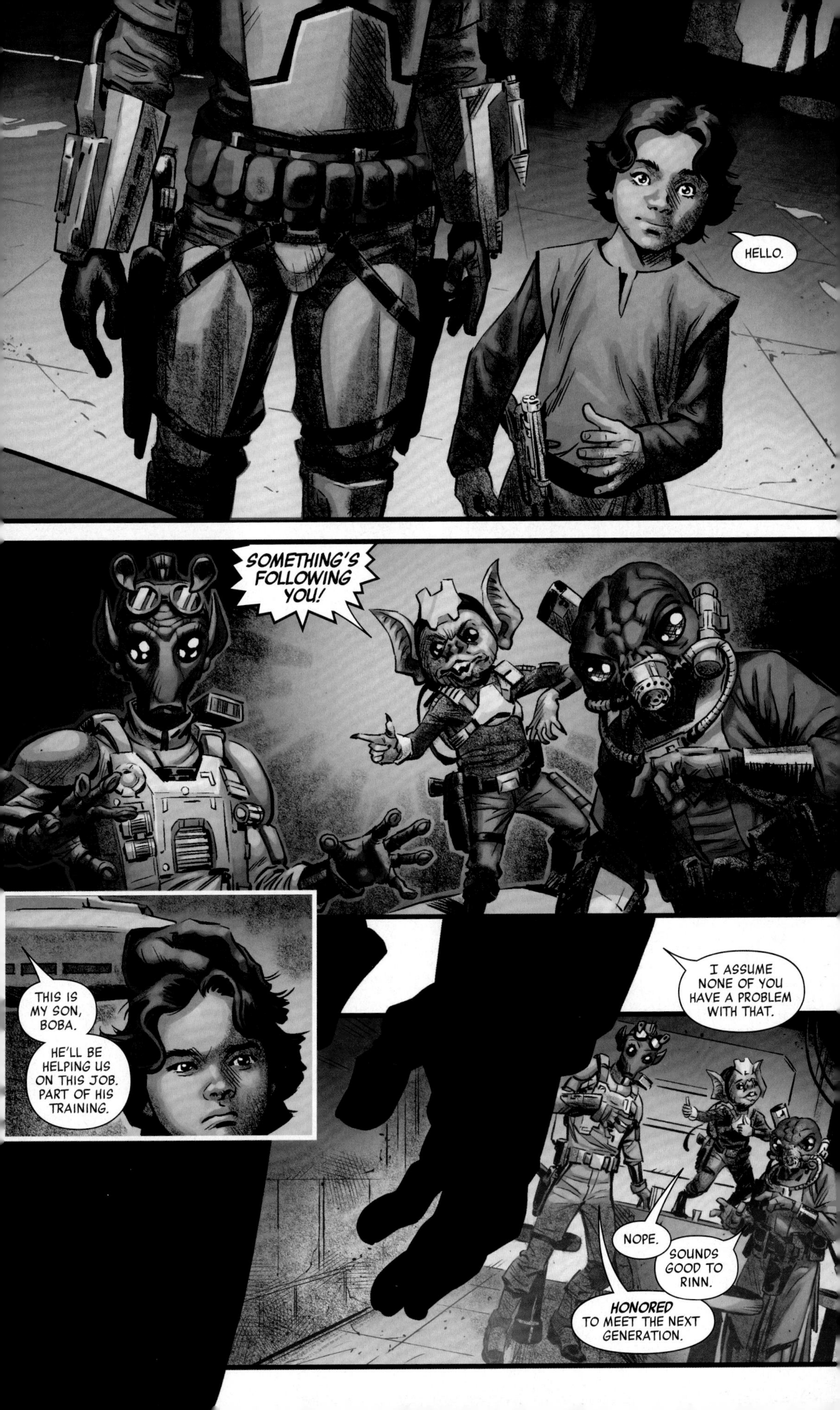
HELLO.
SOMETHING'S FOLLOWING YOU!
THIS IS MY SON, BOBA.
HE'LL BE HELPING US ON THIS JOB. PART OF HIS TRAINING.
I ASSUME NONE OF YOU HAVE A PROBLEM WITH THAT.
NOPE.
SOUNDS GOOD TO RINN.
HONORED TO MEET THE NEXT GENERATION.

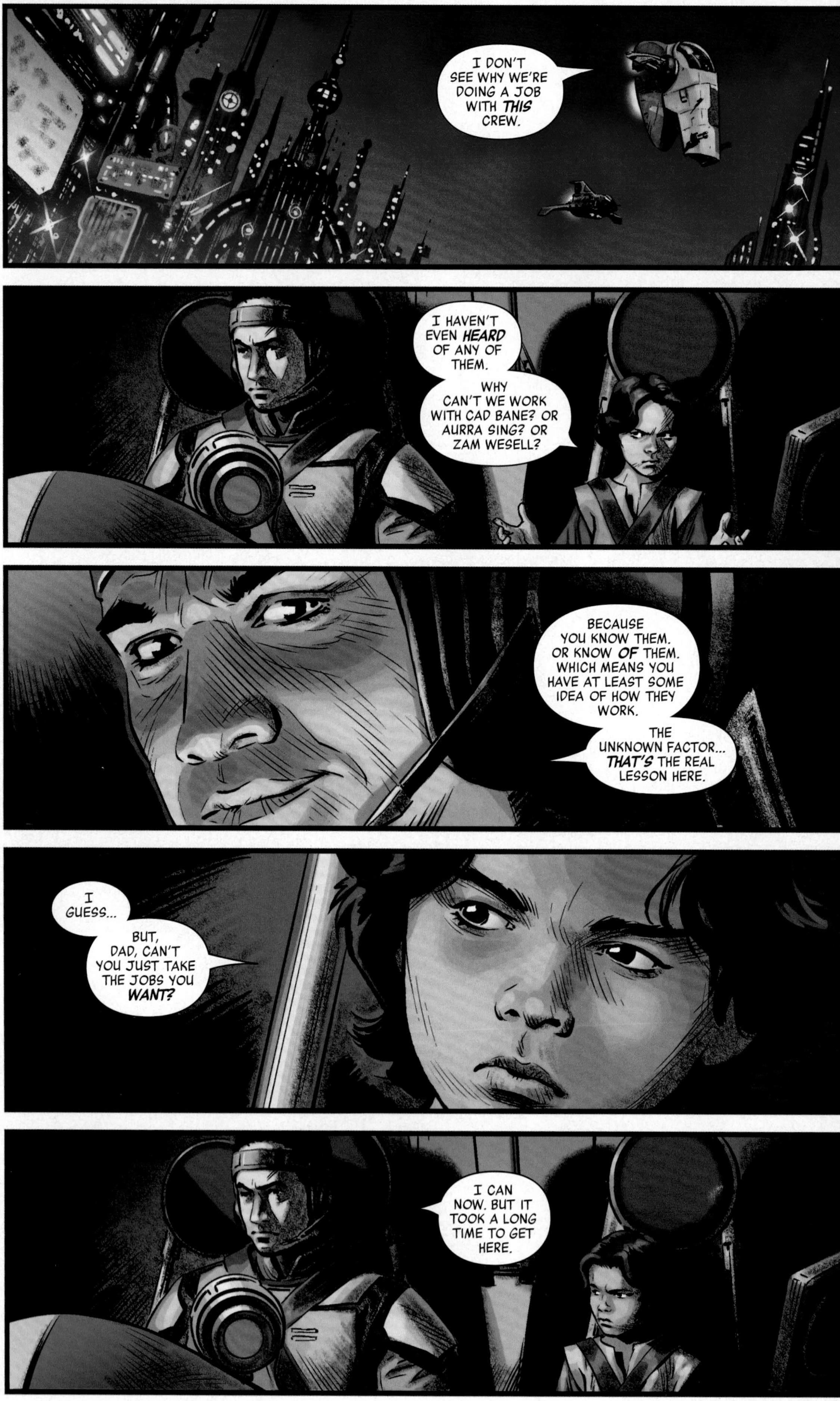
I DON'T SEE WHY WE'RE DOING A JOB WITH *THIS* CREW.
I HAVEN'T EVEN *HEARD* OF ANY OF THEM.
WHY CAN'T WE WORK WITH CAD BANE? OR AURRA SING? OR ZAM WESELL?
BECAUSE YOU KNOW THEM. OR KNOW *OF* THEM. WHICH MEANS YOU HAVE AT LEAST SOME IDEA OF HOW THEY WORK.
THE UNKNOWN FACTOR... *THAT'S* THE REAL LESSON HERE.
I GUESS...
BUT, DAD, CAN'T YOU JUST TAKE THE JOBS YOU *WANT?*
I CAN NOW. BUT IT TOOK A LONG TIME TO GET HERE.

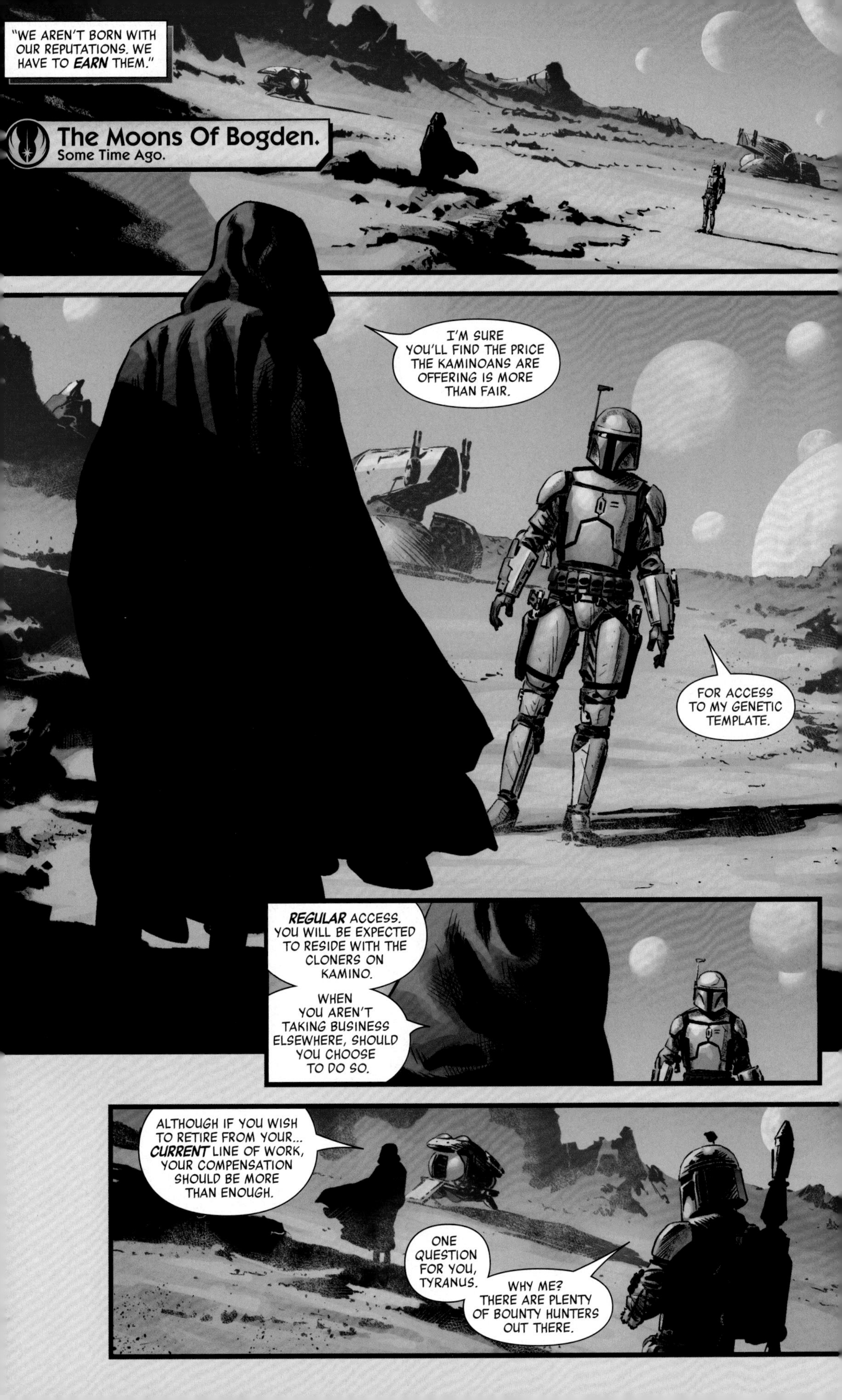
"WE AREN'T BORN WITH OUR REPUTATIONS. WE HAVE TO EARN THEM."
The Moons Of Bogden.
Some Time Ago.
I'M SURE YOU'LL FIND THE PRICE THE KAMINOANS ARE OFFERING IS MORE THAN FAIR.
FOR ACCESS TO MY GENETIC TEMPLATE.
REGULAR ACCESS. YOU WILL BE EXPECTED TO RESIDE WITH THE CLONERS ON KAMINO.
WHEN YOU AREN'T TAKING BUSINESS ELSEWHERE, SHOULD YOU CHOOSE TO DO SO.
ALTHOUGH IF YOU WISH TO RETIRE FROM YOUR... CURRENT LINE OF WORK, YOUR COMPENSATION SHOULD BE MORE THAN ENOUGH.
ONE QUESTION FOR YOU, TYRANUS.
WHY ME? THERE ARE PLENTY OF BOUNTY HUNTERS OUT THERE.

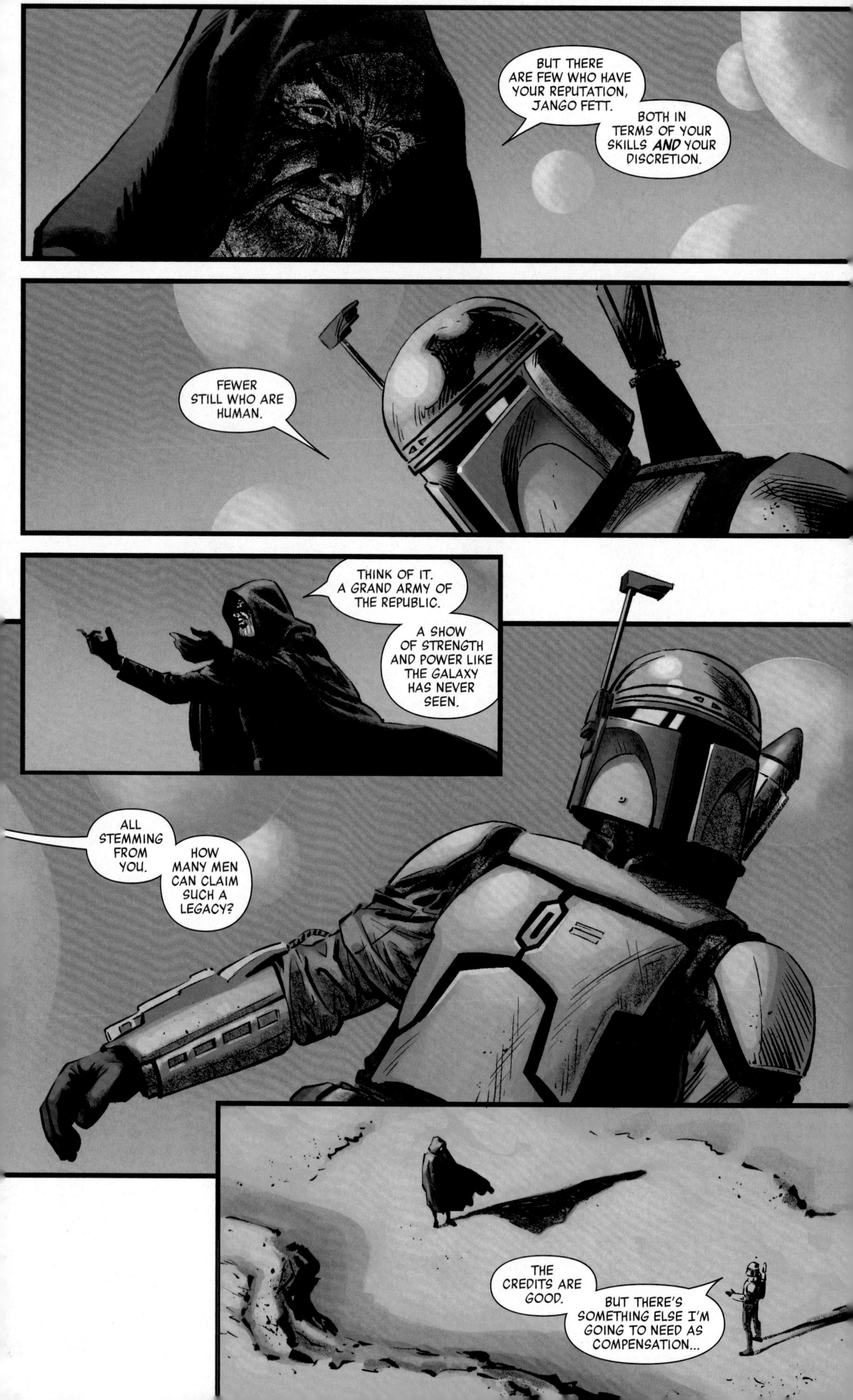
BUT THERE ARE FEW WHO HAVE YOUR REPUTATION, JANGO FETT.
BOTH IN TERMS OF YOUR SKILLS AND YOUR DISCRETION.
FEWER STILL WHO ARE HUMAN.
THINK OF IT. A GRAND ARMY OF THE REPUBLIC.
A SHOW OF STRENGTH AND POWER LIKE THE GALAXY HAS NEVER SEEN.
ALL STEMMING FROM YOU.
HOW MANY MEN CAN CLAIM SUCH A LEGACY?
THE CREDITS ARE GOOD.
BUT THERE'S SOMETHING ELSE I'M GOING TO NEED AS COMPENSATION...

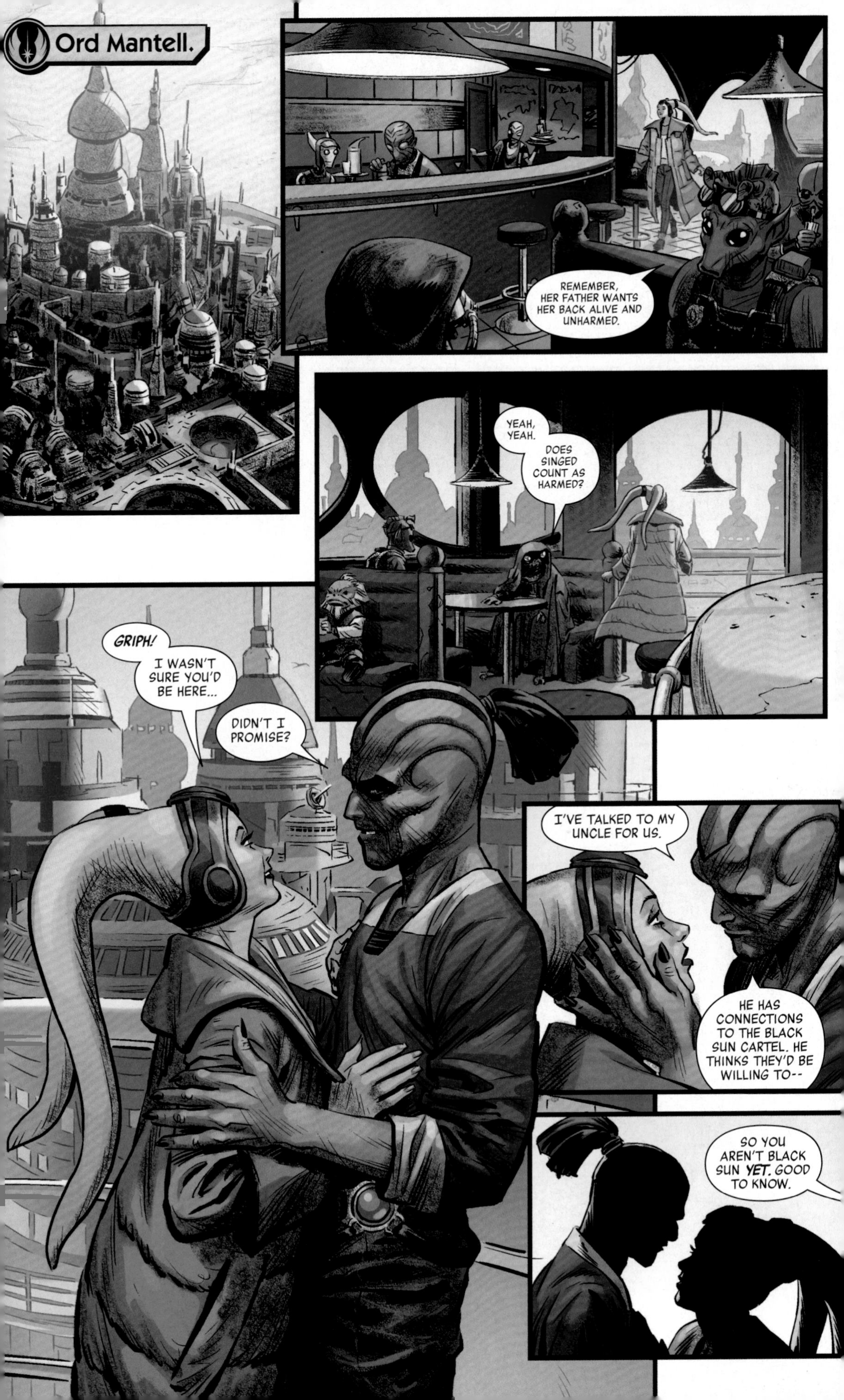
Ord Mantell.
REMEMBER, HER FATHER WANTS HER BACK ALIVE AND UNHARMED.
YEAH, YEAH.
DOES SINGED COUNT AS HARMED?
GRIPH!
I WASN'T SURE YOU'D BE HERE...
DIDN'T I PROMISE?
I'VE TALKED TO MY UNCLE FOR US.
HE HAS CONNECTIONS TO THE BLACK SUN CARTEL. HE THINKS THEY'D BE WILLING TO--
SO YOU AREN'T BLACK SUN *YET.* GOOD TO KNOW.

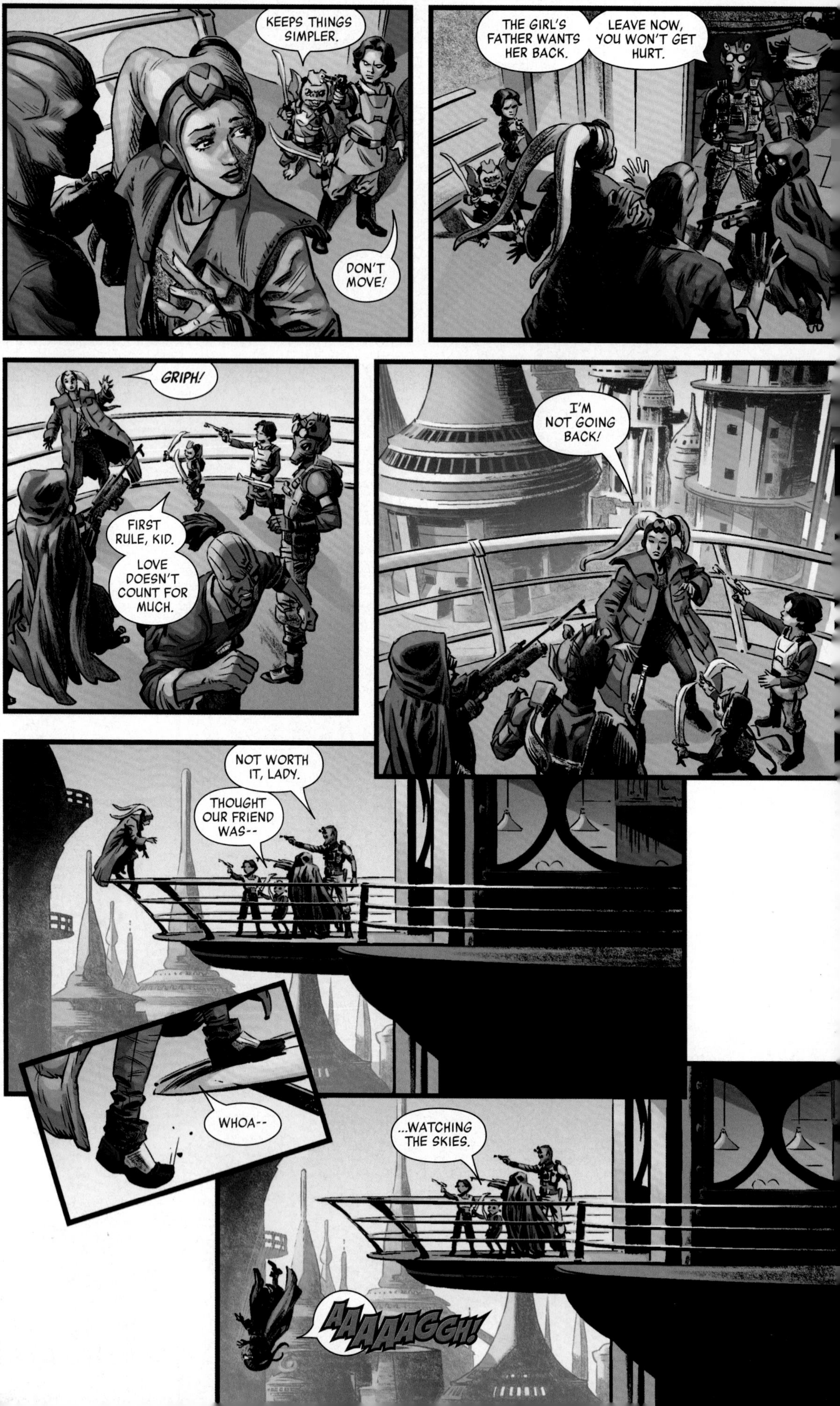
KEEPS THINGS SIMPLER.
DON'T MOVE!
THE GIRL'S FATHER WANTS HER BACK.
LEAVE NOW, YOU WON'T GET HURT.
GRIPH!
FIRST RULE, KID.
LOVE DOESN'T COUNT FOR MUCH.
I'M NOT GOING BACK!
NOT WORTH IT, LADY.
THOUGHT OUR FRIEND WAS--
WHOA--
...WATCHING THE SKIES.
AAAAAAGGH!

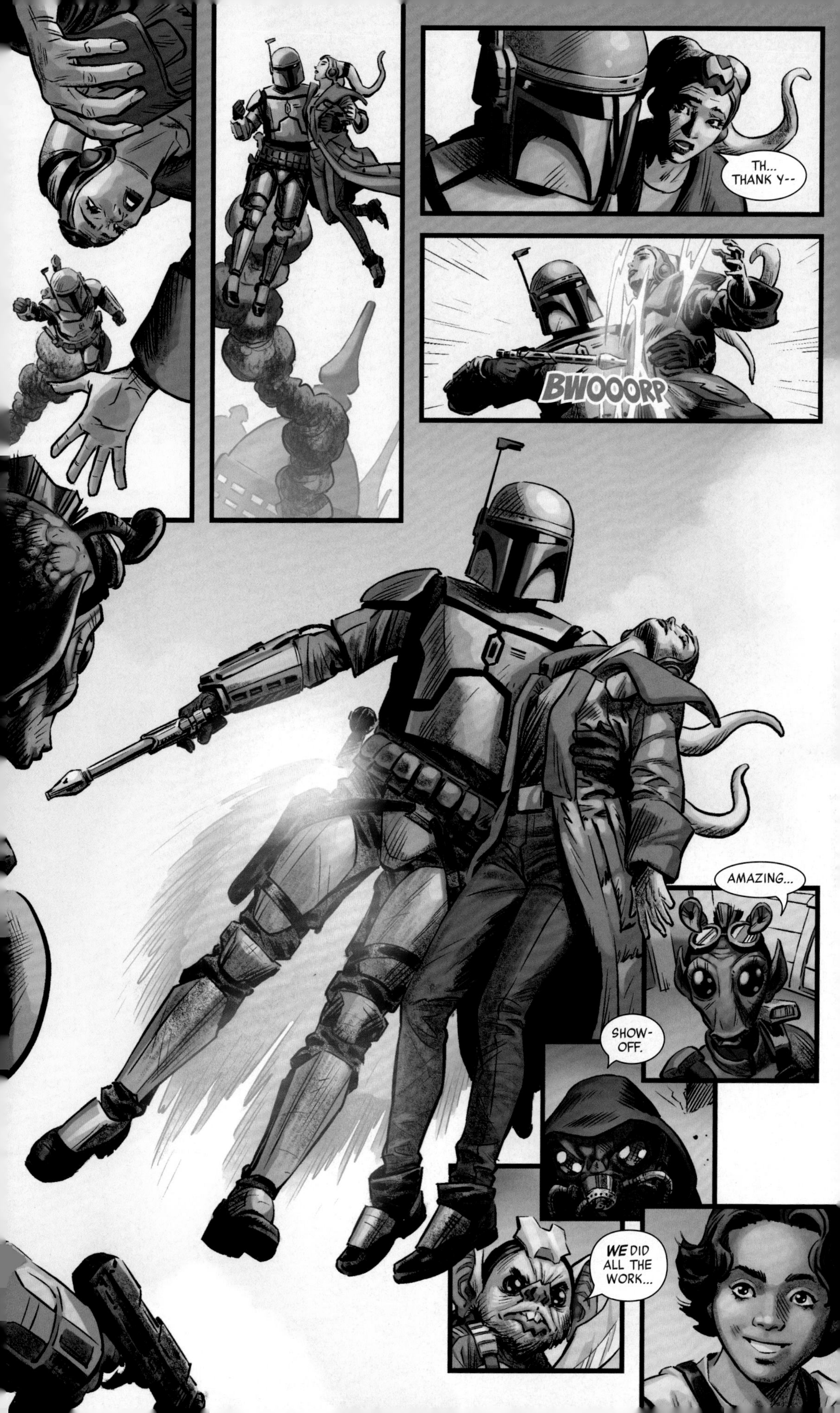
TH... THANK Y--
BWOOORP
AMAZING...
SHOW-OFF.
WE DID ALL THE WORK...

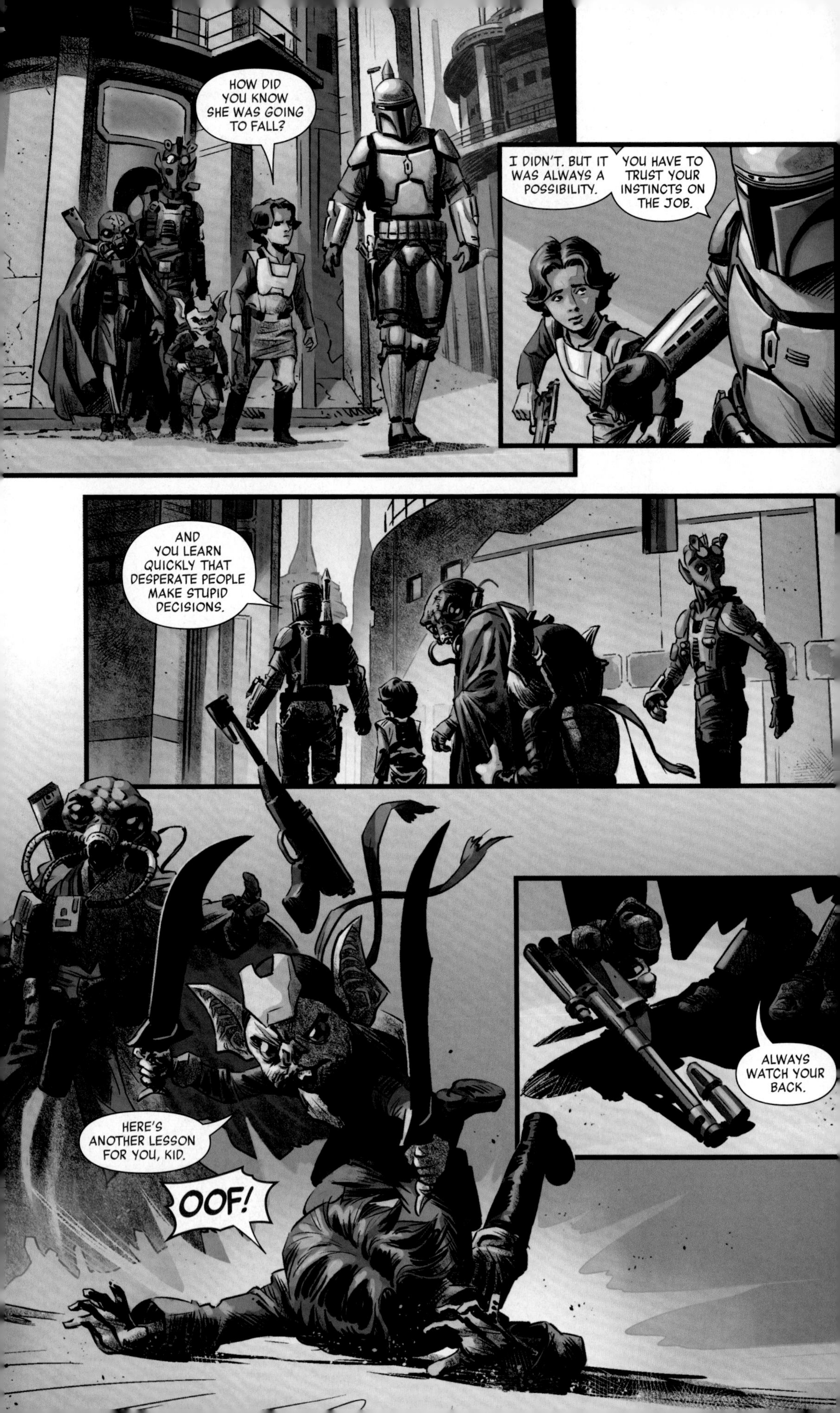
HOW DID YOU KNOW SHE WAS GOING TO FALL?
I DIDN'T. BUT IT WAS ALWAYS A POSSIBILITY.
YOU HAVE TO TRUST YOUR INSTINCTS ON THE JOB.
AND YOU LEARN QUICKLY THAT DESPERATE PEOPLE MAKE STUPID DECISIONS.
HERE'S ANOTHER LESSON FOR YOU, KID.
OOF!
ALWAYS WATCH YOUR BACK.

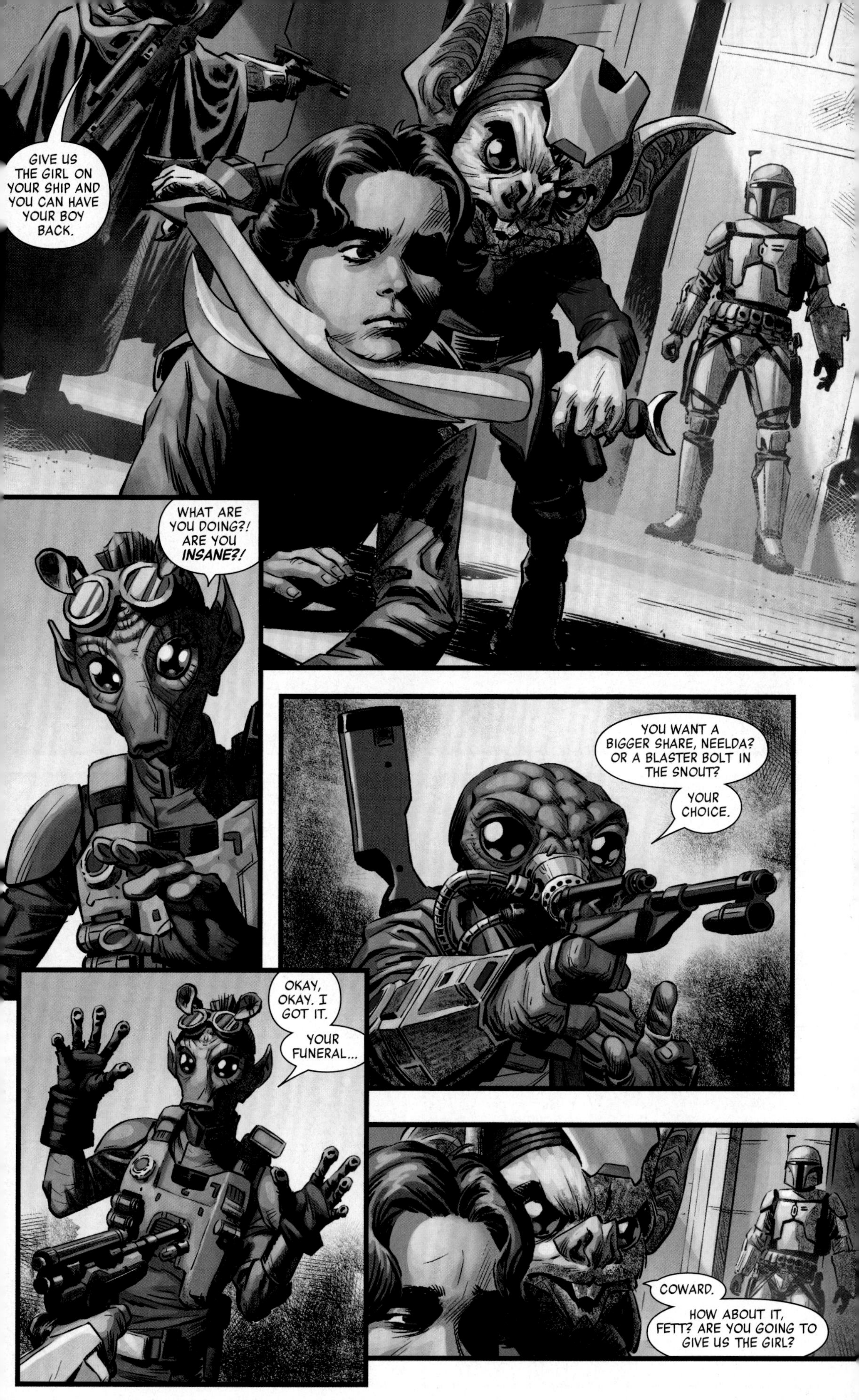

GIVE US THE GIRL ON YOUR SHIP AND YOU CAN HAVE YOUR BOY BACK.
WHAT ARE YOU DOING?! ARE YOU INSANE?!
YOU WANT A BIGGER SHARE, NEELDA? OR A BLASTER BOLT IN THE SNOUT?
YOUR CHOICE.
OKAY, OKAY. I GOT IT.
YOUR FUNERAL...
COWARD.
HOW ABOUT IT, FETT? ARE YOU GOING TO GIVE US THE GIRL?

"ARE YOU GOING TO SAVE YOUR SON?"

Kamino.
Before.

I DO BELIEVE THAT THIS ARMY WILL BE OUR FINEST CREATION YET.

NOT A SINGLE CLONE UNIT HAS FALLEN BELOW COMBAT PARAMETERS.

YOU MUST BE VERY PROUD.

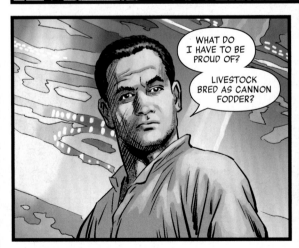

WHAT DO I HAVE TO BE PROUD OF?

LIVESTOCK BRED AS CANNON FODDER?

LIKE YOU SAID, THEY'RE YOUR CREATIONS.

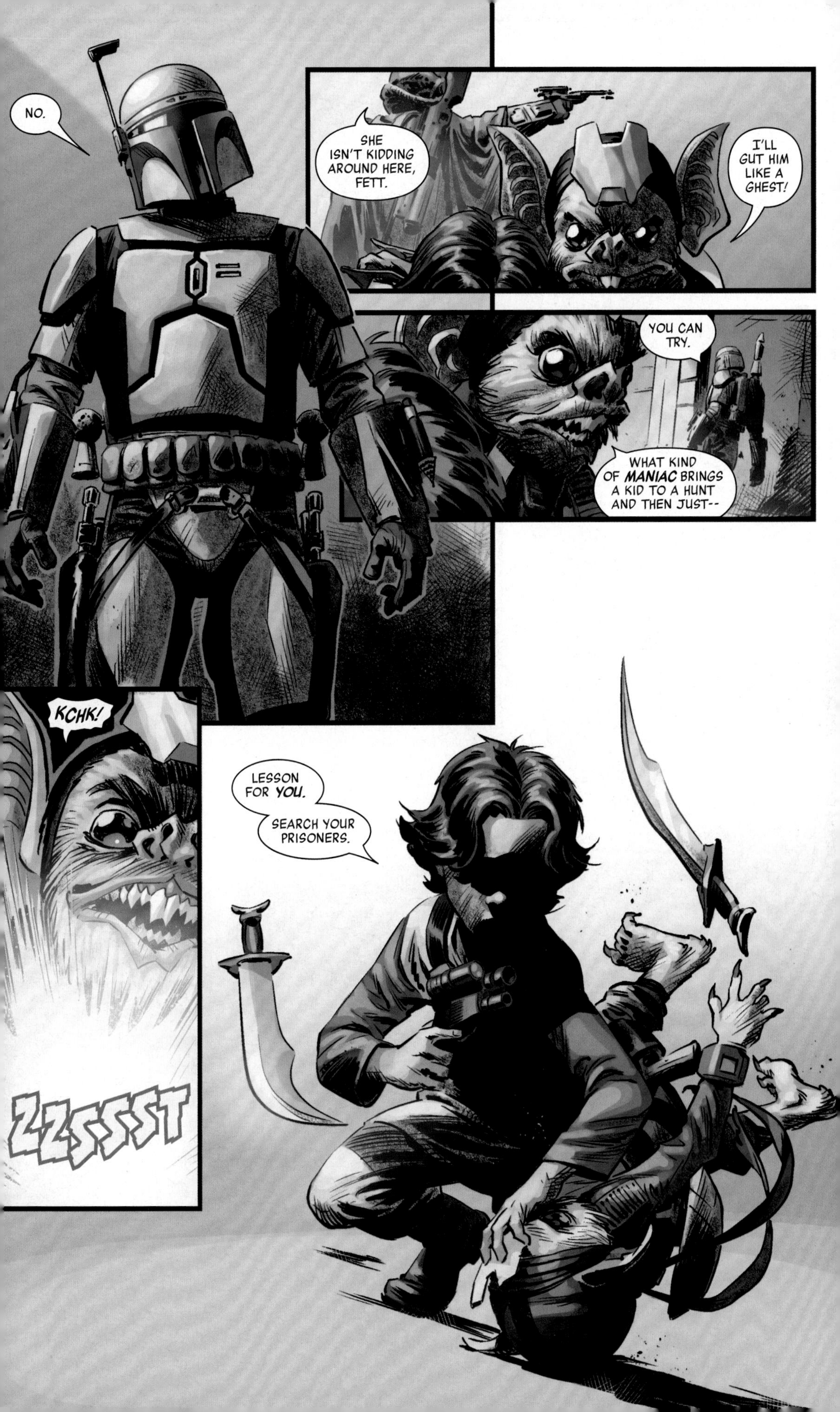

NO.
SHE ISN'T KIDDING AROUND HERE, FETT.
I'LL GUT HIM LIKE A GHEST!
YOU CAN TRY.
WHAT KIND OF MANIAC BRINGS A KID TO A HUNT AND THEN JUST--
KCHK!
ZZSSST
LESSON FOR YOU.
SEARCH YOUR PRISONERS.

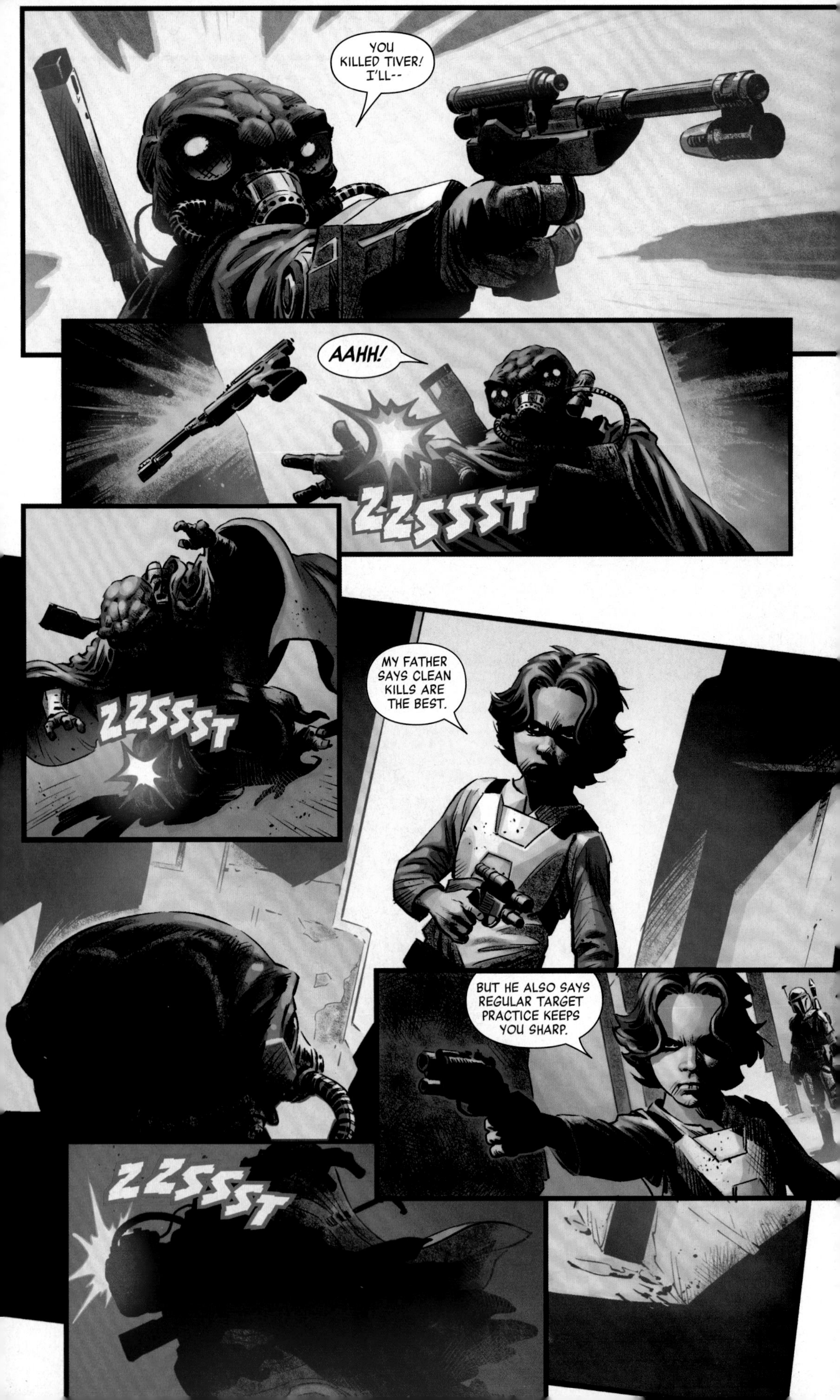
YOU KILLED TIVER! I'LL--
AAHH!
ZZSSST
ZZSSST
MY FATHER SAYS CLEAN KILLS ARE THE BEST.
BUT HE ALSO SAYS REGULAR TARGET PRACTICE KEEPS YOU SHARP.
ZZSSST

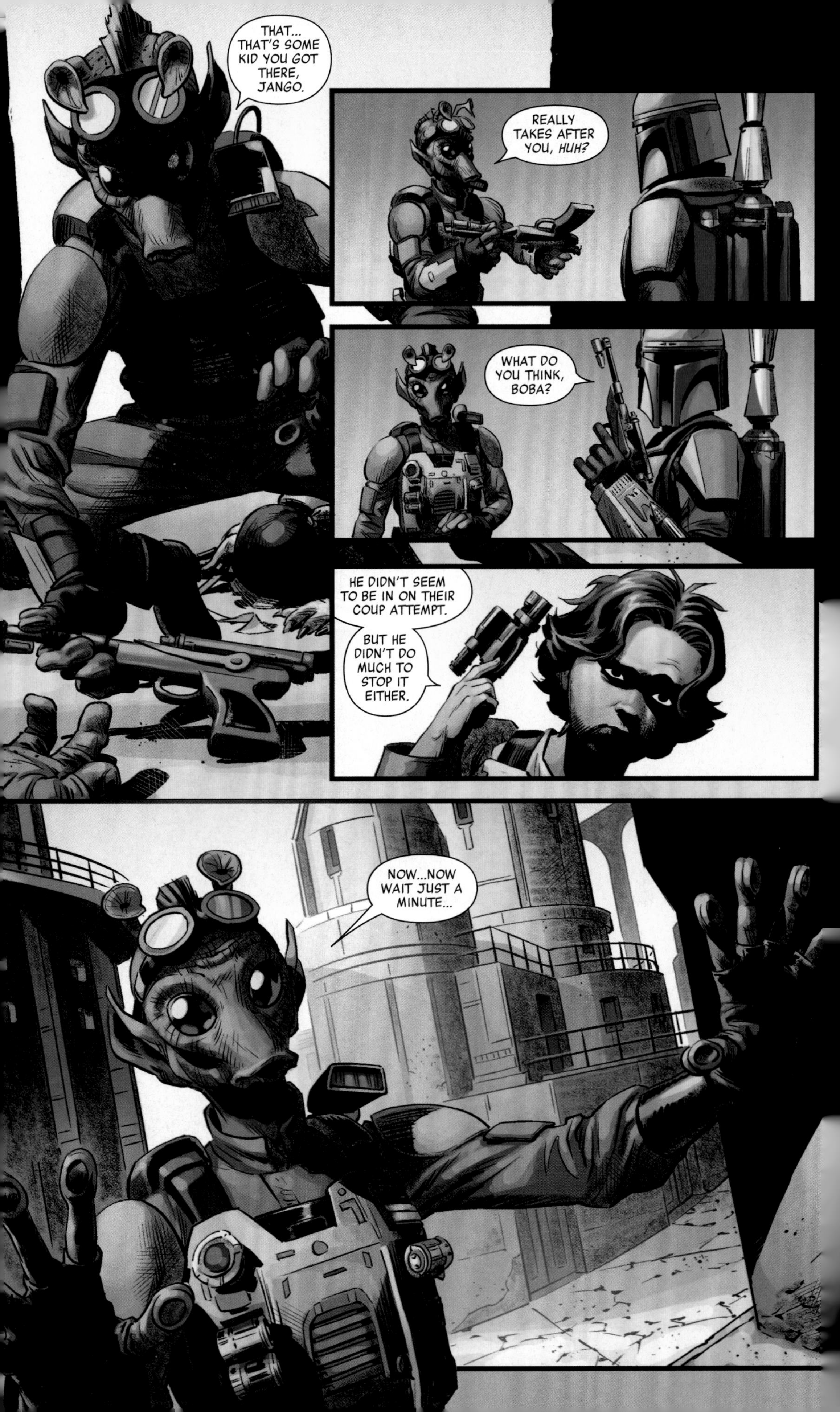
THAT... THAT'S SOME KID YOU GOT THERE, JANGO.
REALLY TAKES AFTER YOU, *HUH?*
WHAT DO YOU THINK, BOBA?
HE DIDN'T SEEM TO BE IN ON THEIR COUP ATTEMPT.
BUT HE DIDN'T DO MUCH TO STOP IT EITHER.
NOW...NOW WAIT JUST A MINUTE...

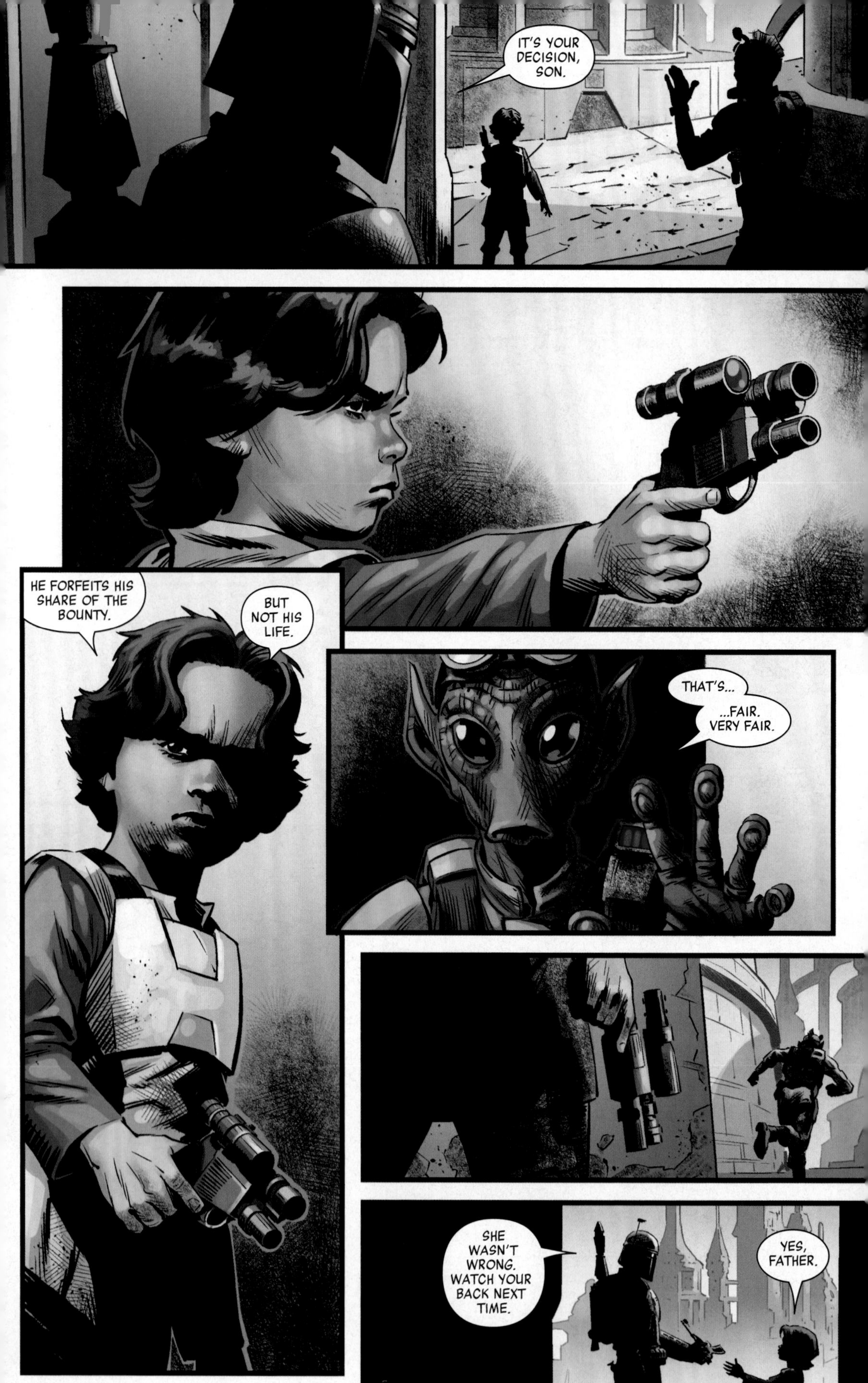
IT'S YOUR DECISION, SON.
HE FORFEITS HIS SHARE OF THE BOUNTY.
BUT NOT HIS LIFE.
THAT'S...
...FAIR. VERY FAIR.
SHE WASN'T WRONG. WATCH YOUR BACK NEXT TIME.
YES, FATHER.

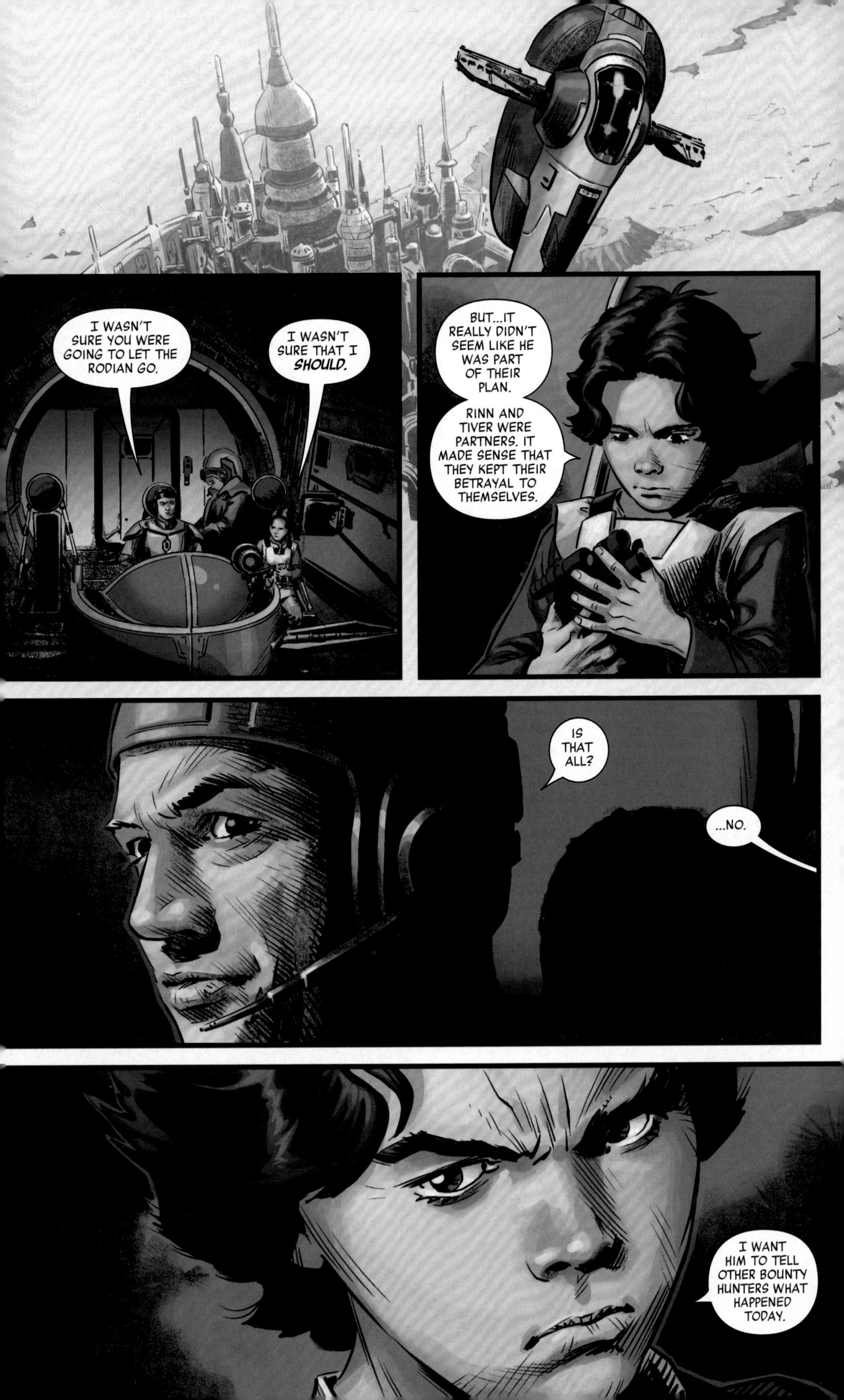

I WASN'T SURE YOU WERE GOING TO LET THE RODIAN GO.
I WASN'T SURE THAT I *SHOULD.*
BUT...IT REALLY DIDN'T SEEM LIKE HE WAS PART OF THEIR PLAN.
RINN AND TIVER WERE PARTNERS. IT MADE SENSE THAT THEY KEPT THEIR BETRAYAL TO THEMSELVES.
IS THAT ALL?
...NO.
I WANT HIM TO TELL OTHER BOUNTY HUNTERS WHAT HAPPENED TODAY.

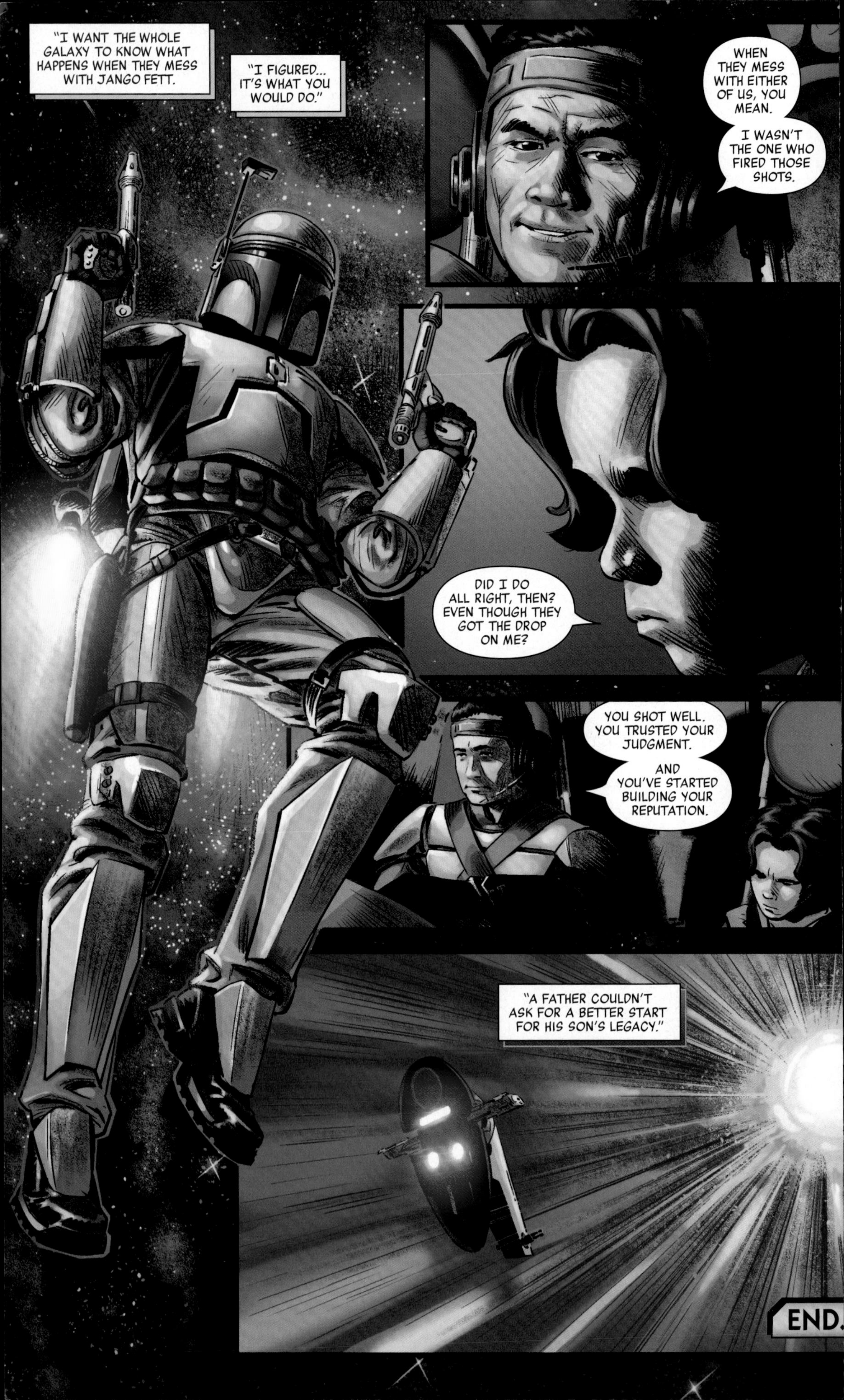
"I WANT THE WHOLE GALAXY TO KNOW WHAT HAPPENS WHEN THEY MESS WITH JANGO FETT.
"I FIGURED... IT'S WHAT YOU WOULD DO."
WHEN THEY MESS WITH EITHER OF US, YOU MEAN.
I WASN'T THE ONE WHO FIRED THOSE SHOTS.
DID I DO ALL RIGHT, THEN? EVEN THOUGH THEY GOT THE DROP ON ME?
YOU SHOT WELL. YOU TRUSTED YOUR JUDGMENT.
AND YOU'VE STARTED BUILDING YOUR REPUTATION.
"A FATHER COULDN'T ASK FOR A BETTER START FOR HIS SON'S LEGACY."
END.

JANGO FETT:
Bounty Hunter, Father, Unrivaled Legacy
By Bria LaVorgna

"I'm just a simple man trying to make my way in the universe."

For a supposedly simple man, Jango Fett left behind quite a legacy. No other *Star Wars* character can say there were over a million identical soldiers created from his genetic code and that he had a son who one day becomes the best bounty hunter in the galaxy just like his father before him. And he did it all with just a single film appearance.

In 2002, the Prequel Trilogy pulled back the curtains on the origins of a fan-favorite character from the Original Trilogy: Boba Fett. While Legends books published in the 1990s had dabbled in his past, most fans just thought of him as being a really cool-looking bounty hunter. *Attack of the Clones* let us meet not only a very young version of Boba but also his father, Jango. It's almost ironic how we now know so much about Boba's origin and yet so little about Jango Fett, as his own background is still shrouded in mystery.

One thing we do know? Jango Fett isn't even Mandalorian. He might wear their armor--and the distinctive diamond in his armor inspired *The Clone Wars* designers for Mandalore's architecture--but that doesn't make Jango one of them. "The idea that

Jango Fett is not a Mandalorian…that's something that comes directly from George [Lucas]," Dave Filoni explained in a behind-the-scenes featurette for *The Clone Wars* about creating Mandalore. "There was this early assumption that Jango must be a Mandalorian… He's always just referred to as a bounty hunter [in *Attack of the Clones*]." Jango claims to be from the Mandalorian planet Concord Dawn, but whether this is true remains to be seen. At the very least, the Prime Minister of Mandalore dismissed him as just being a "common bounty hunter" when Obi-Wan brought him up.

Origin story aside, Jango's reputation as an efficient and honorable bounty hunter grew until Darth Tyranus recruited him to be the genetic template for a clone army. In return, Jango asked for only two things: a very large stack of credits and an unaltered clone whom he would raise as his son. A decade later, Count Dooku was back with another request: assassinate Senator Amidala. It was a request that would ultimately lead to Jango losing his head in the arena on Geonosis, falling in battle against Jedi Master Mace Windu.

Regardless of whether Jango had the right to wear his armor, it's become integral to our image of the character and to how we picture Mandalorians.

Initially, his armor scheme was intended to be white like Boba Fett's original concept art as well as the clone troopers in *Attack of the Clones* but was changed during production to the now-iconic silver-and-blue to help make him stand out. As anyone who's worn Mandalorian armor can tell you, the costume did present some unique challenges for actor Temuera Morrison while filming. "You couldn't see anything!" Morrison said, recounting his time in the *beskar* armor plates. "I'm standing there and can't see or hear anything because [my helmet] was fogged up from my breathing, and I'm the idiot standing there doing nothing while they're yelling out 'Action!'"

Whether he's a simple man is very much up for debate, but Jango Fett *is* proof of one simple concept: You don't have to be part of something greater than you in the galaxy. You just need to be good at your job, look cool doing it and the fans will remember you forever.

All quotes sourced from behind the scenes featurettes from The Clone Wars *and written interviews with StarWars.com Australia.*

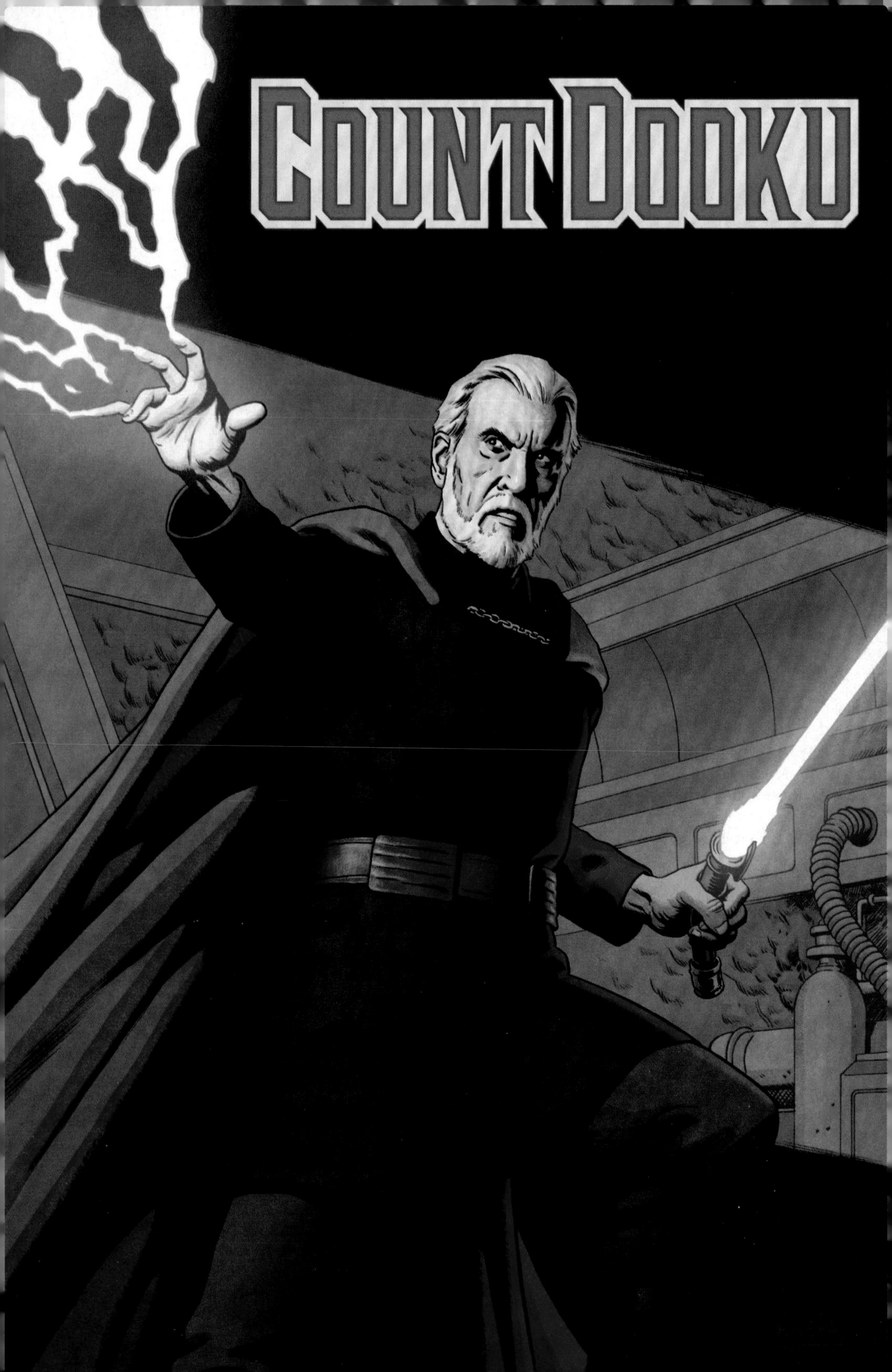
COUNT DOOKU

"THE COST"

Count Dooku was one of the wisest and most revered Jedi in the galaxy. But during his long years of service he became disgusted by the rampant corruption poisoning the Republic and disillusioned with the archaic and dogmatic views of the Jedi. Finally, Dooku left the Order to follow a new path in the hope of saving the galaxy from itself.

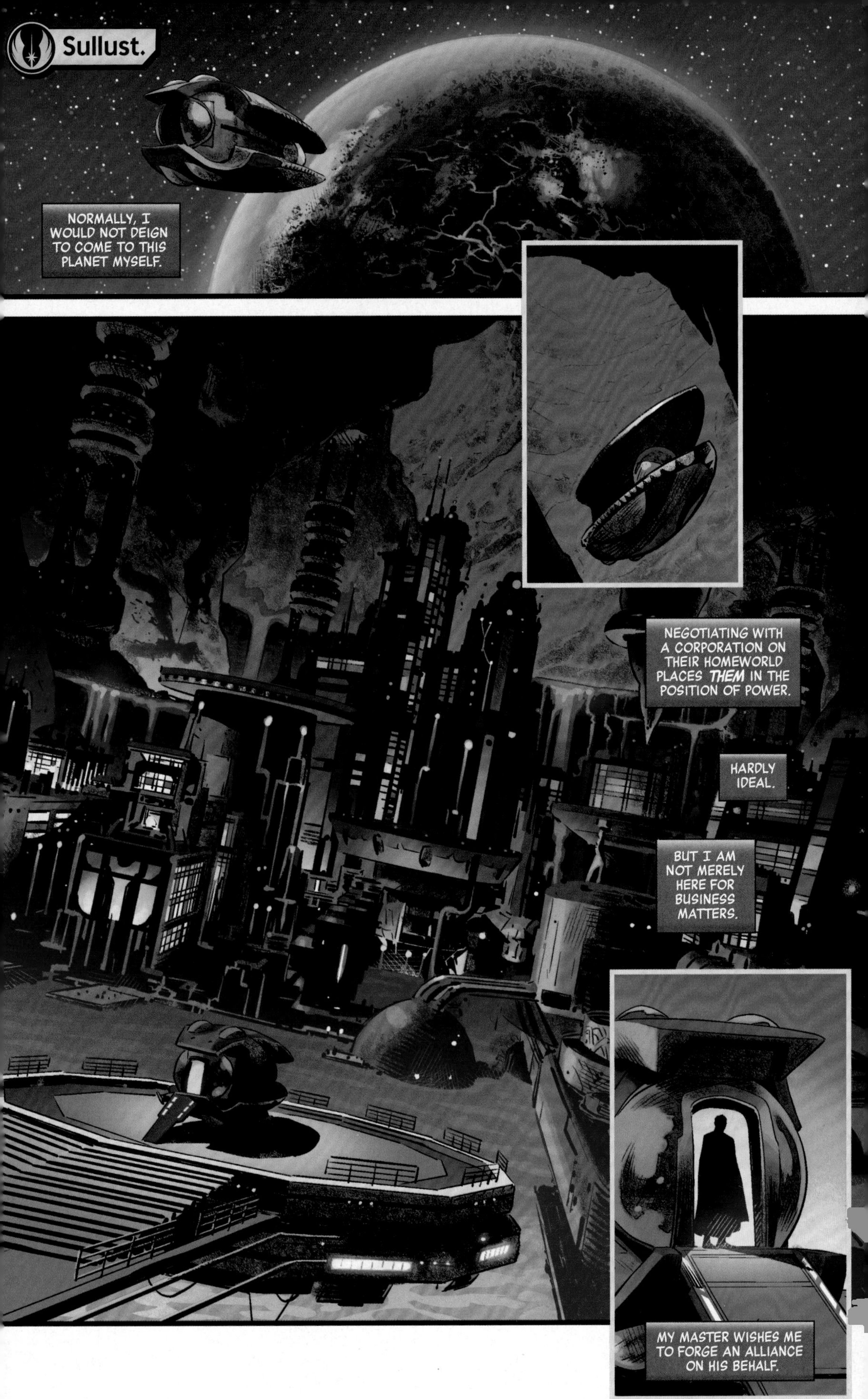
Sullust.
NORMALLY, I WOULD NOT DEIGN TO COME TO THIS PLANET MYSELF.
NEGOTIATING WITH A CORPORATION ON THEIR HOMEWORLD PLACES *THEM* IN THE POSITION OF POWER.
HARDLY IDEAL.
BUT I AM NOT MERELY HERE FOR BUSINESS MATTERS.
MY MASTER WISHES ME TO FORGE AN ALLIANCE ON HIS BEHALF.

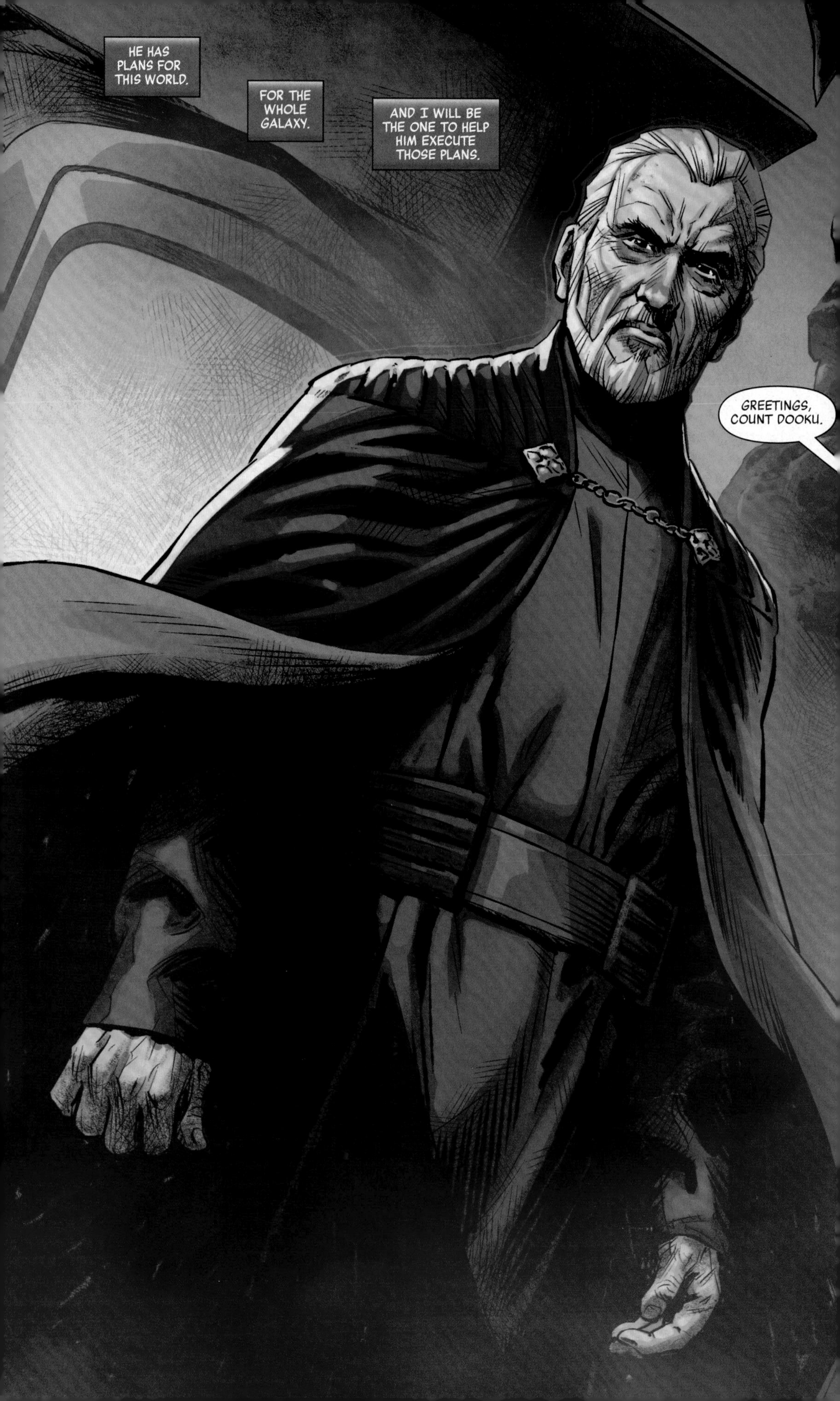
HE HAS PLANS FOR THIS WORLD.
FOR THE WHOLE GALAXY.
AND I WILL BE THE ONE TO HELP HIM EXECUTE THOSE PLANS.
GREETINGS, COUNT DOOKU.

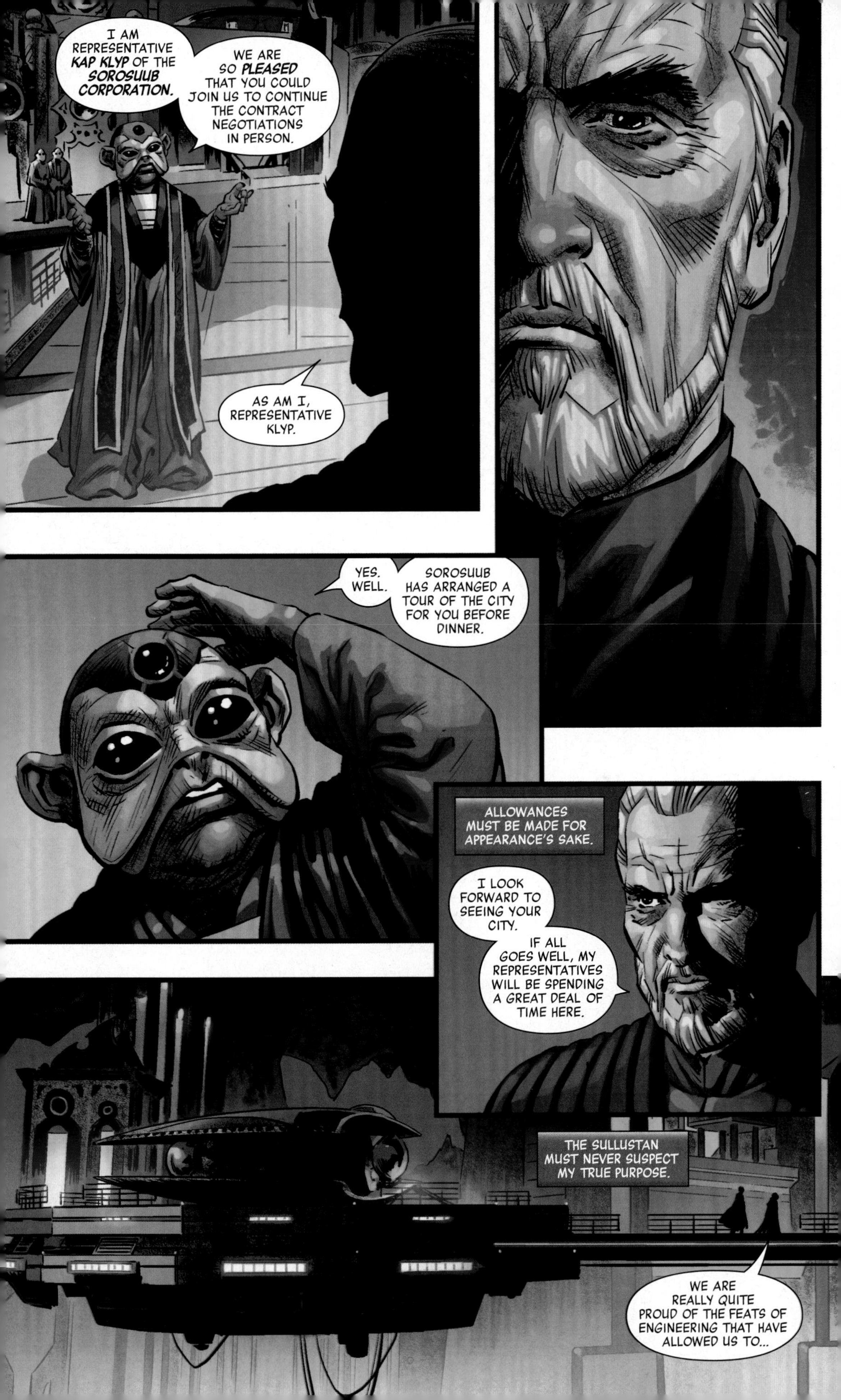
I AM REPRESENTATIVE KAP KLYP OF THE SOROSUUB CORPORATION.
WE ARE SO PLEASED THAT YOU COULD JOIN US TO CONTINUE THE CONTRACT NEGOTIATIONS IN PERSON.
AS AM I, REPRESENTATIVE KLYP.
YES. WELL.
SOROSUUB HAS ARRANGED A TOUR OF THE CITY FOR YOU BEFORE DINNER.
ALLOWANCES MUST BE MADE FOR APPEARANCE'S SAKE.
I LOOK FORWARD TO SEEING YOUR CITY.
IF ALL GOES WELL, MY REPRESENTATIVES WILL BE SPENDING A GREAT DEAL OF TIME HERE.
THE SULLUSTAN MUST NEVER SUSPECT MY TRUE PURPOSE.
WE ARE REALLY QUITE PROUD OF THE FEATS OF ENGINEERING THAT HAVE ALLOWED US TO...

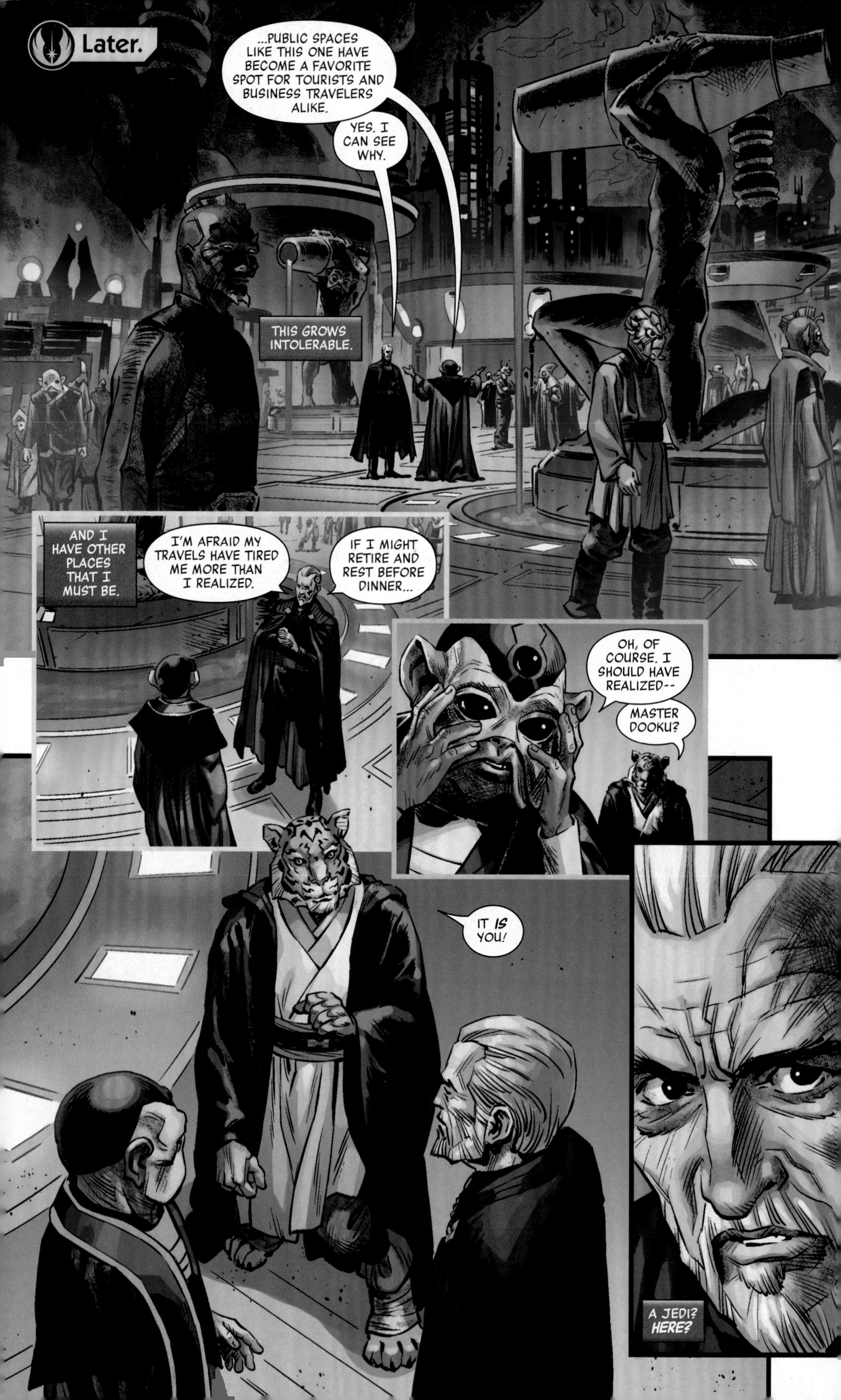
Later.
...PUBLIC SPACES LIKE THIS ONE HAVE BECOME A FAVORITE SPOT FOR TOURISTS AND BUSINESS TRAVELERS ALIKE.
YES. I CAN SEE WHY.
THIS GROWS INTOLERABLE.
AND I HAVE OTHER PLACES THAT I MUST BE.
I'M AFRAID MY TRAVELS HAVE TIRED ME MORE THAN I REALIZED.
IF I MIGHT RETIRE AND REST BEFORE DINNER...
OH, OF COURSE. I SHOULD HAVE REALIZED--
MASTER DOOKU?
IT *IS* YOU!
A JEDI? *HERE?*

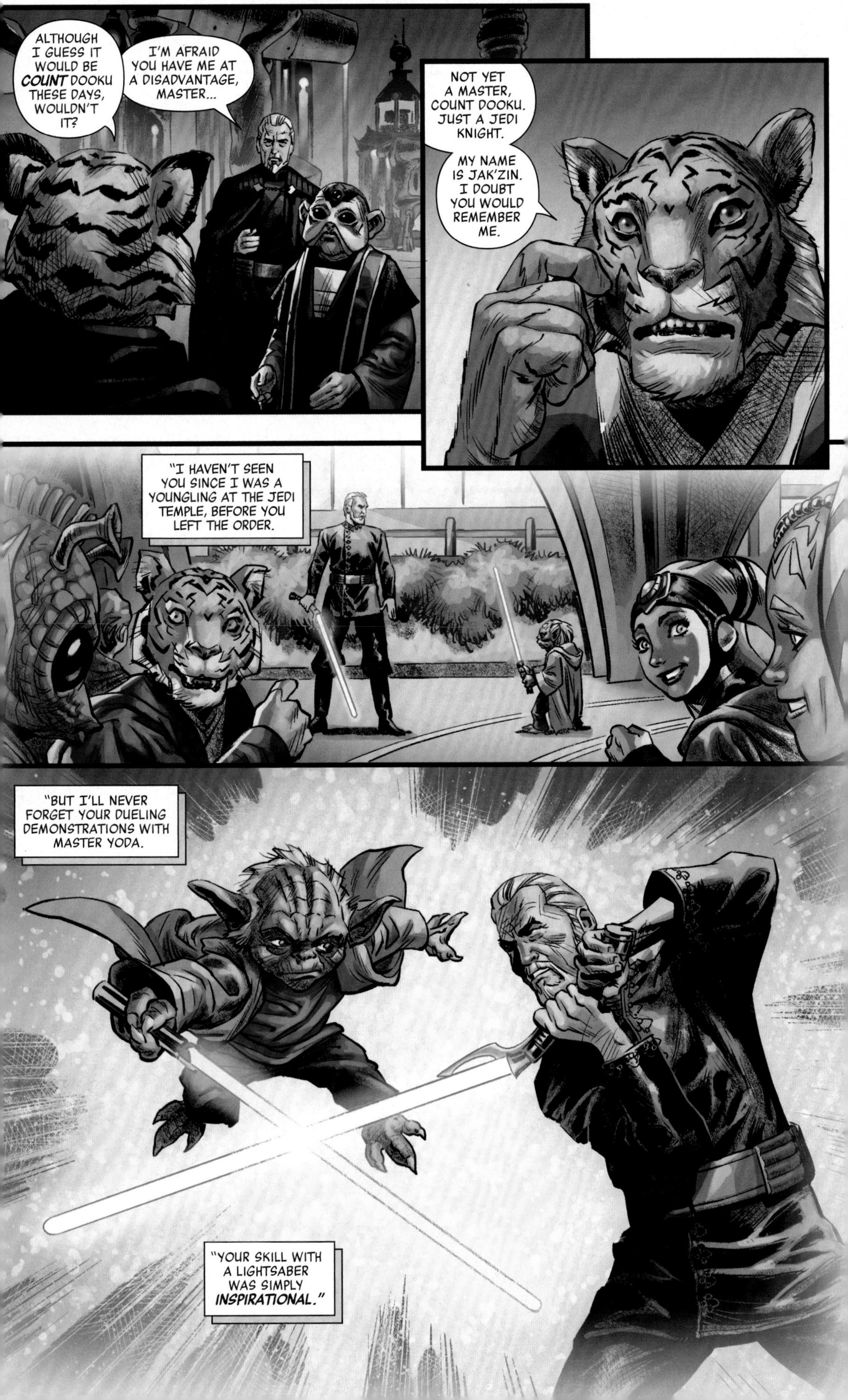

ALTHOUGH I GUESS IT WOULD BE COUNT DOOKU THESE DAYS, WOULDN'T IT?
I'M AFRAID YOU HAVE ME AT A DISADVANTAGE, MASTER...
NOT YET A MASTER, COUNT DOOKU. JUST A JEDI KNIGHT.
MY NAME IS JAK'ZIN. I DOUBT YOU WOULD REMEMBER ME.
"I HAVEN'T SEEN YOU SINCE I WAS A YOUNGLING AT THE JEDI TEMPLE, BEFORE YOU LEFT THE ORDER.
"BUT I'LL NEVER FORGET YOUR DUELING DEMONSTRATIONS WITH MASTER YODA.
"YOUR SKILL WITH A LIGHTSABER WAS SIMPLY INSPIRATIONAL."

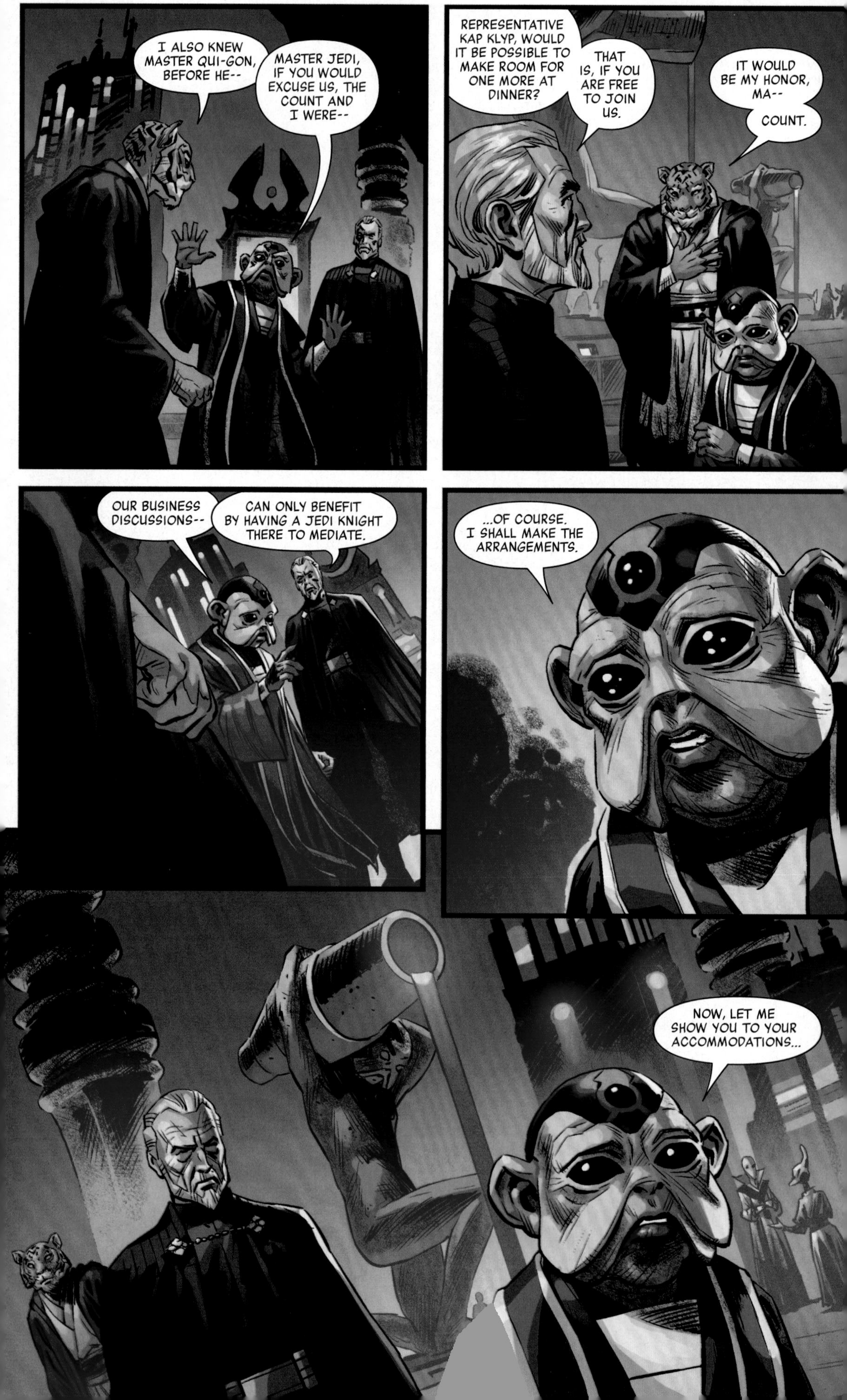
I ALSO KNEW MASTER QUI-GON, BEFORE HE--
MASTER JEDI, IF YOU WOULD EXCUSE US, THE COUNT AND I WERE--
REPRESENTATIVE KAP KLYP, WOULD IT BE POSSIBLE TO MAKE ROOM FOR ONE MORE AT DINNER?
THAT IS, IF YOU ARE FREE TO JOIN US.
IT WOULD BE MY HONOR, MA--
COUNT.
OUR BUSINESS DISCUSSIONS--
CAN ONLY BENEFIT BY HAVING A JEDI KNIGHT THERE TO MEDIATE.
...OF COURSE. I SHALL MAKE THE ARRANGEMENTS.
NOW, LET ME SHOW YOU TO YOUR ACCOMMODATIONS...

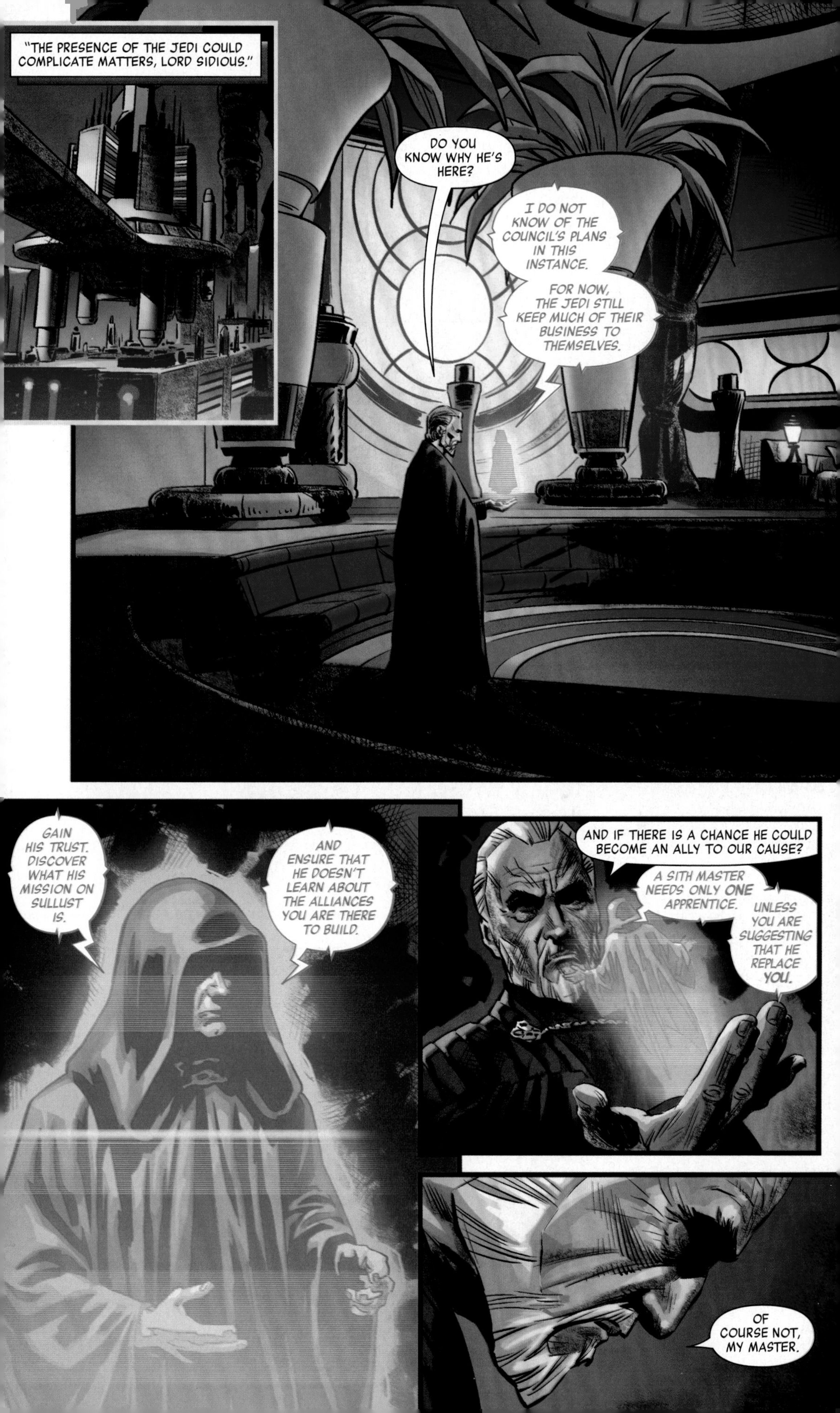
"THE PRESENCE OF THE JEDI COULD COMPLICATE MATTERS, LORD SIDIOUS."
DO YOU KNOW WHY HE'S HERE?
I DO NOT KNOW OF THE COUNCIL'S PLANS IN THIS INSTANCE.
FOR NOW, THE JEDI STILL KEEP MUCH OF THEIR BUSINESS TO THEMSELVES.
GAIN HIS TRUST. DISCOVER WHAT HIS MISSION ON SULLUST IS.
AND ENSURE THAT HE DOESN'T LEARN ABOUT THE ALLIANCES YOU ARE THERE TO BUILD.
AND IF THERE IS A CHANCE HE COULD BECOME AN ALLY TO OUR CAUSE?
A SITH MASTER NEEDS ONLY ONE APPRENTICE.
UNLESS YOU ARE SUGGESTING THAT HE REPLACE YOU.
OF COURSE NOT, MY MASTER.

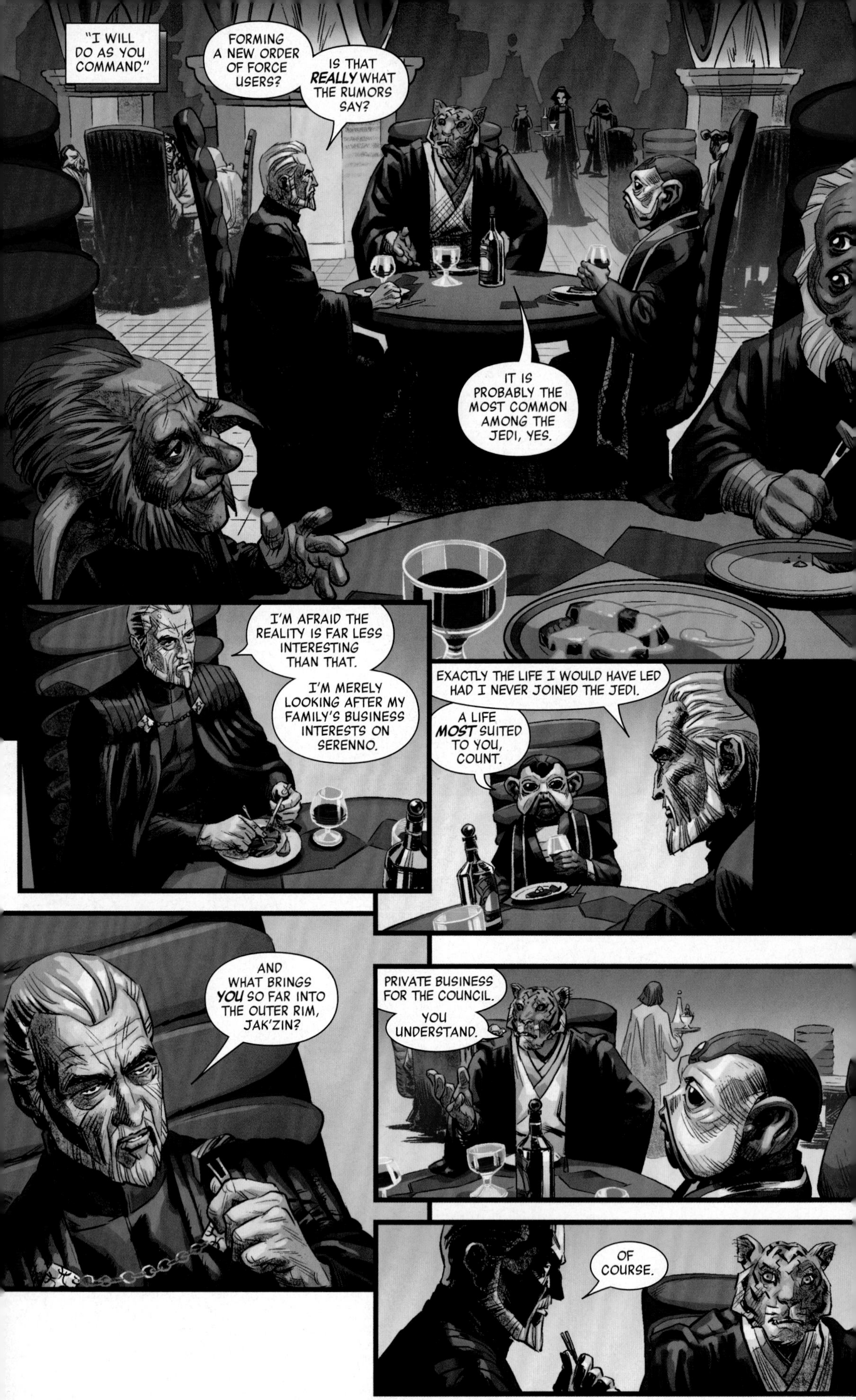
"I WILL DO AS YOU COMMAND."
FORMING A NEW ORDER OF FORCE USERS?
IS THAT REALLY WHAT THE RUMORS SAY?
IT IS PROBABLY THE MOST COMMON AMONG THE JEDI, YES.
I'M AFRAID THE REALITY IS FAR LESS INTERESTING THAN THAT.
I'M MERELY LOOKING AFTER MY FAMILY'S BUSINESS INTERESTS ON SERENNO.
EXACTLY THE LIFE I WOULD HAVE LED HAD I NEVER JOINED THE JEDI.
A LIFE MOST SUITED TO YOU, COUNT.
AND WHAT BRINGS YOU SO FAR INTO THE OUTER RIM, JAK'ZIN?
PRIVATE BUSINESS FOR THE COUNCIL.
YOU UNDERSTAND.
OF COURSE.

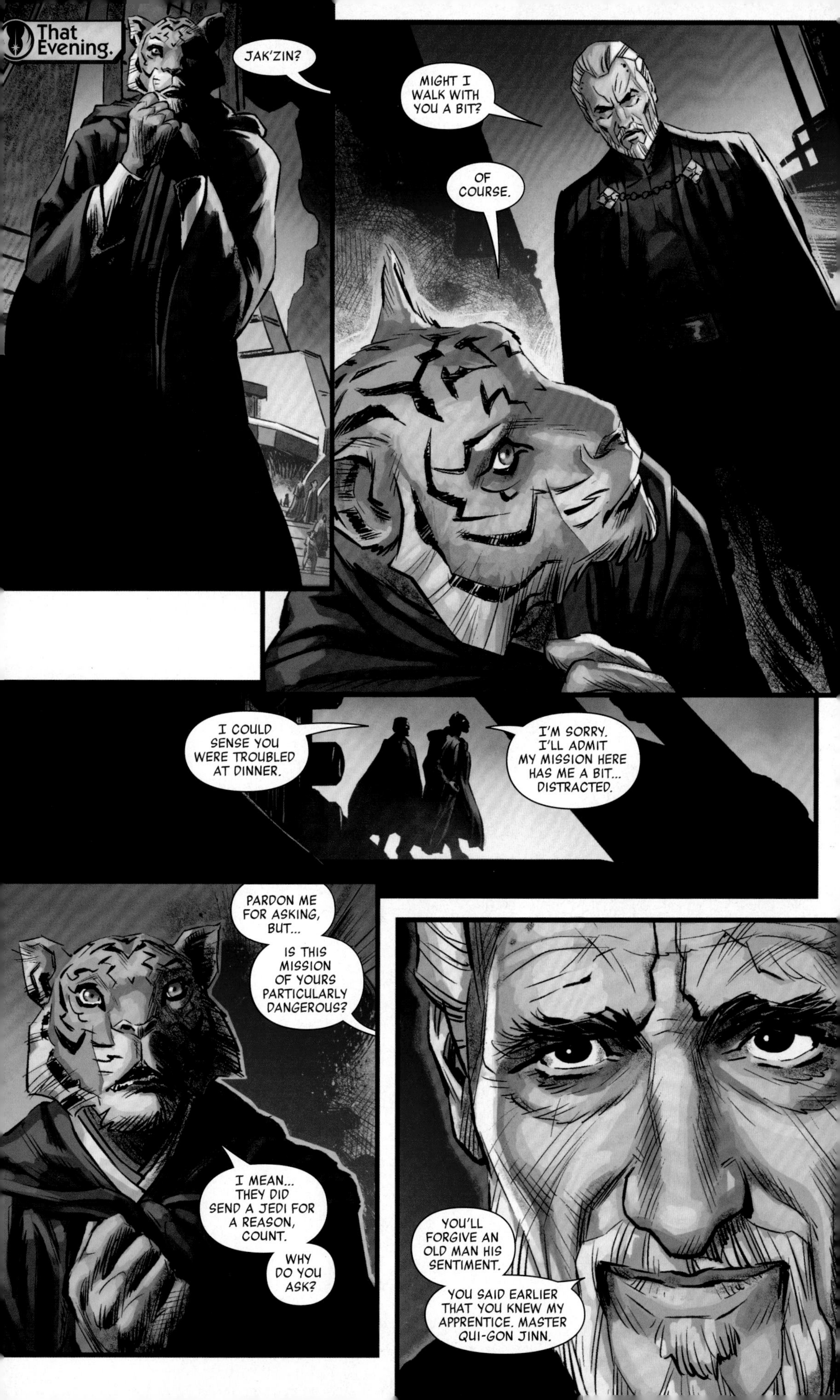
That Evening.
JAK'ZIN?
MIGHT I WALK WITH YOU A BIT?
OF COURSE.
I COULD SENSE YOU WERE TROUBLED AT DINNER.
I'M SORRY. I'LL ADMIT MY MISSION HERE HAS ME A BIT... DISTRACTED.
PARDON ME FOR ASKING, BUT...
IS THIS MISSION OF YOURS PARTICULARLY DANGEROUS?
I MEAN... THEY DID SEND A JEDI FOR A REASON, COUNT.
WHY DO YOU ASK?
YOU'LL FORGIVE AN OLD MAN HIS SENTIMENT.
YOU SAID EARLIER THAT YOU KNEW MY APPRENTICE. MASTER QUI-GON JINN.

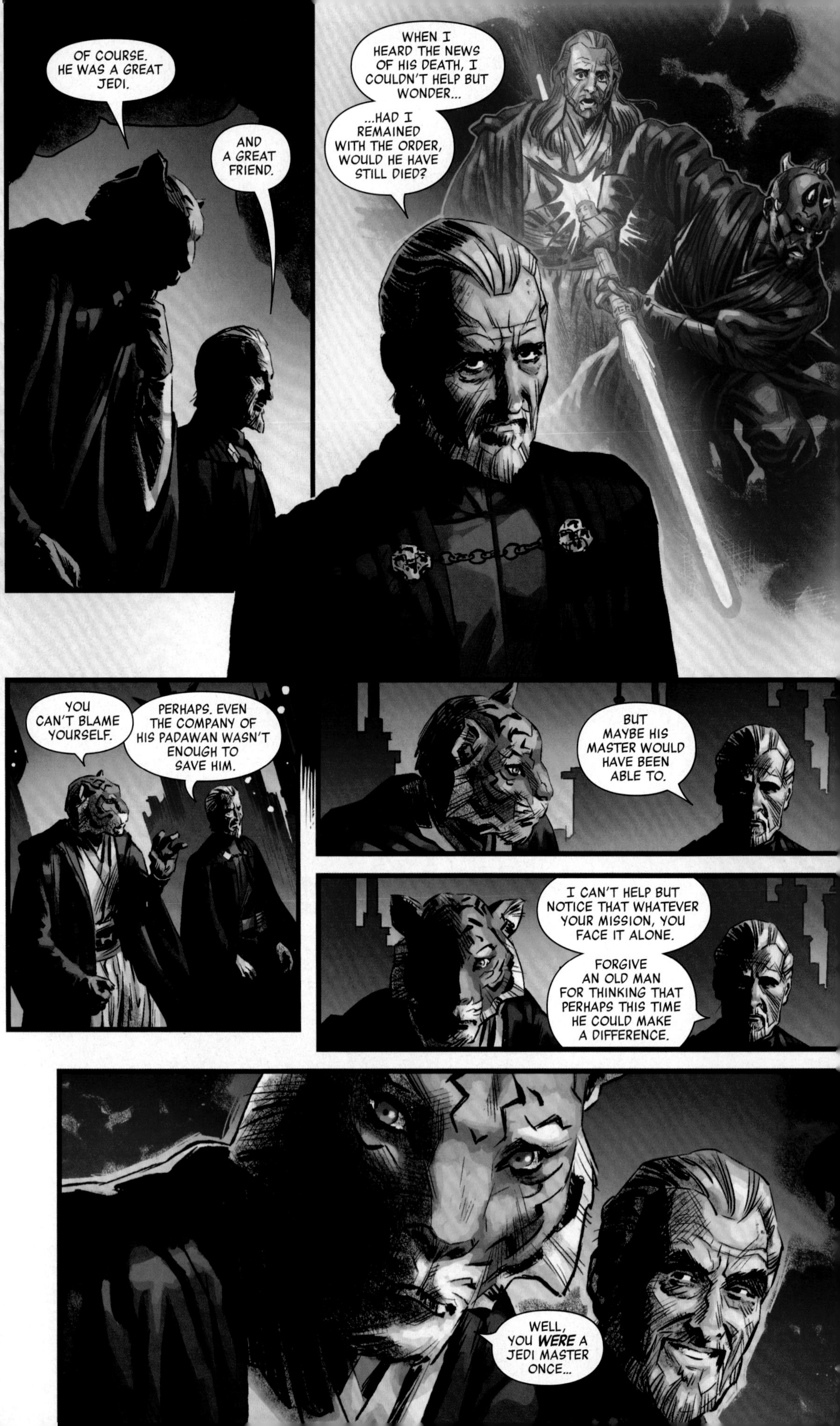
OF COURSE. HE WAS A GREAT JEDI.
AND A GREAT FRIEND.
WHEN I HEARD THE NEWS OF HIS DEATH, I COULDN'T HELP BUT WONDER...
...HAD I REMAINED WITH THE ORDER, WOULD HE HAVE STILL DIED?
YOU CAN'T BLAME YOURSELF.
PERHAPS. EVEN THE COMPANY OF HIS PADAWAN WASN'T ENOUGH TO SAVE HIM.
BUT MAYBE HIS MASTER WOULD HAVE BEEN ABLE TO.
I CAN'T HELP BUT NOTICE THAT WHATEVER YOUR MISSION, YOU FACE IT ALONE.
FORGIVE AN OLD MAN FOR THINKING THAT PERHAPS THIS TIME HE COULD MAKE A DIFFERENCE.
WELL, YOU WERE A JEDI MASTER ONCE...

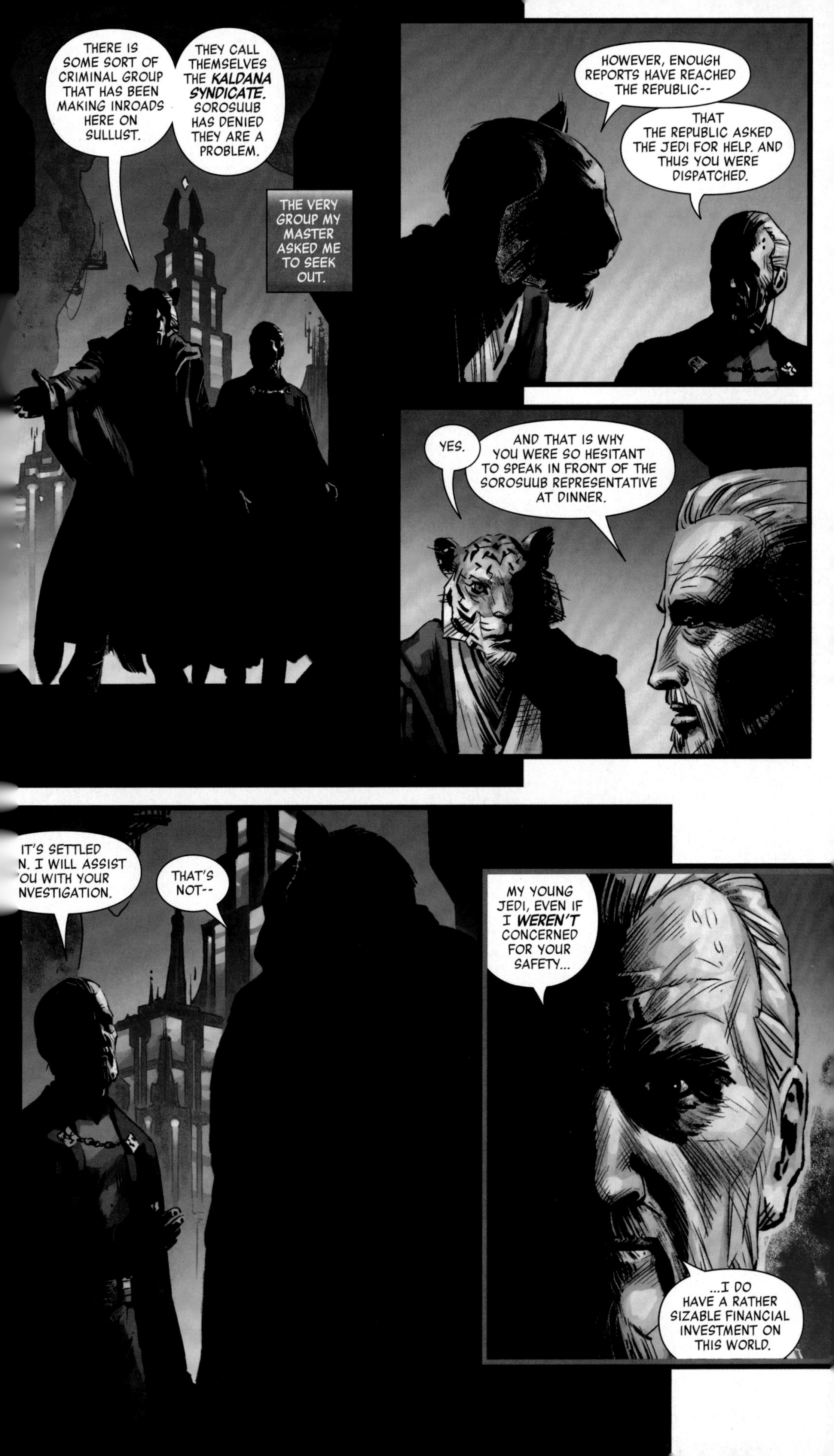
THERE IS SOME SORT OF CRIMINAL GROUP THAT HAS BEEN MAKING INROADS HERE ON SULLUST.
THEY CALL THEMSELVES THE ***KALDANA SYNDICATE.*** SOROSUUB HAS DENIED THEY ARE A PROBLEM.
THE VERY GROUP MY MASTER ASKED ME TO SEEK OUT.
HOWEVER, ENOUGH REPORTS HAVE REACHED THE REPUBLIC--
THAT THE REPUBLIC ASKED THE JEDI FOR HELP. AND THUS YOU WERE DISPATCHED.
YES.
AND THAT IS WHY YOU WERE SO HESITANT TO SPEAK IN FRONT OF THE SOROSUUB REPRESENTATIVE AT DINNER.
IT'S SETTLED N. I WILL ASSIST OU WITH YOUR NVESTIGATION.
THAT'S NOT--
MY YOUNG JEDI, EVEN IF I ***WEREN'T*** CONCERNED FOR YOUR SAFETY...
...I DO HAVE A RATHER SIZABLE FINANCIAL INVESTMENT ON THIS WORLD.

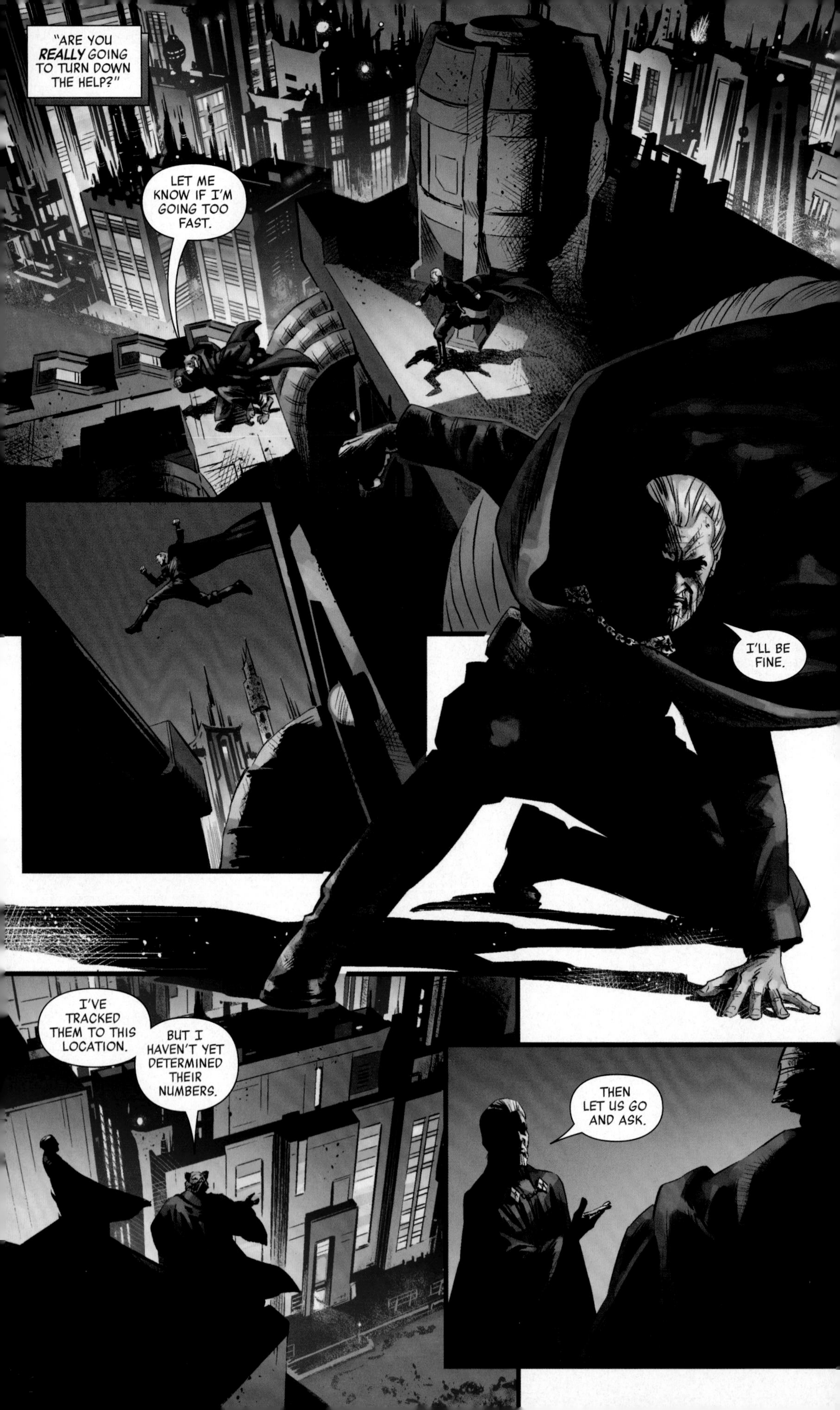
"ARE YOU REALLY GOING TO TURN DOWN THE HELP?"
LET ME KNOW IF I'M GOING TOO FAST.
I'LL BE FINE.
I'VE TRACKED THEM TO THIS LOCATION.
BUT I HAVEN'T YET DETERMINED THEIR NUMBERS.
THEN LET US GO AND ASK.

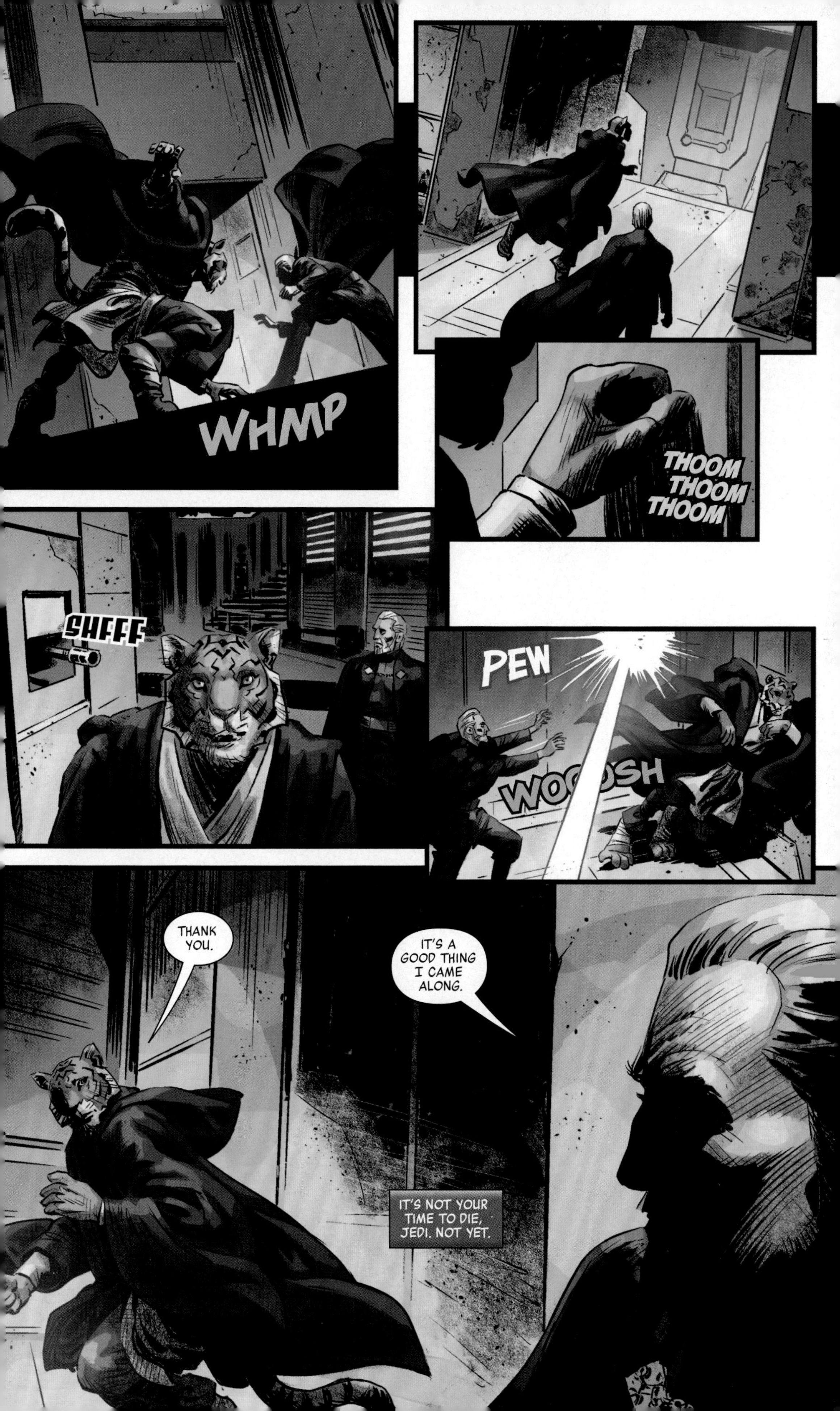
WHMP
THOOM THOOM THOOM
SHFFF
PEW
WOOOSH
THANK YOU.
IT'S A GOOD THING I CAME ALONG.
IT'S NOT YOUR TIME TO DIE, JEDI. NOT YET.

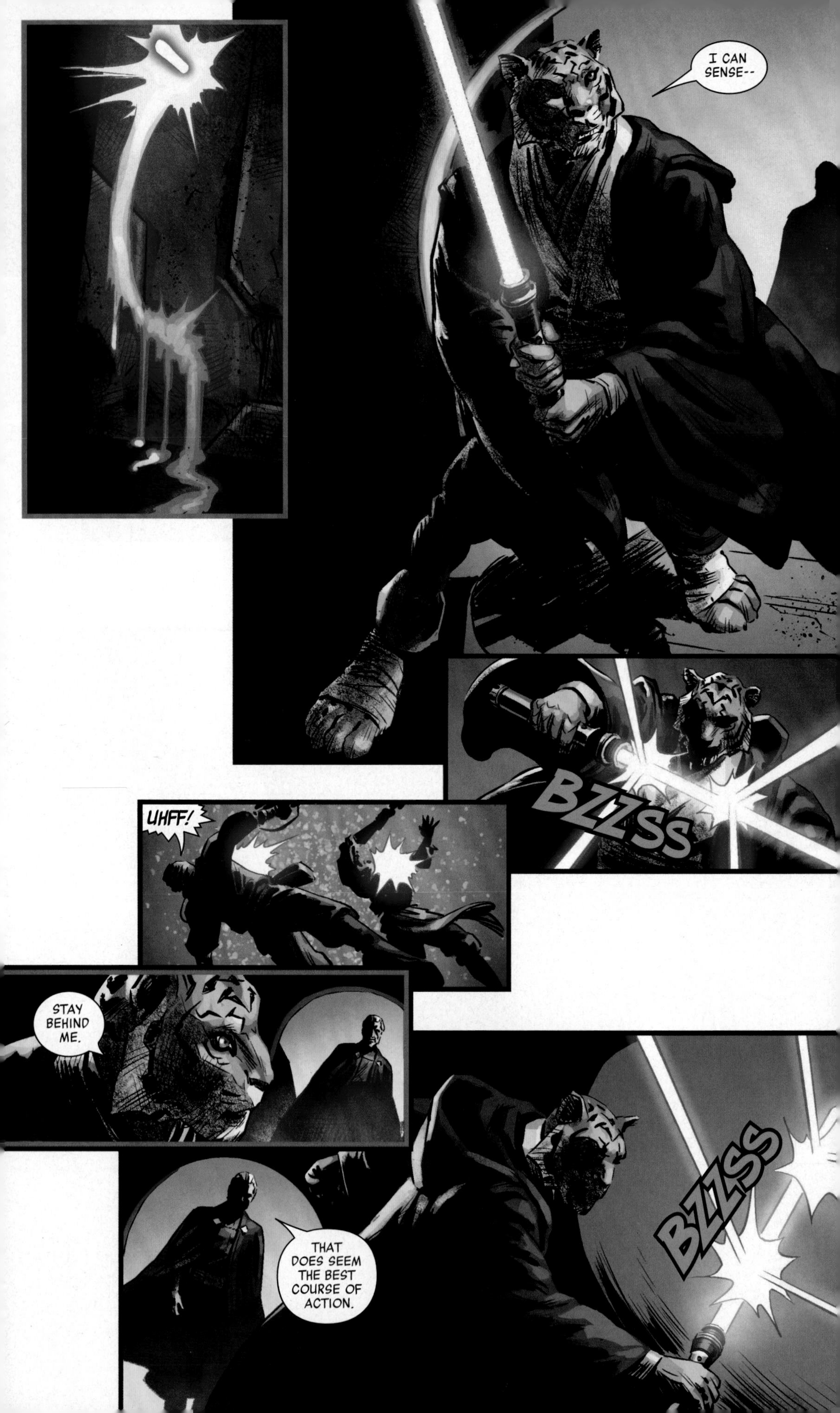
I CAN SENSE--
BZZSS
UHFF!
STAY BEHIND ME.
THAT DOES SEEM THE BEST COURSE OF ACTION.
BZZSS

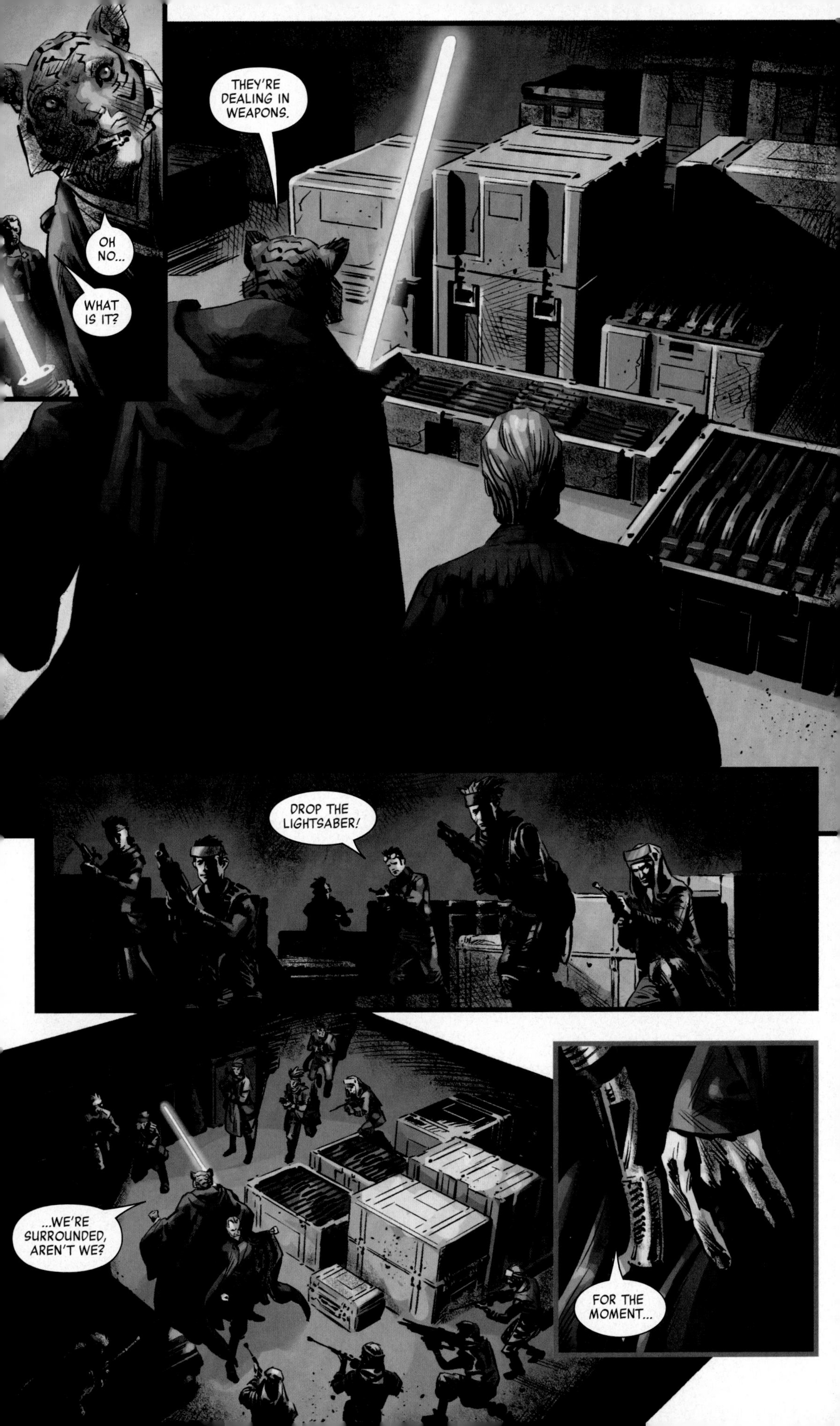
THEY'RE DEALING IN WEAPONS.
OH NO...
WHAT IS IT?
DROP THE LIGHTSABER!
...WE'RE SURROUNDED, AREN'T WE?
FOR THE MOMENT...

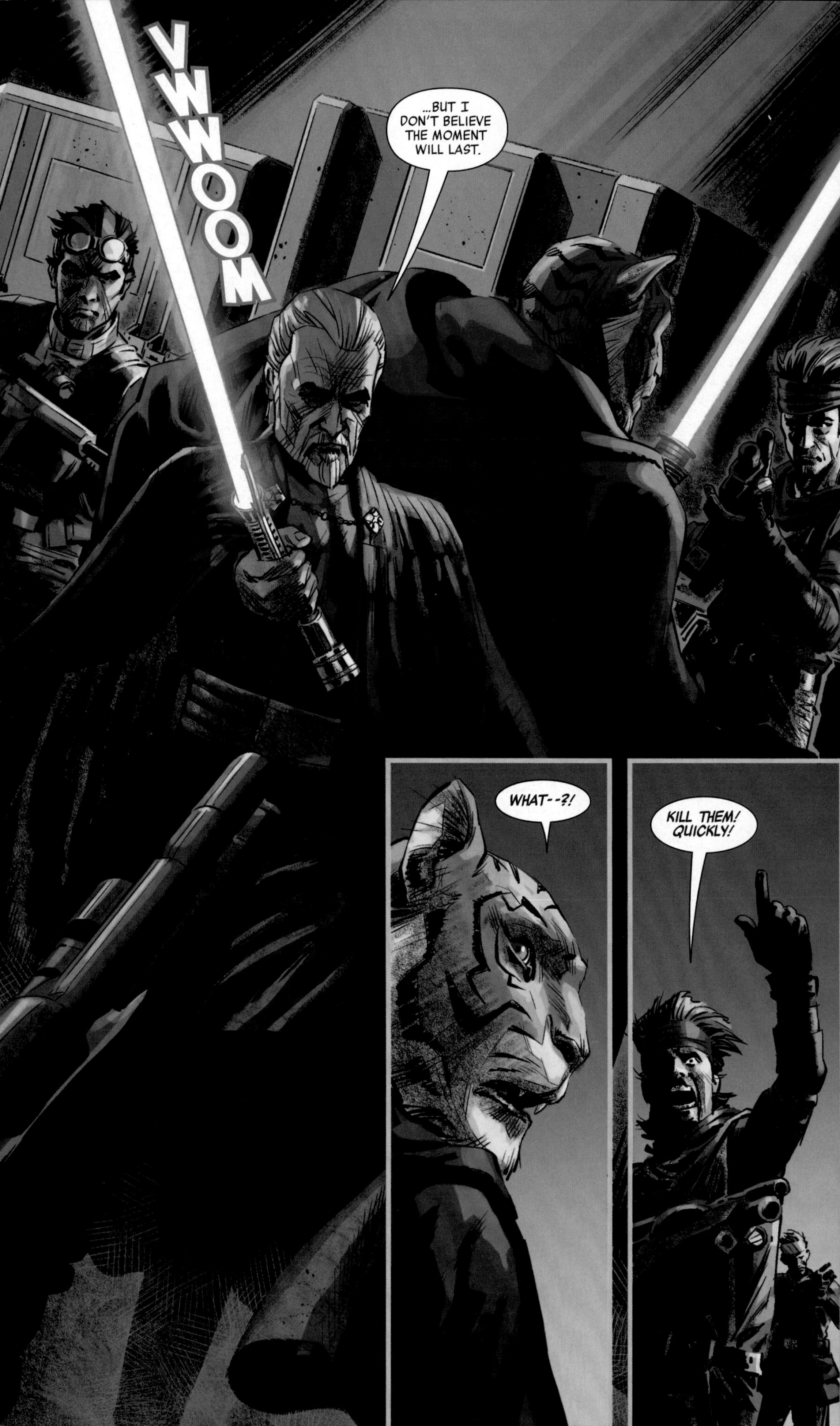
VWWOOM
...BUT I DON'T BELIEVE THE MOMENT WILL LAST.
WHAT--?!
KILL THEM! QUICKLY!

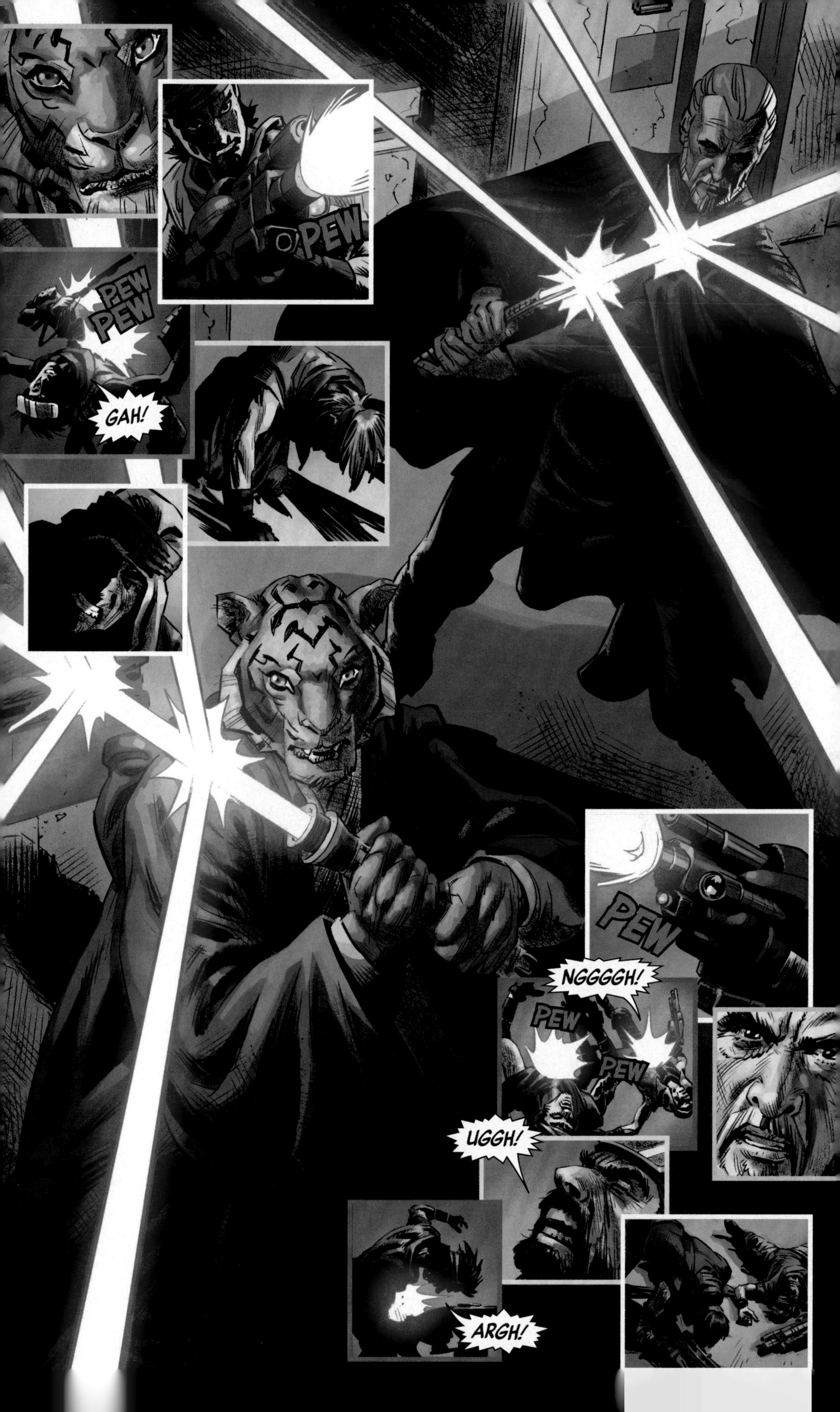
PEW
PEW
PEW
GAH!
PEW
NGGGGH!
PEW
PEW
UGGH!
ARGH!

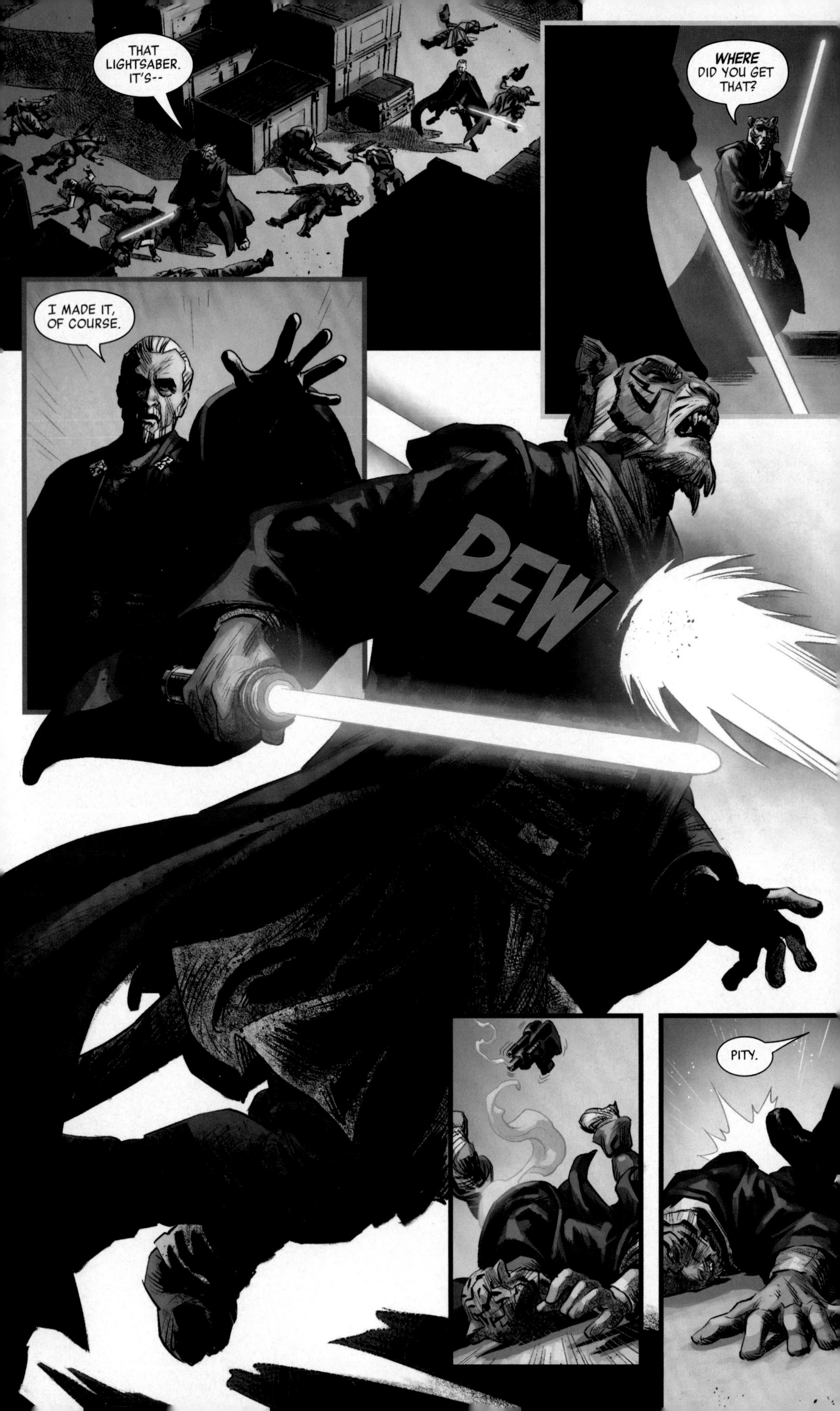
THAT LIGHTSABER. IT'S--
WHERE DID YOU GET THAT?
I MADE IT, OF COURSE.
PEW
PITY.

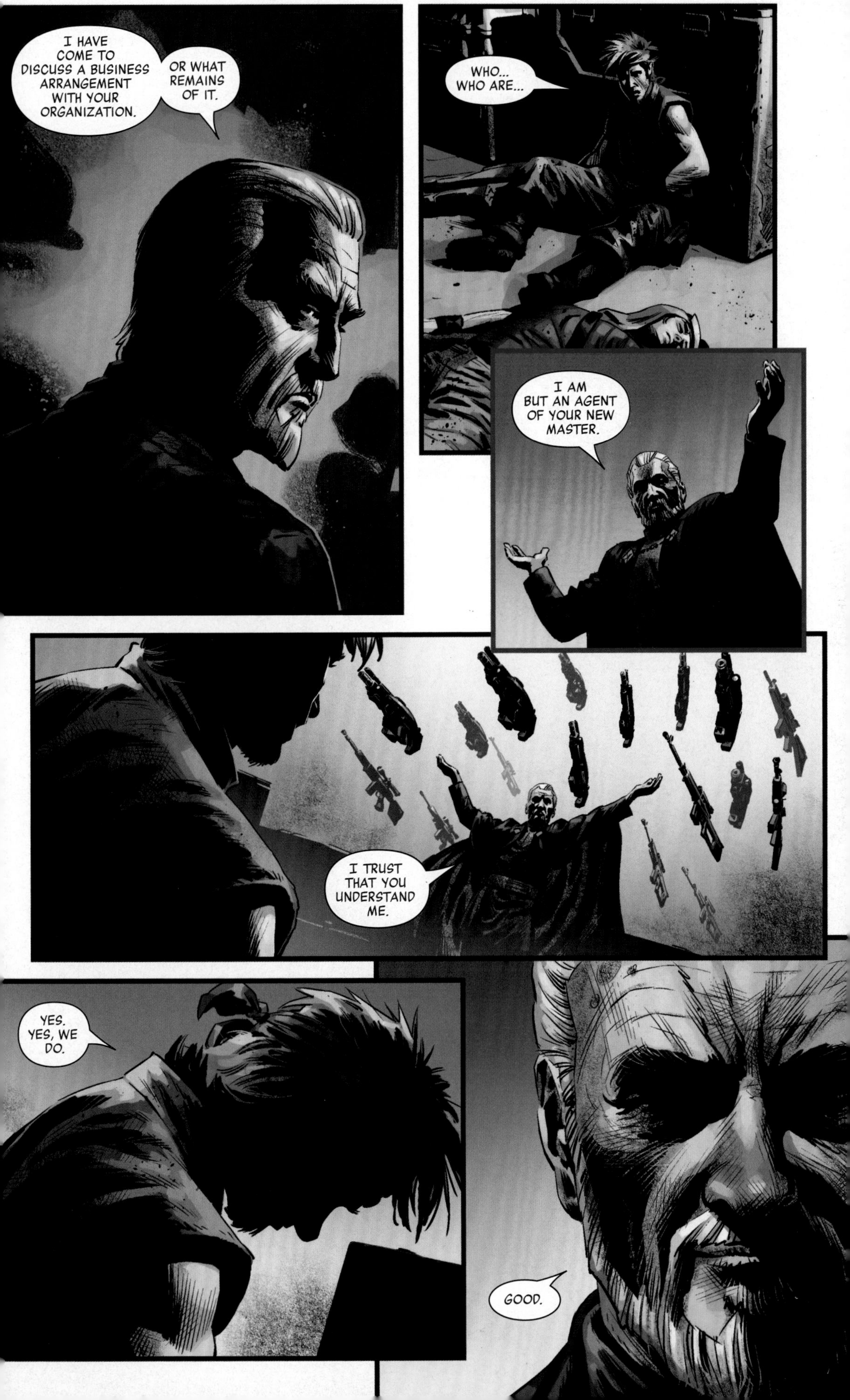
I HAVE COME TO DISCUSS A BUSINESS ARRANGEMENT WITH YOUR ORGANIZATION.
OR WHAT REMAINS OF IT.
WHO... WHO ARE...
I AM BUT AN AGENT OF YOUR NEW MASTER.
I TRUST THAT YOU UNDERSTAND ME.
YES. YES, WE DO.
GOOD.

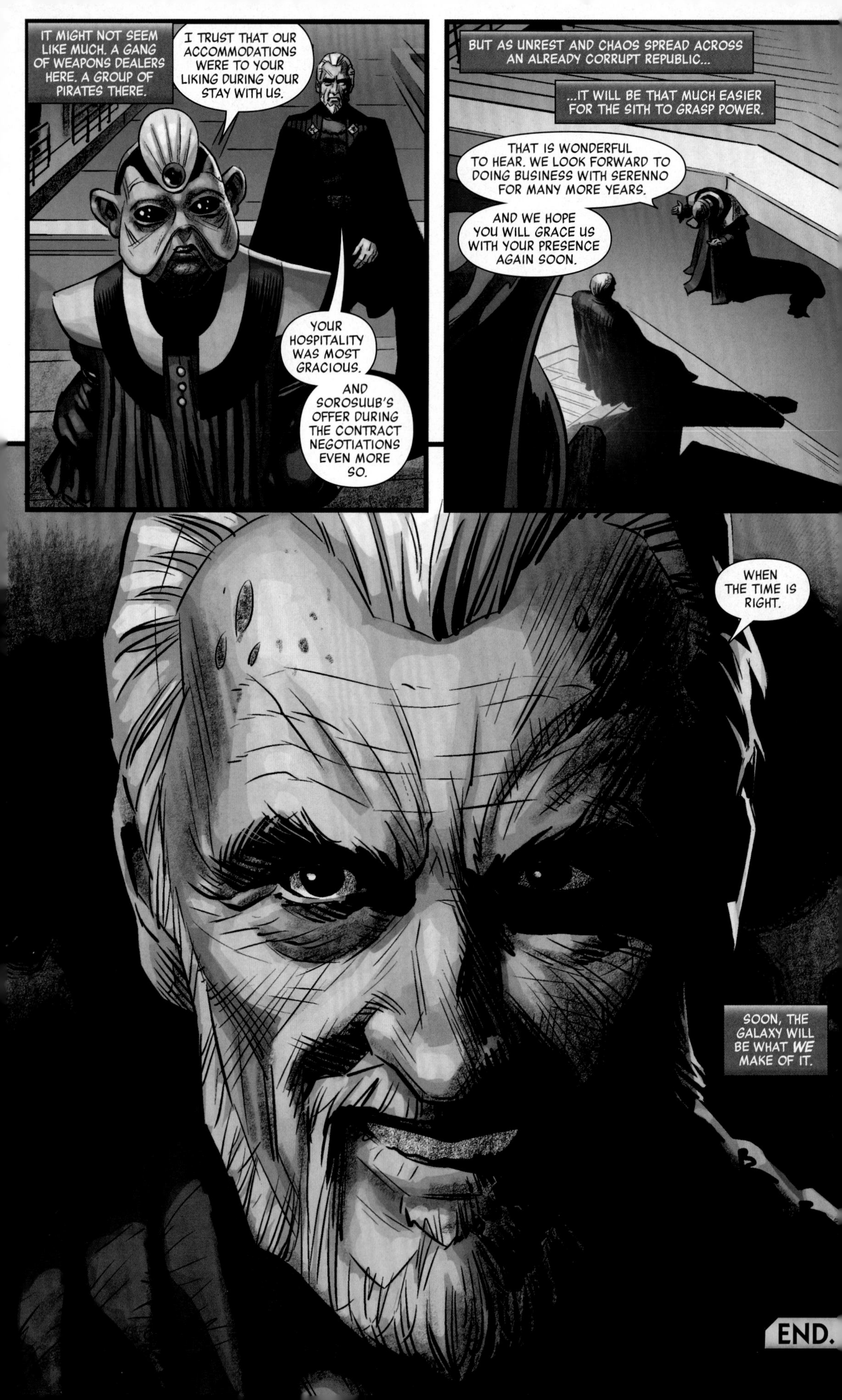

IT MIGHT NOT SEEM LIKE MUCH. A GANG OF WEAPONS DEALERS HERE. A GROUP OF PIRATES THERE.
I TRUST THAT OUR ACCOMMODATIONS WERE TO YOUR LIKING DURING YOUR STAY WITH US.
YOUR HOSPITALITY WAS MOST GRACIOUS.
AND SOROSUUB'S OFFER DURING THE CONTRACT NEGOTIATIONS EVEN MORE SO.
BUT AS UNREST AND CHAOS SPREAD ACROSS AN ALREADY CORRUPT REPUBLIC...
...IT WILL BE THAT MUCH EASIER FOR THE SITH TO GRASP POWER.
THAT IS WONDERFUL TO HEAR. WE LOOK FORWARD TO DOING BUSINESS WITH SERENNO FOR MANY MORE YEARS.
AND WE HOPE YOU WILL GRACE US WITH YOUR PRESENCE AGAIN SOON.
WHEN THE TIME IS RIGHT.
SOON, THE GALAXY WILL BE WHAT *WE* MAKE OF IT.
END.

AGE OF REPUBLIC
Count Dooku: A Sith for a More Civilized Age
By Bria LaVorgna

Every good villain is the hero of his or her own story, and *Star Wars* embraces this concept wholeheartedly from Vader to Ventress. However, the villains in *Star Wars* movies tend to be easily visually identified as such. Darth Vader is a monster clad in black, Emperor Palpatine's face is far from beautiful and Maul's look could have been ripped from someone's nightmare. This holds mostly true in the films right up until *Attack of the Clones*, when we meet Count Dooku, who couldn't appear more different from the other villains. At first glance, Dooku exudes nobility and elegance; someone who looks more like a senator, or perhaps the hero, than a dark lord of the Sith, and yet he's very much on the evil Darth Sidious' side.

Or is he? When Dooku first meets Obi-Wan Kenobi, he tells the Jedi Knight the truth: the Senate is corrupt and under the control of the Sith. The Count is even honest about how Sidious manipulated the Trade Federation into forming a blockade around Naboo. Dooku asks Obi-Wan to join him and destroy the Sith, but Kenobi turns him down and, ultimately, Dooku falls to Anakin Skywalker's blade when Sidious betrays his onetime apprentice. It's hard not to wonder what might have been if Obi-Wan had taken the

invitation or whether Dooku's offer had even been sincere. His villainy grows deeper the longer the Clone Wars continue, yet one thing is clear: Dooku, an idealist, believes he's doing the right thing for the galaxy. He just might not be going about it in the most light side way.

While the character may not have looked like one of the bad guys, his actor was well known for playing villains. Perhaps more than most characters, Count Dooku's identity is intimately entwined with his actor, Sir Christopher Lee, in voice, appearance and presence. A prolific and respected actor, Lee already had ties to *Star Wars* via his close friendship with Peter Cushing. The pair appeared in over twenty films together and, while their appearances in the saga were twenty-five years apart and in separate films, it was, in a way, their final collaboration. Like Cushing once had with Grand Moff Tarkin, Lee brought a certain gravitas to his role. His presence on the screen demands the viewer's attention, as does his distinct voice, and Lee's influence on the character is unmistakable.

One such way was by utilizing his experience. "I've probably done more sword fights on celluloid than any actor in history," Lee said in the making-of

documentary for *Attack of the Clones*, "and I've got the scars to prove it." Whereas most of the Jedi and Sith use a two-handed grip, Stunt Coordinator Nick Gillard has Dooku favor a distinct single-handed grip. The style, combined with a curved lightsaber hilt, hints at a different sort of Jedi lightsaber training and plays to Lee's strengths and how comfortable he was fencing on-screen (although he did still require a stunt double for some scenes). Dooku handily defeats both Obi-Wan and Anakin on Geonosis and holds his own for much of the duel aboard the Capital starship *Invisible Hand*, proving alongside Master Yoda that for a Force user, age is only a number.

From his elegant cape to his unique fighting style, Count Dooku is proof that you don't always have to choose when it comes to style versus substance. Dooku and Sir Christopher Lee have given *Star Wars* a different sort of Sith, adding to the ever-growing mythos of the galaxy far, far away.

SOURCES: From Puppets to Pixels: Digital Characters *in* Episode II *featurette.*

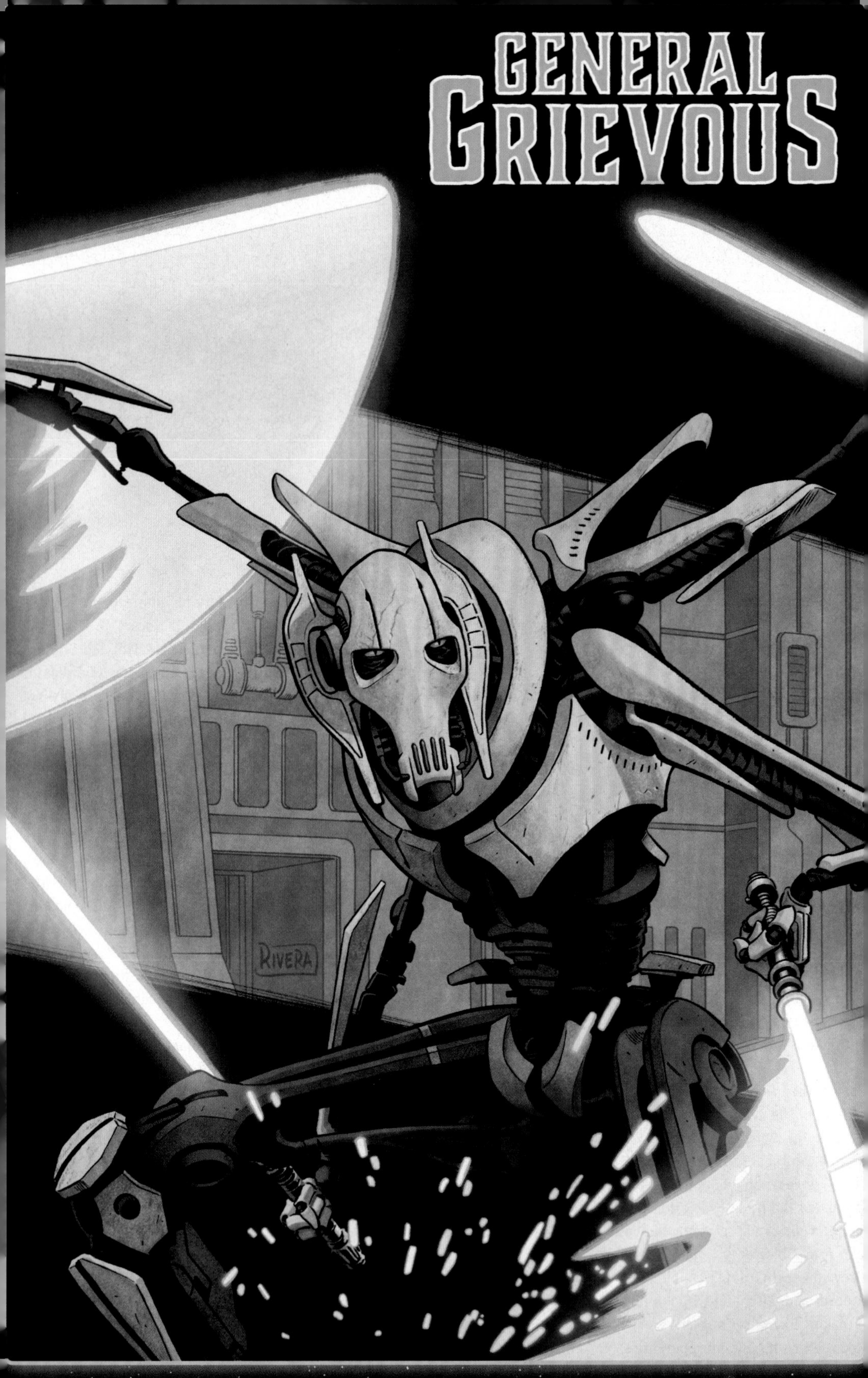

GENERAL GRIEVOUS
RIVERA

"BURN"

The Clone War rages! The Jedi Order leads the armies of the Republic in battle against the endless Separatist droid legions. The Jedi may have finally met their match in the fearsome and merciless General Grievous! Countless Jedi have fallen to Grievous' blades but no matter how many Jedi he slaughters nothing can sate the cyborg's appetite for destruction.

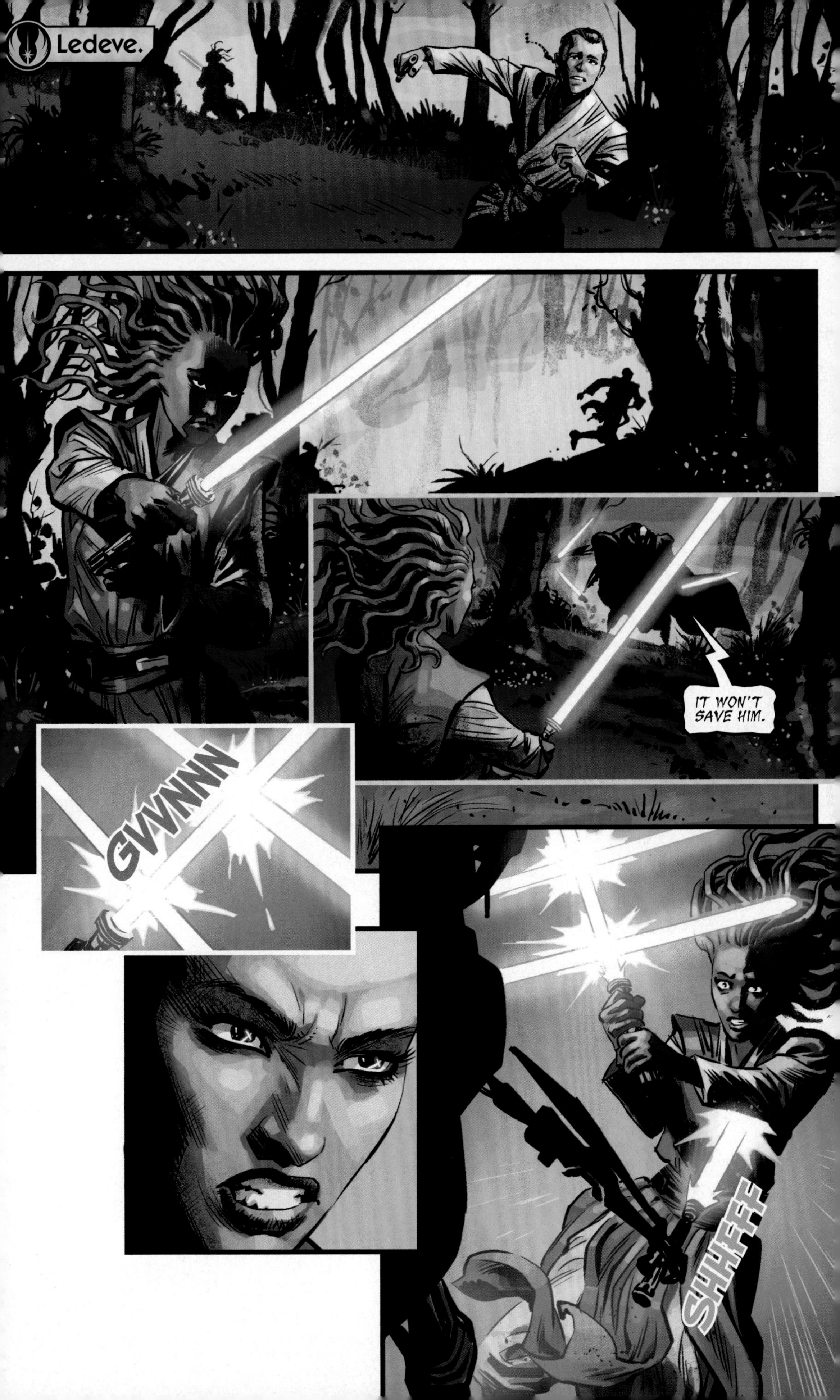
Ledeve.
IT WON'T SAVE HIM.
GVVNNN
SHHFFF

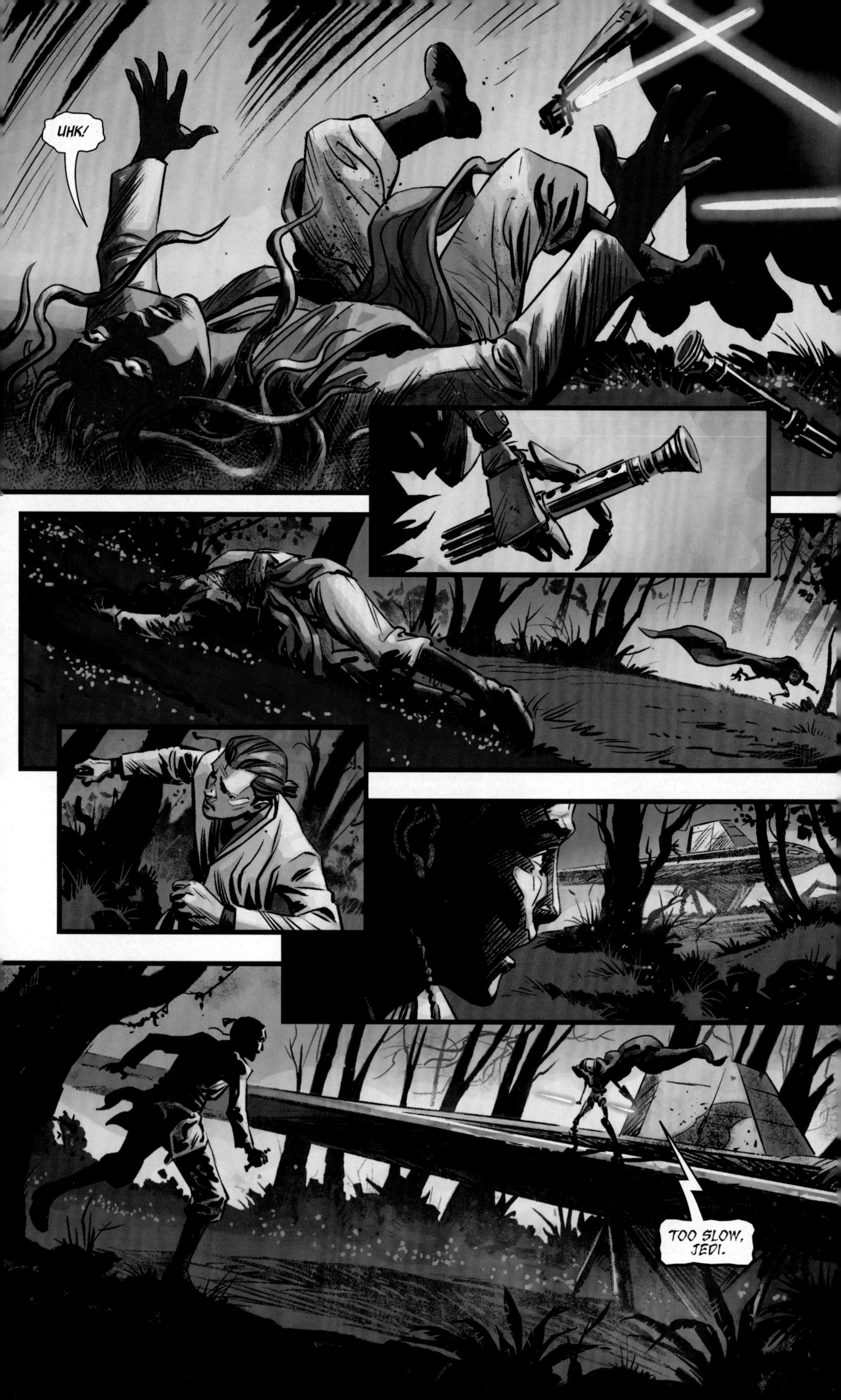
UHK!
TOO SLOW, JEDI.

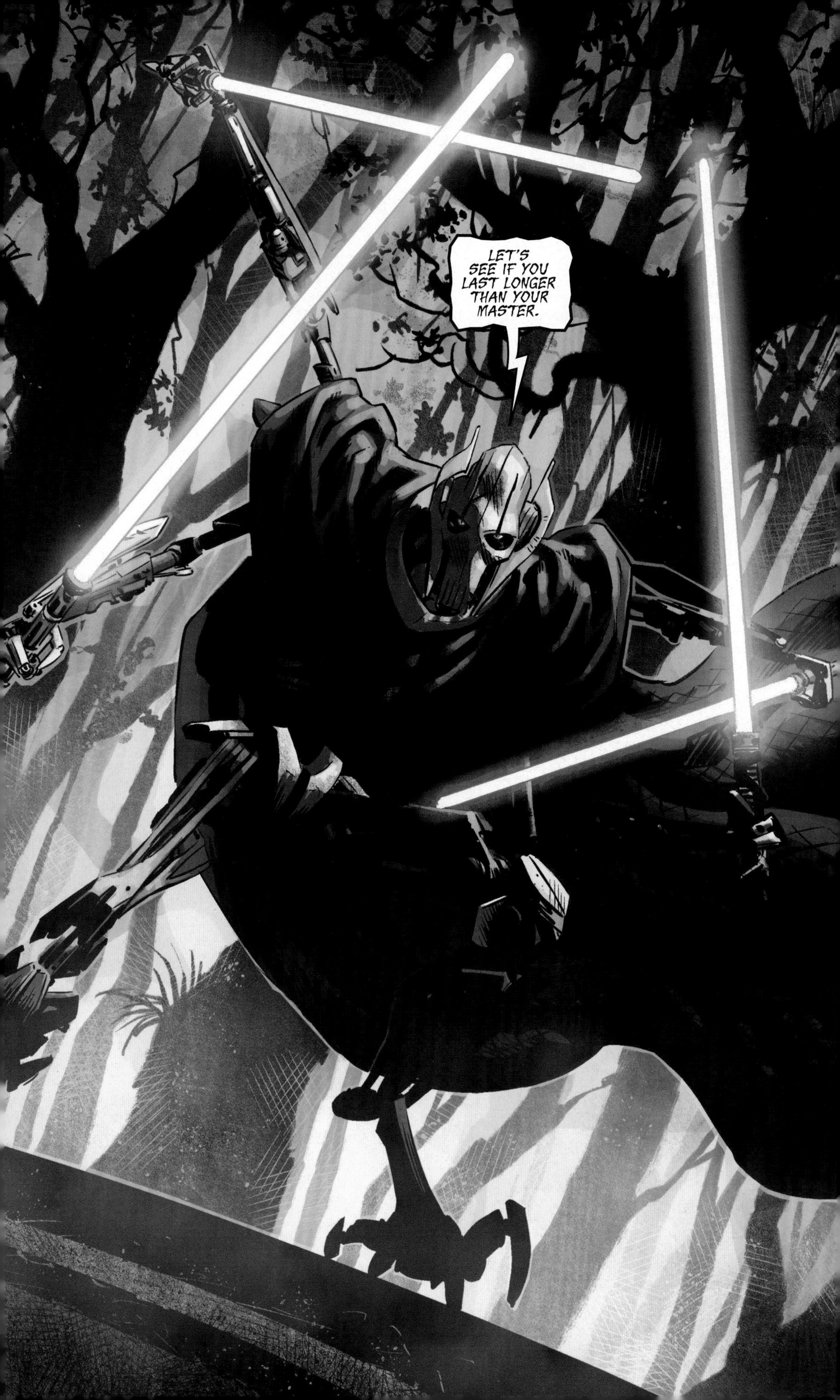
LET'S SEE IF YOU LAST LONGER THAN YOUR MASTER.

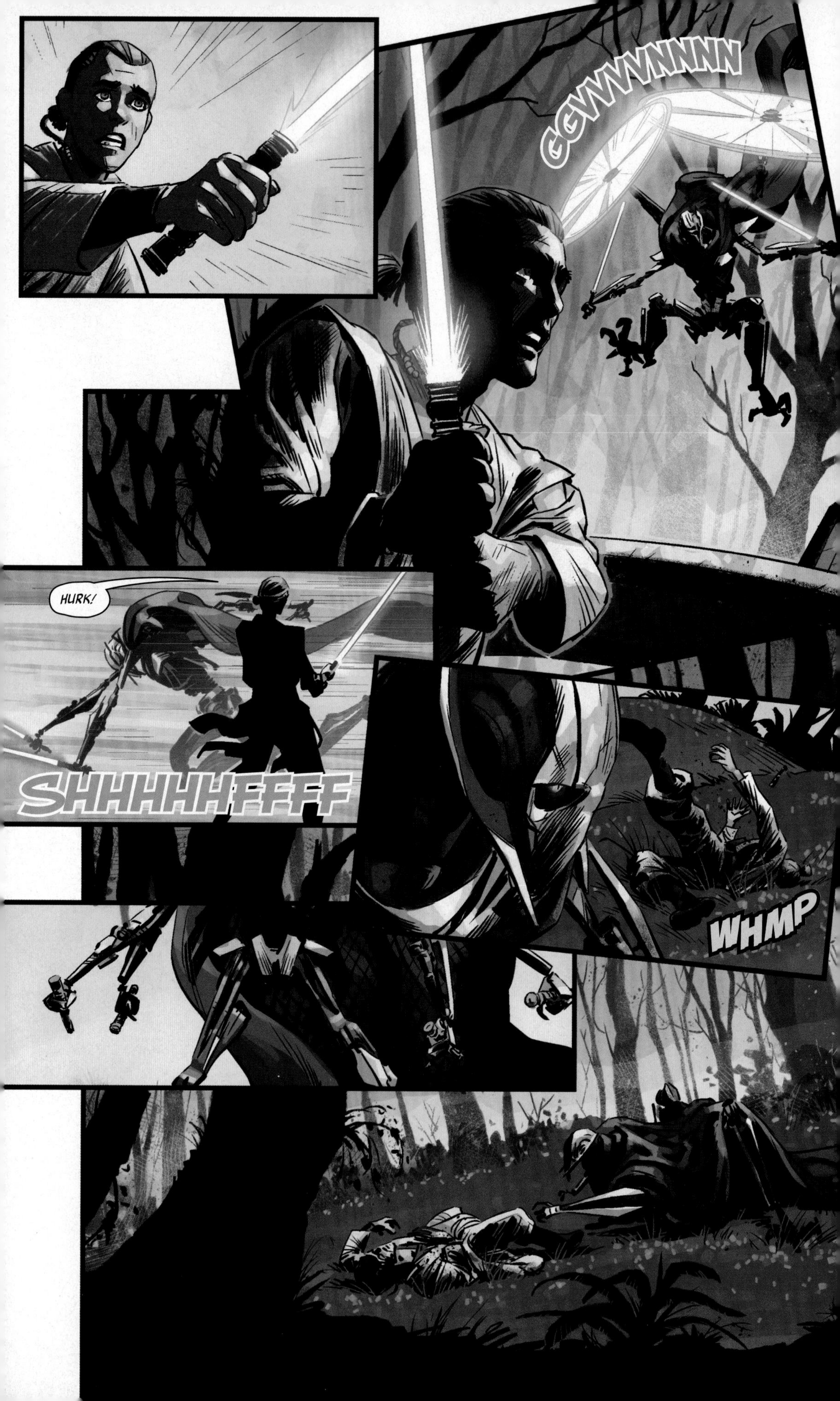
GGVVVVNNNN
HURK!
SHHHHHFFFF
WHMP

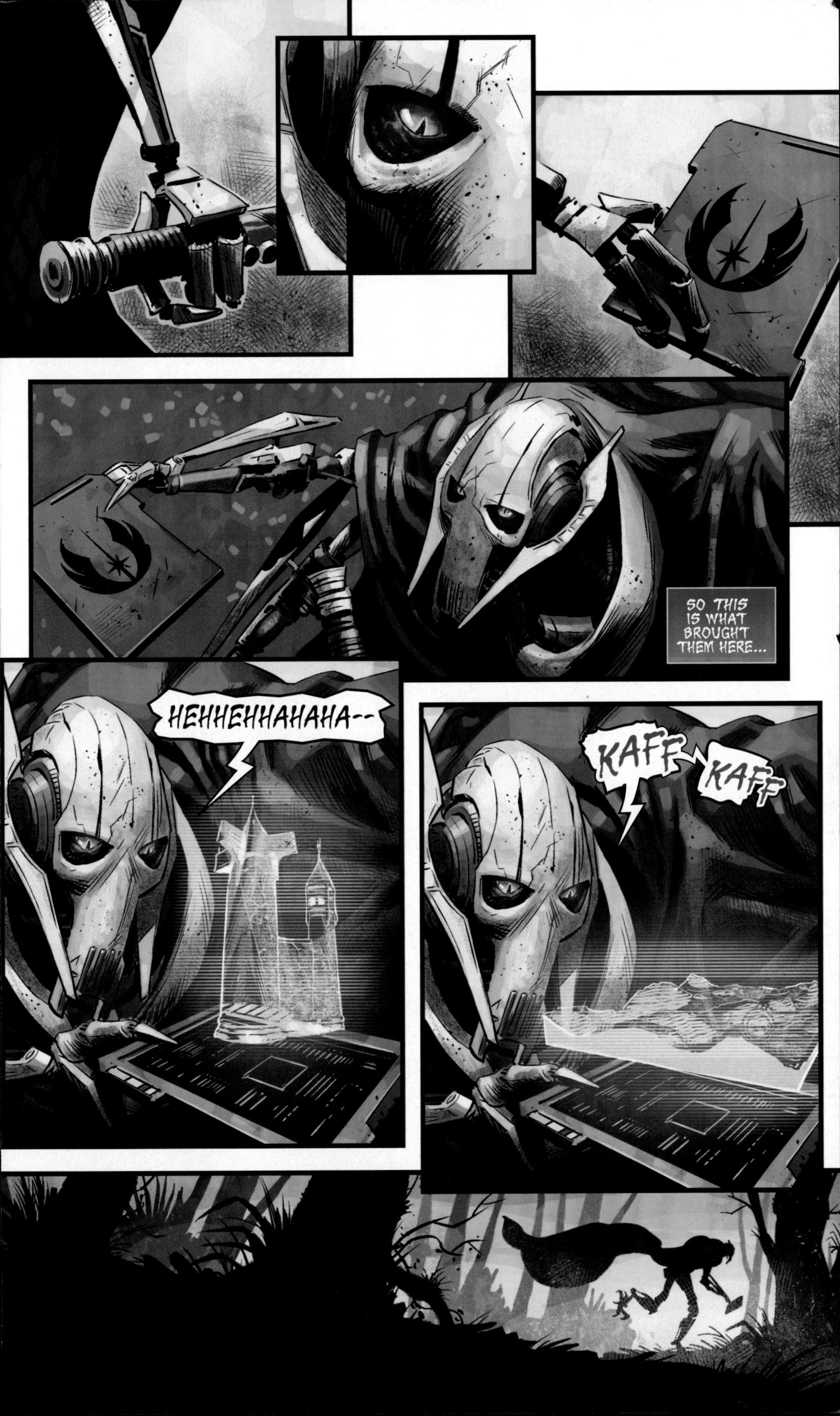
SO THIS IS WHAT BROUGHT THEM HERE...
HEHHEHHAHAHA--
KAFF
KAFF

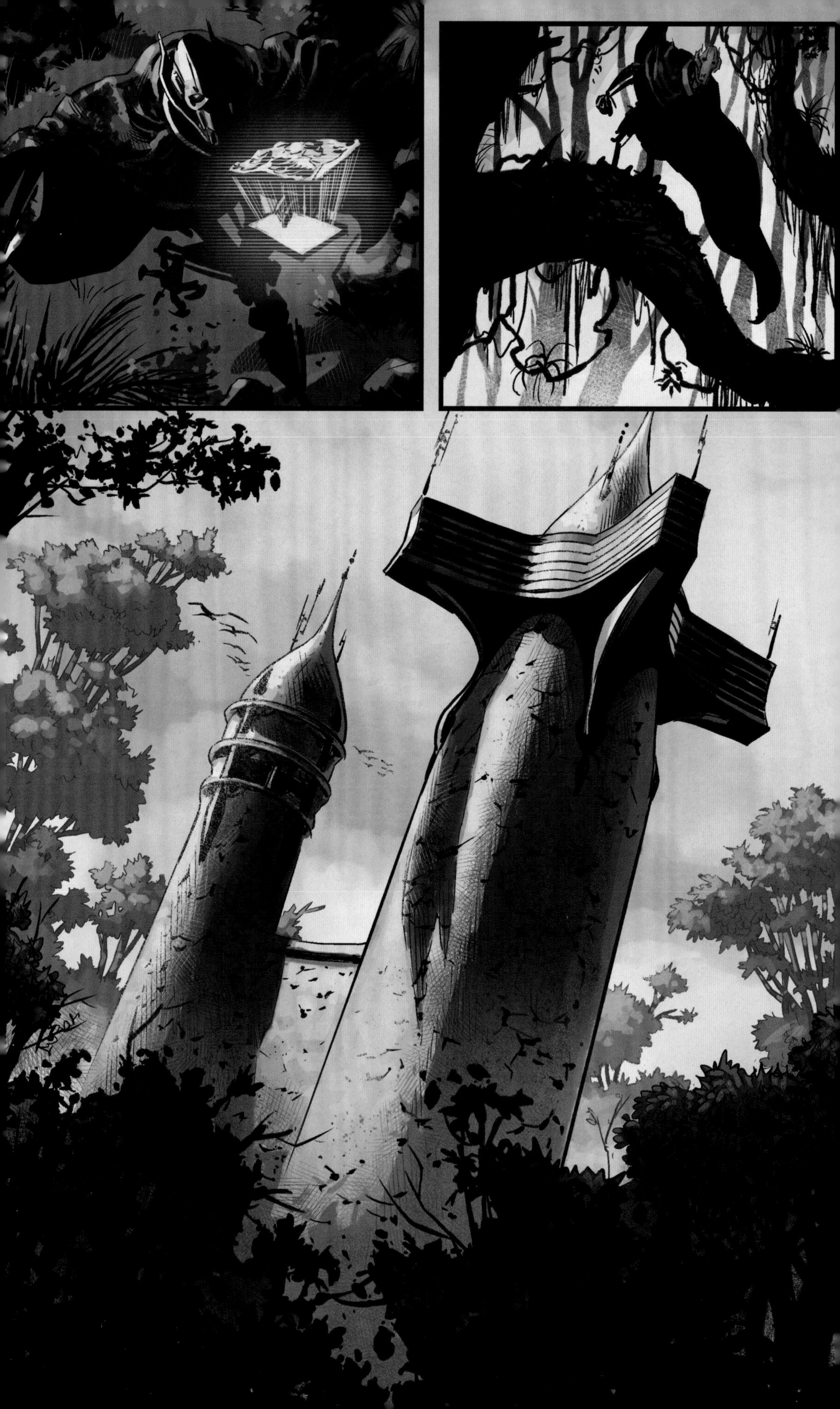

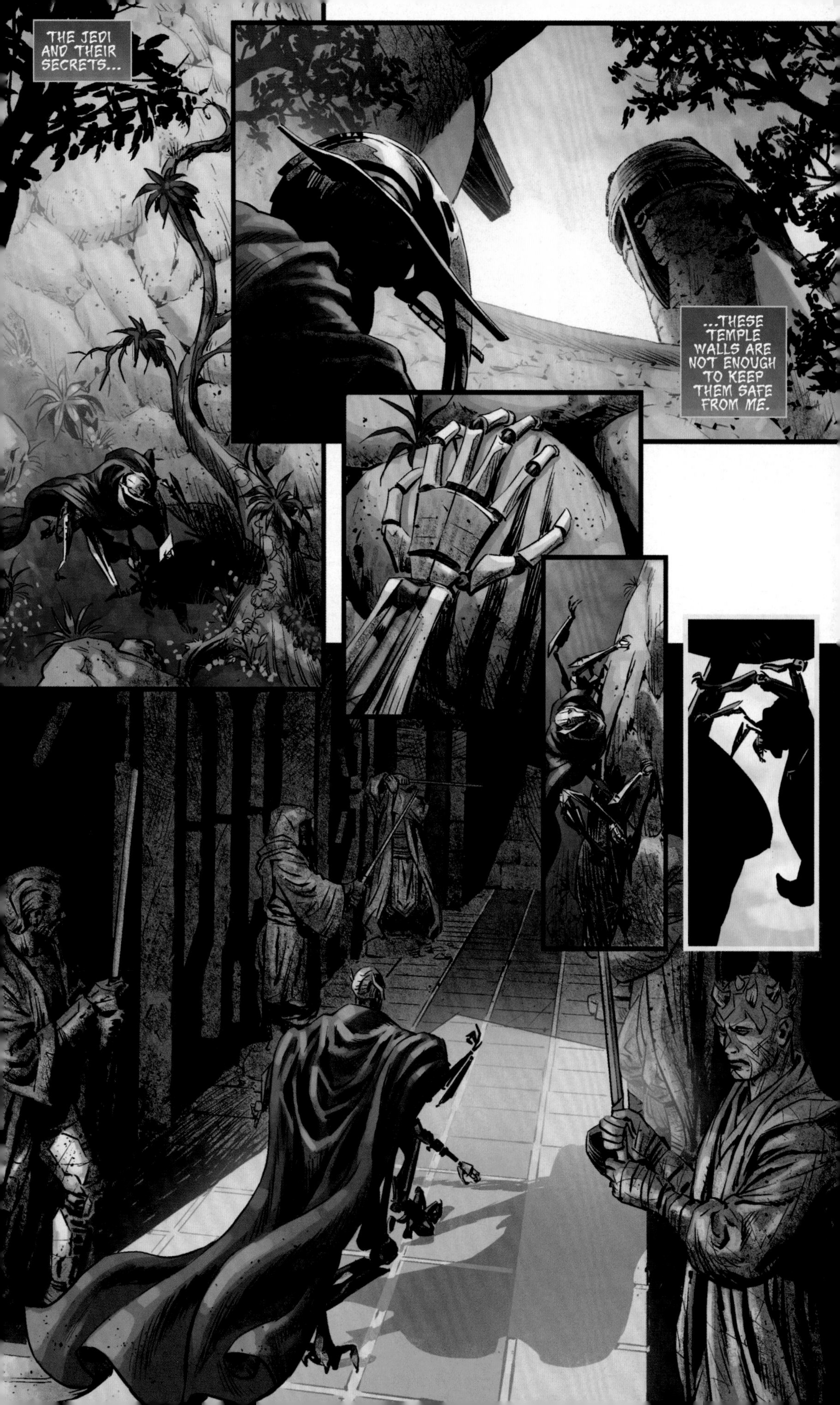
THE JEDI AND THEIR SECRETS...
...THESE TEMPLE WALLS ARE NOT ENOUGH TO KEEP THEM SAFE FROM ME.

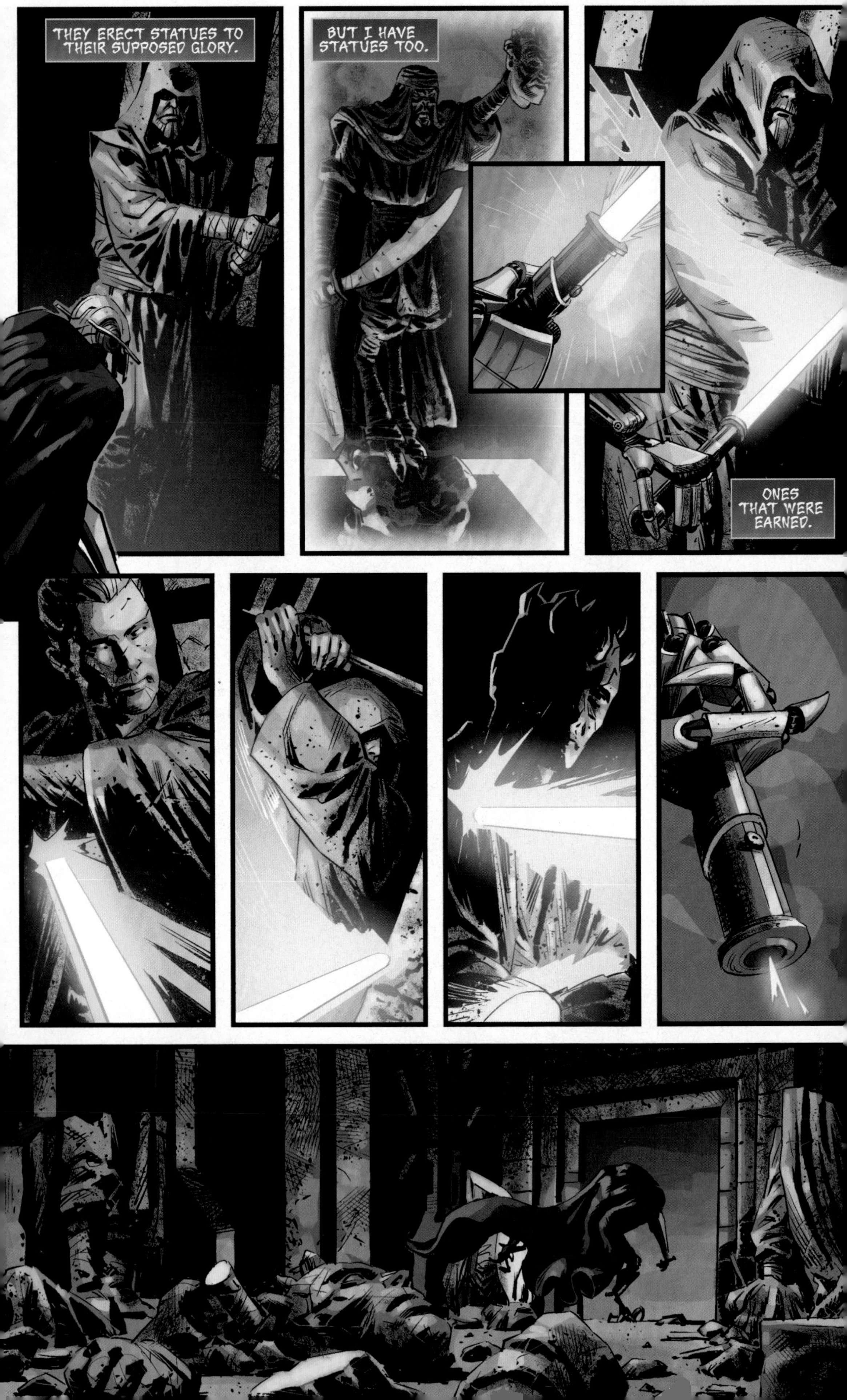
THEY ERECT STATUES TO THEIR SUPPOSED GLORY.
BUT I HAVE STATUES TOO.
ONES THAT WERE EARNED.

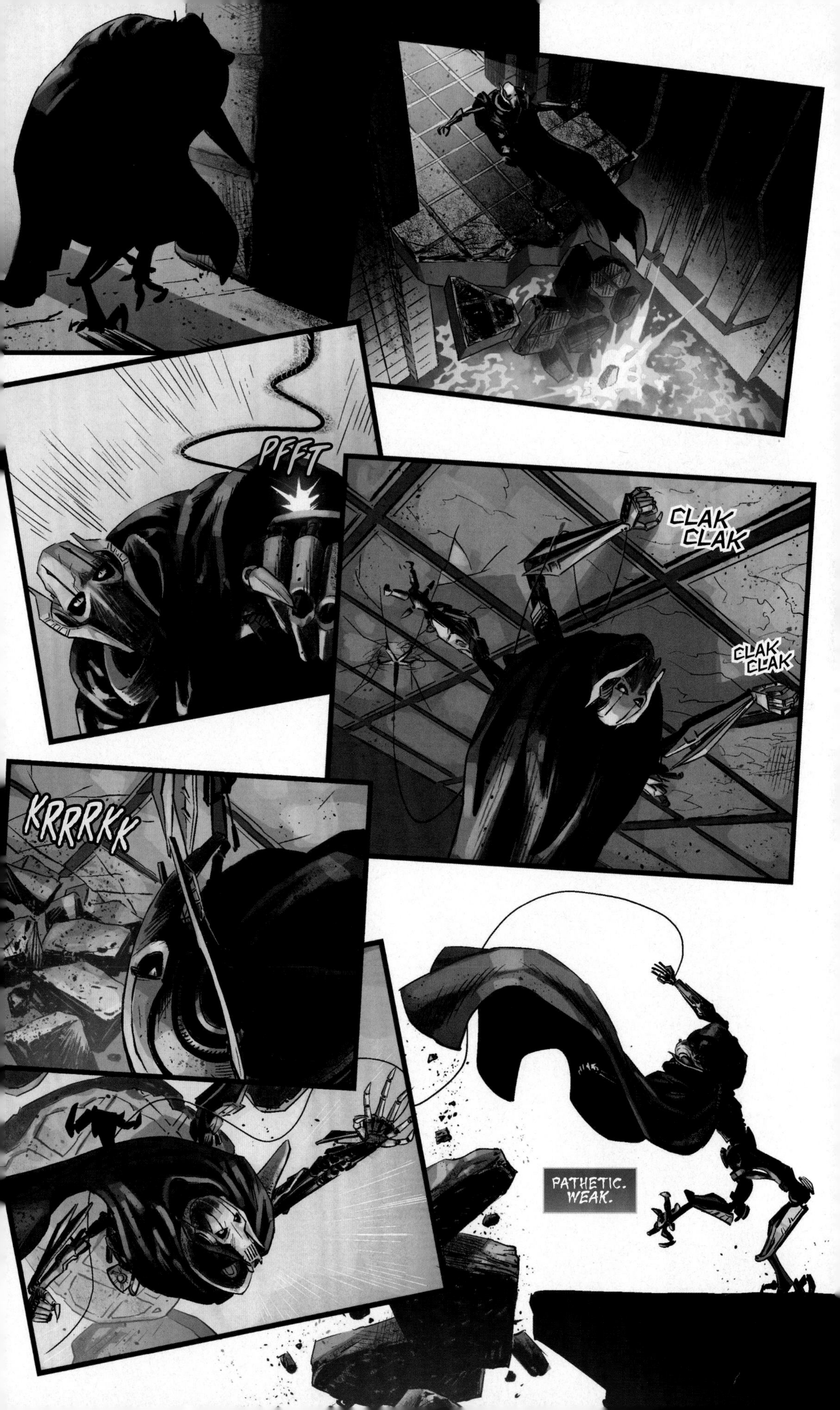
PFFT
CLAK
CLAK
CLAK
CLAK
KRRRKK
PATHETIC.
WEAK.

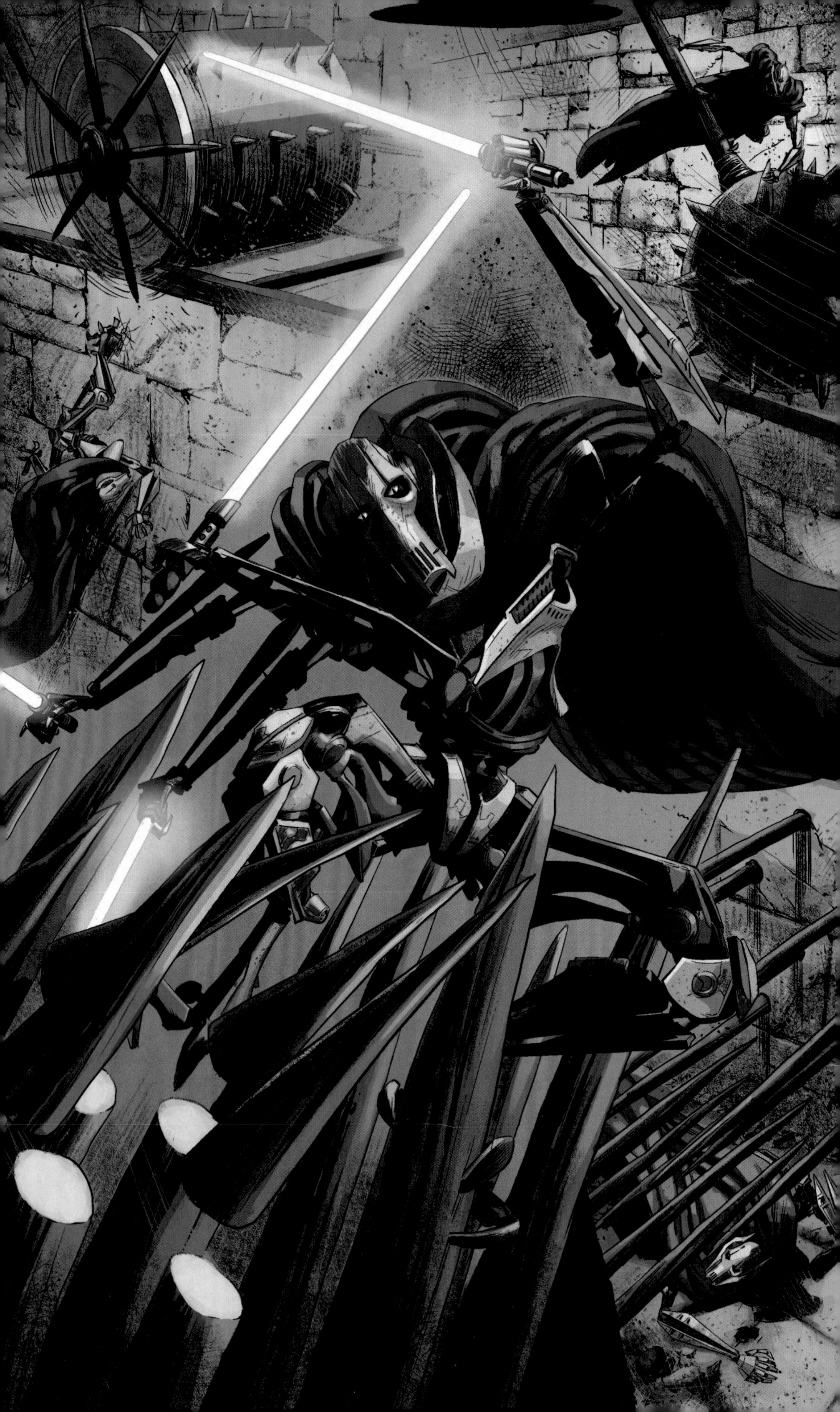

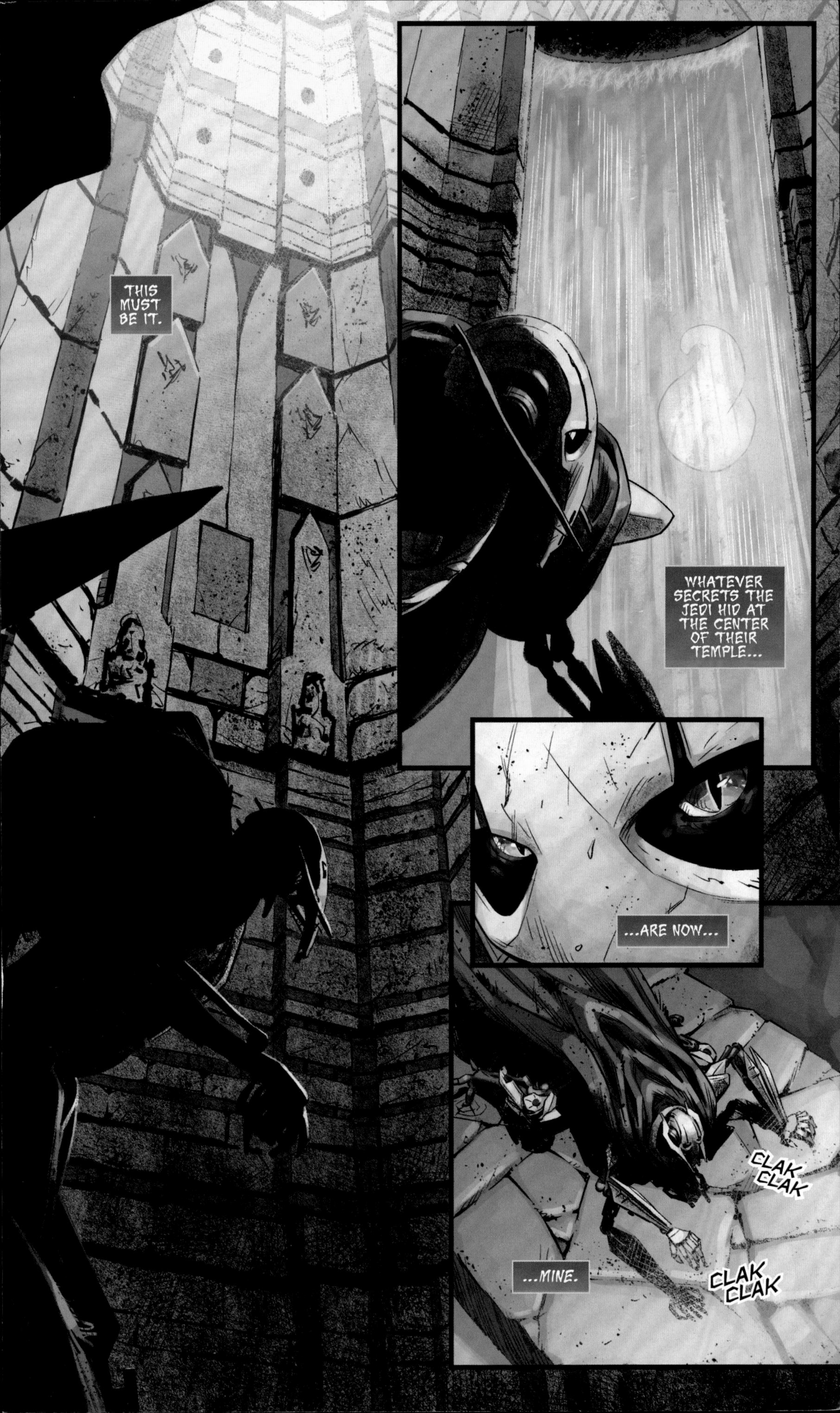
THIS MUST BE IT.
WHATEVER SECRETS THE JEDI HID AT THE CENTER OF THEIR TEMPLE...
...ARE NOW...
CLAK CLAK
...MINE.
CLAK CLAK

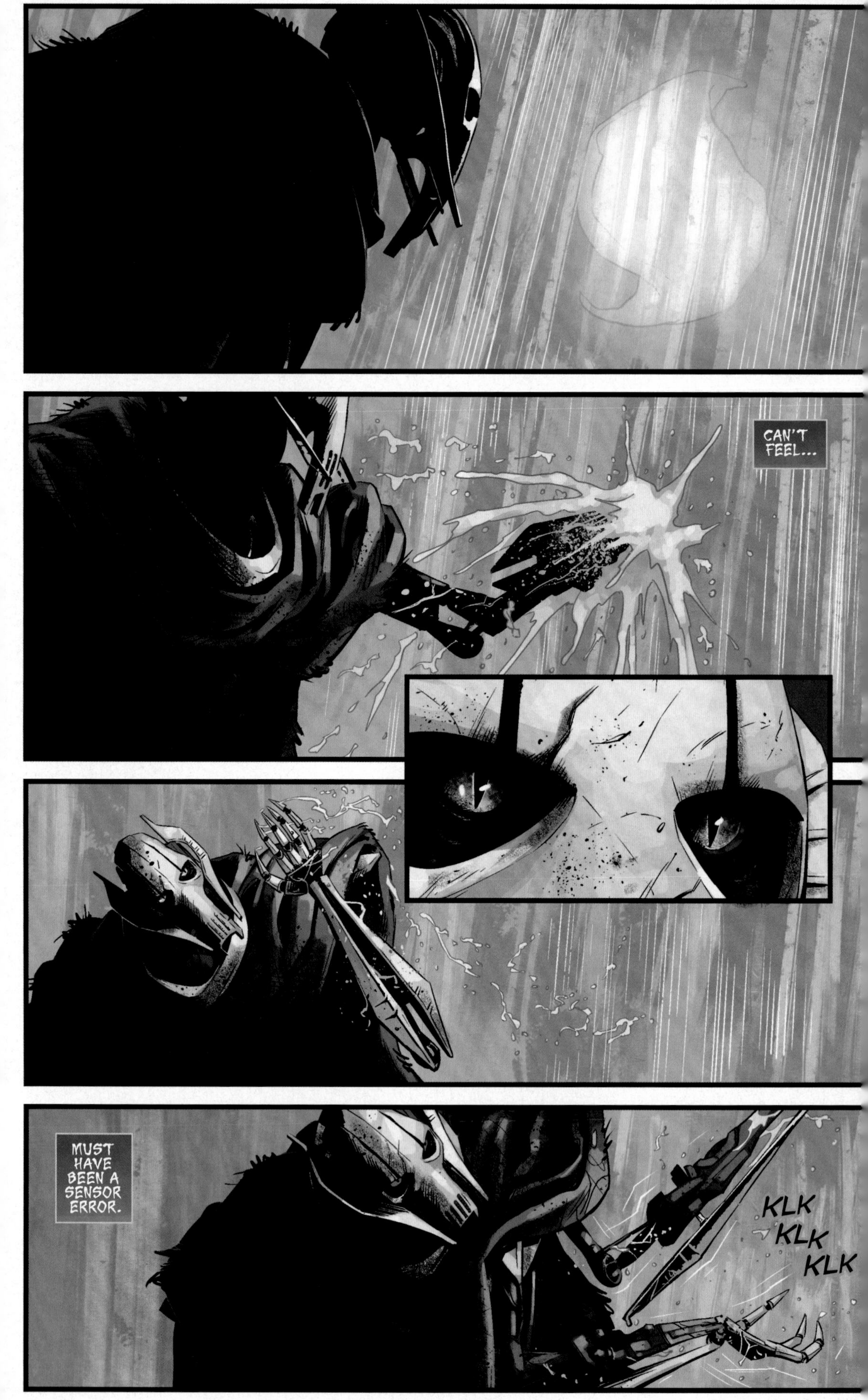
CAN'T FEEL...
MUST HAVE BEEN A SENSOR ERROR.
KLK
KLK
KLK

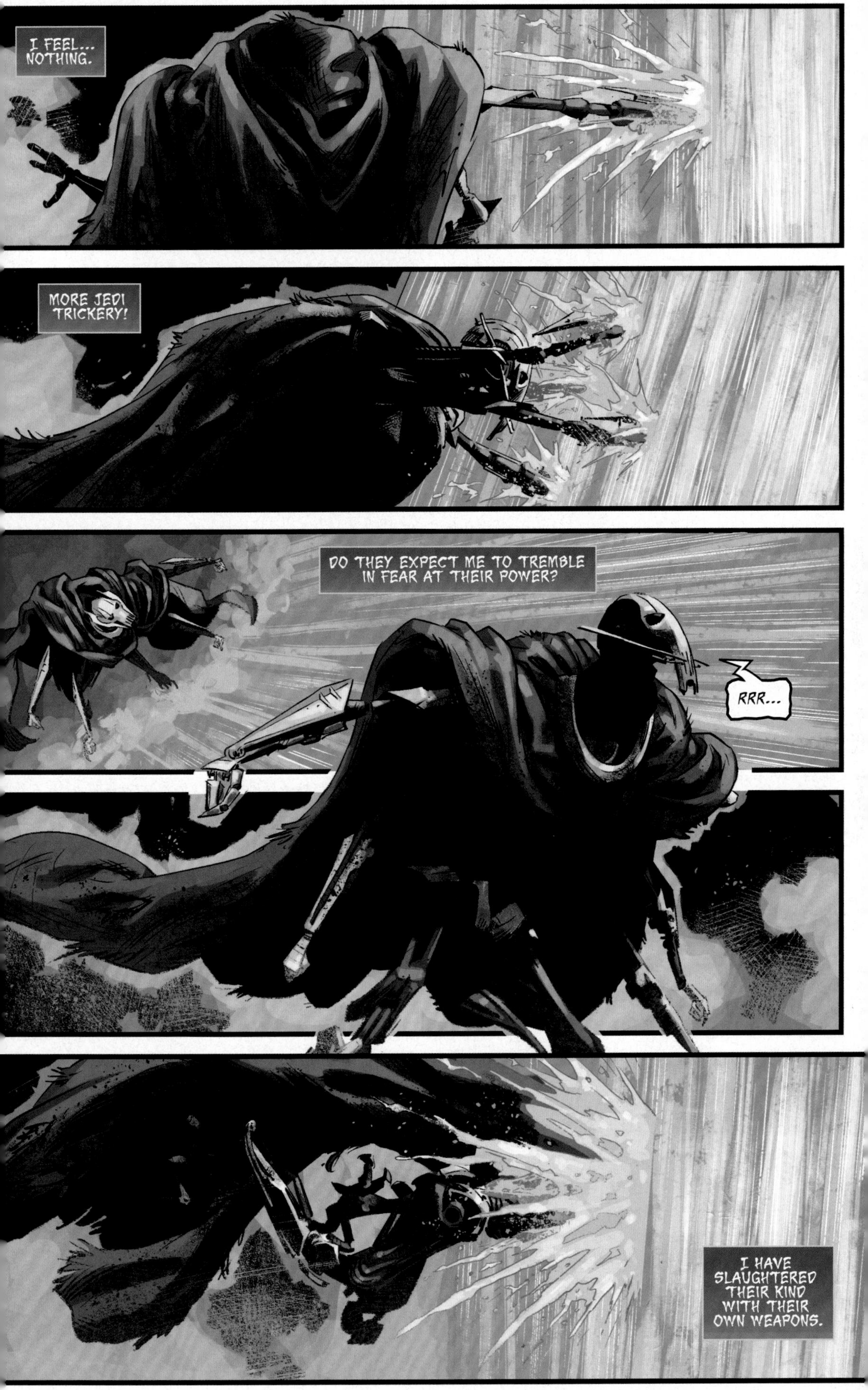
I FEEL... NOTHING.
MORE JEDI TRICKERY!
DO THEY EXPECT ME TO TREMBLE IN FEAR AT THEIR POWER?
RRR...
I HAVE SLAUGHTERED THEIR KIND WITH THEIR OWN WEAPONS.

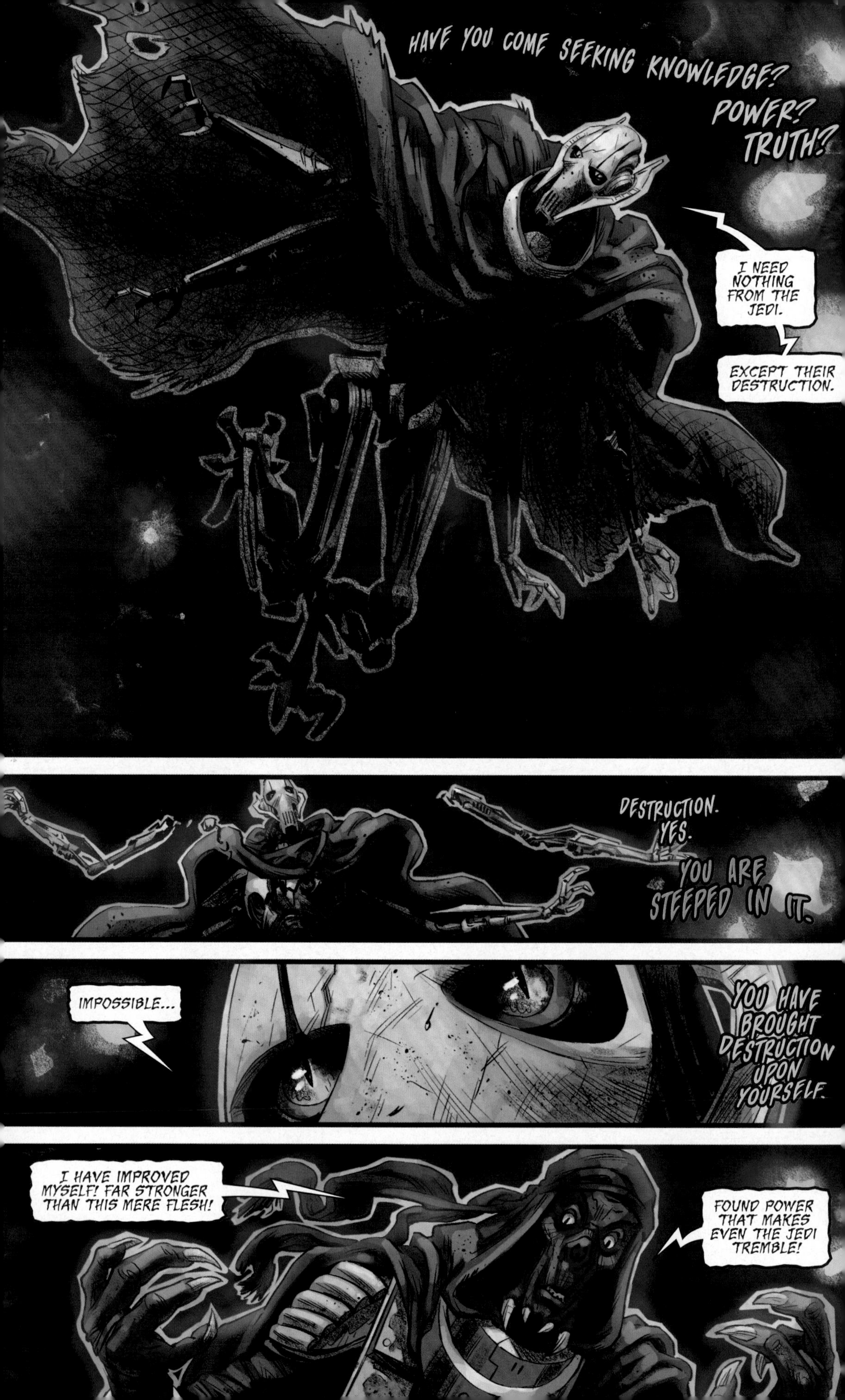
HAVE YOU COME SEEKING KNOWLEDGE?
POWER? TRUTH?
I NEED NOTHING FROM THE JEDI.
EXCEPT THEIR DESTRUCTION.
DESTRUCTION. YES.
YOU ARE STEEPED IN IT.
IMPOSSIBLE...
YOU HAVE BROUGHT DESTRUCTION UPON YOURSELF.
I HAVE IMPROVED MYSELF! FAR STRONGER THAN THIS MERE FLESH!
FOUND POWER THAT MAKES EVEN THE JEDI TREMBLE!

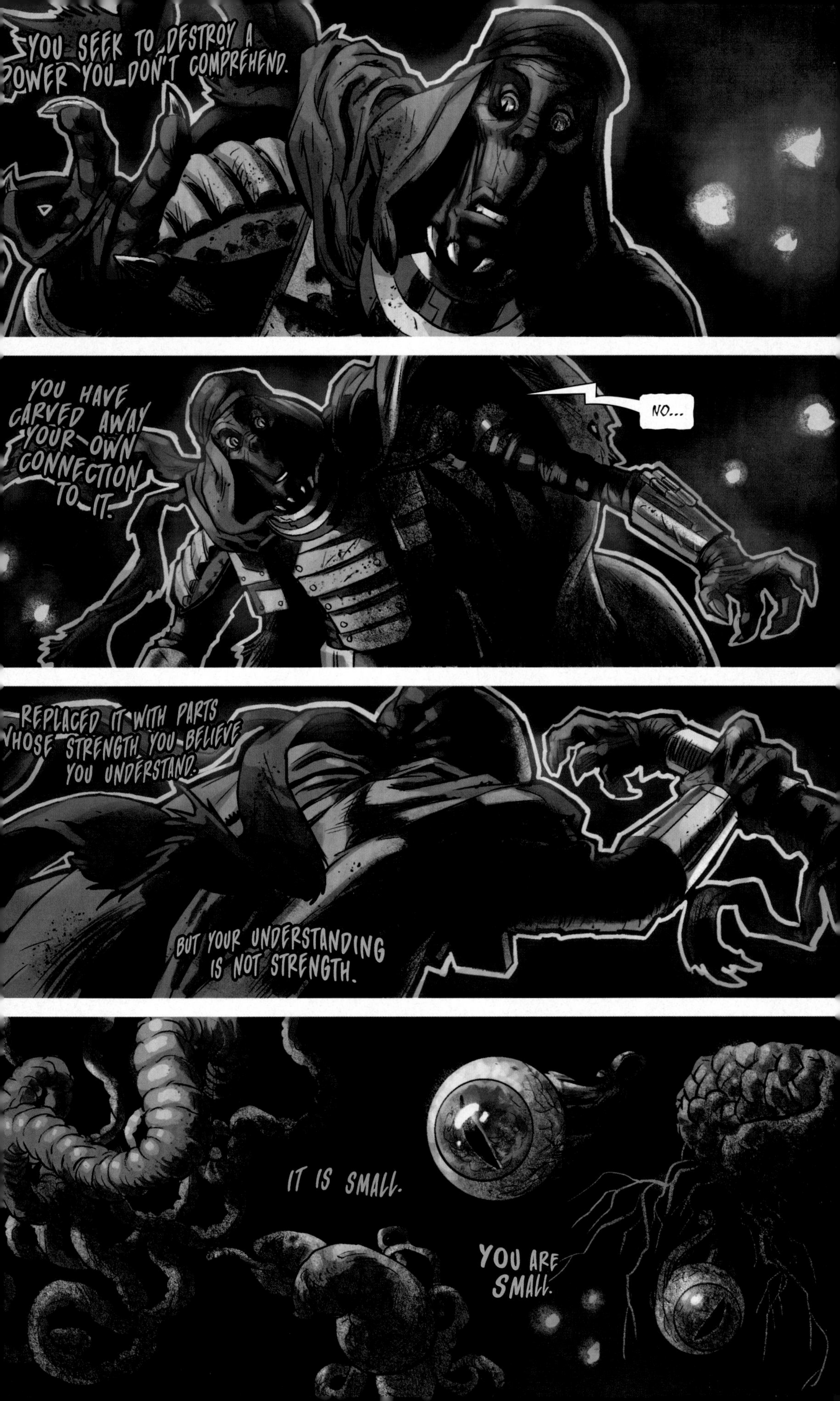
YOU SEEK TO DESTROY A POWER YOU DON'T COMPREHEND.
YOU HAVE CARVED AWAY YOUR OWN CONNECTION TO IT.
NO...
REPLACED IT WITH PARTS WHOSE STRENGTH YOU BELIEVE YOU UNDERSTAND.
BUT YOUR UNDERSTANDING IS NOT STRENGTH.
IT IS SMALL.
YOU ARE SMALL.

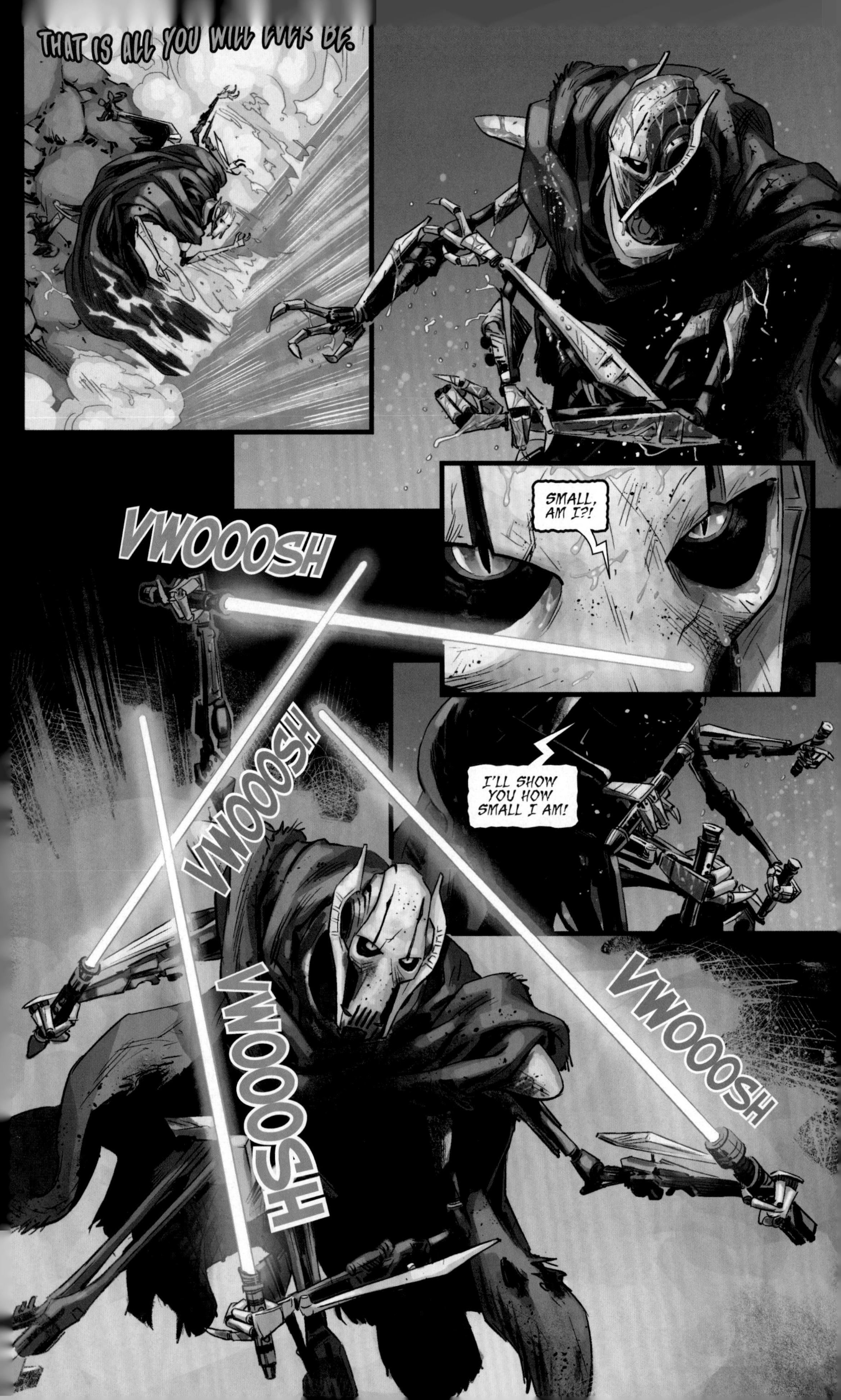
THAT IS ALL YOU WILL EVER BE.
SMALL, AM I?!
VWOOOSH
I'LL SHOW YOU HOW SMALL I AM!
VWOOOSH
VWOOOSH
VWOOOSH

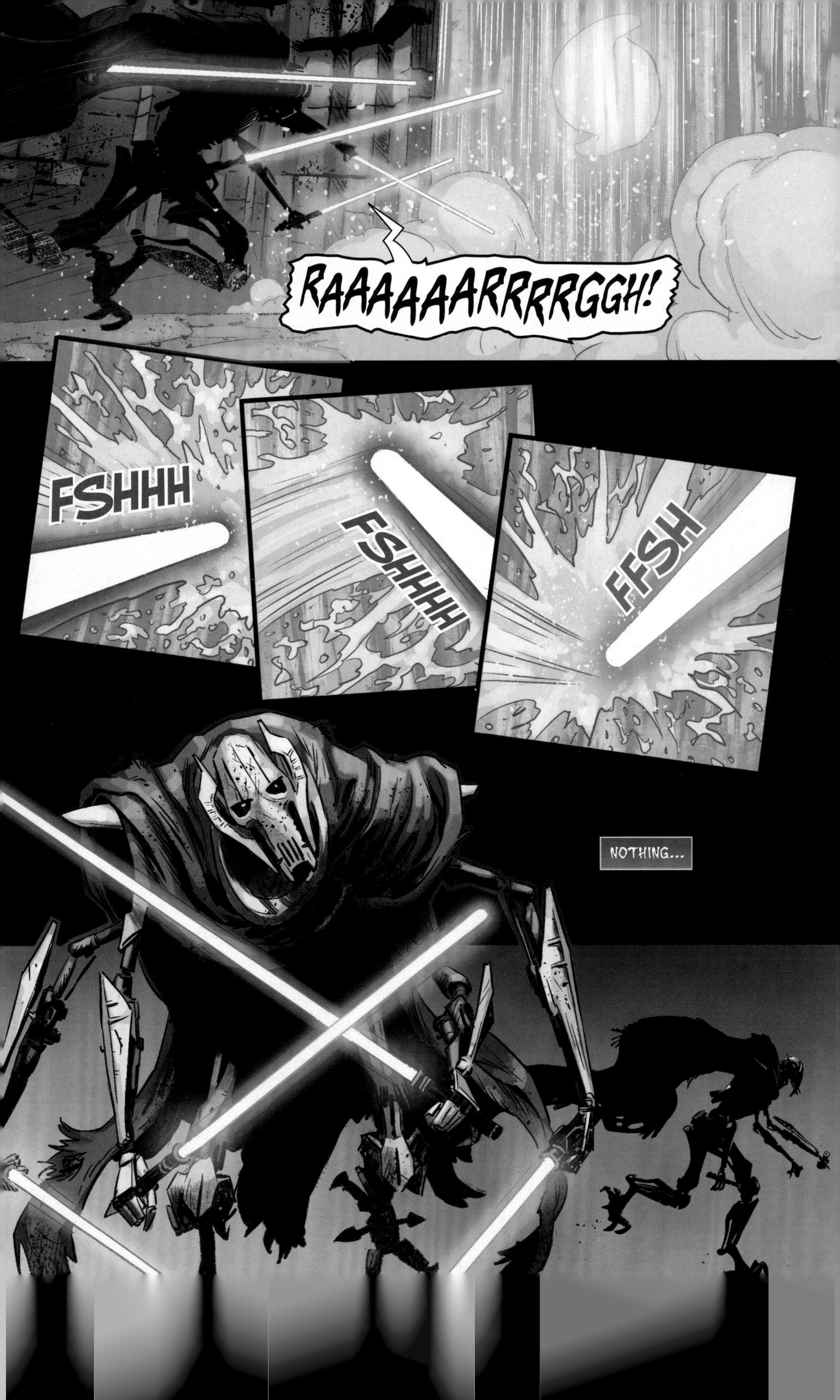
RAAAAAARRRRGGH!
FSHHH
FSHHHH
FFSH
NOTHING...

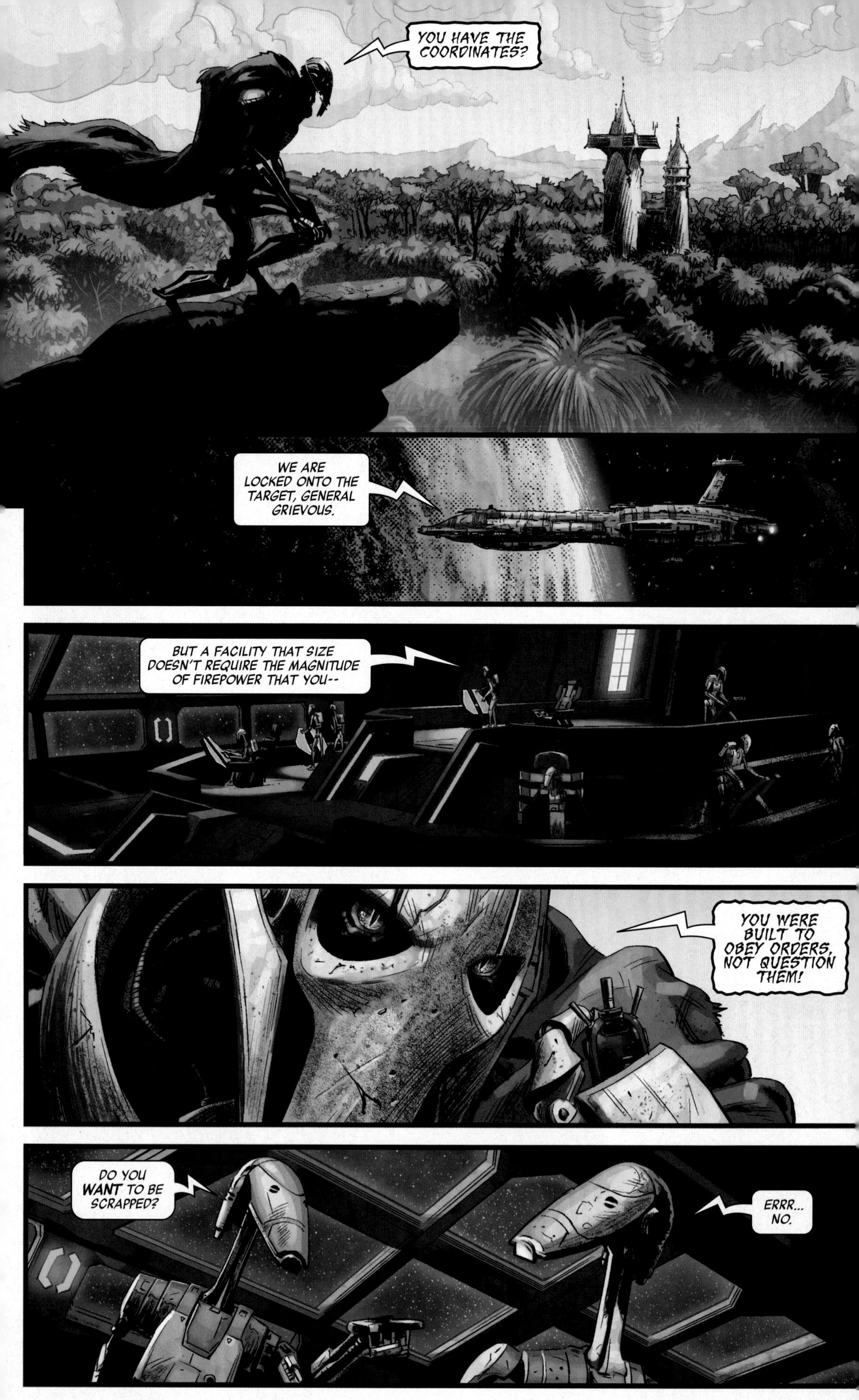
YOU HAVE THE COORDINATES?
WE ARE LOCKED ONTO THE TARGET, GENERAL GRIEVOUS.
BUT A FACILITY THAT SIZE DOESN'T REQUIRE THE MAGNITUDE OF FIREPOWER THAT YOU--
YOU WERE BUILT TO OBEY ORDERS, NOT QUESTION THEM!
DO YOU WANT TO BE SCRAPPED?
ERRR... NO.

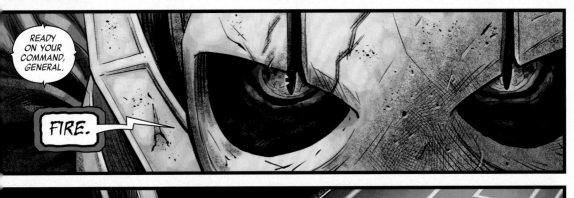

READY ON YOUR COMMAND, GENERAL.

FIRE.

ROGER ROGER.

FTOOM FTOOM FTOOM

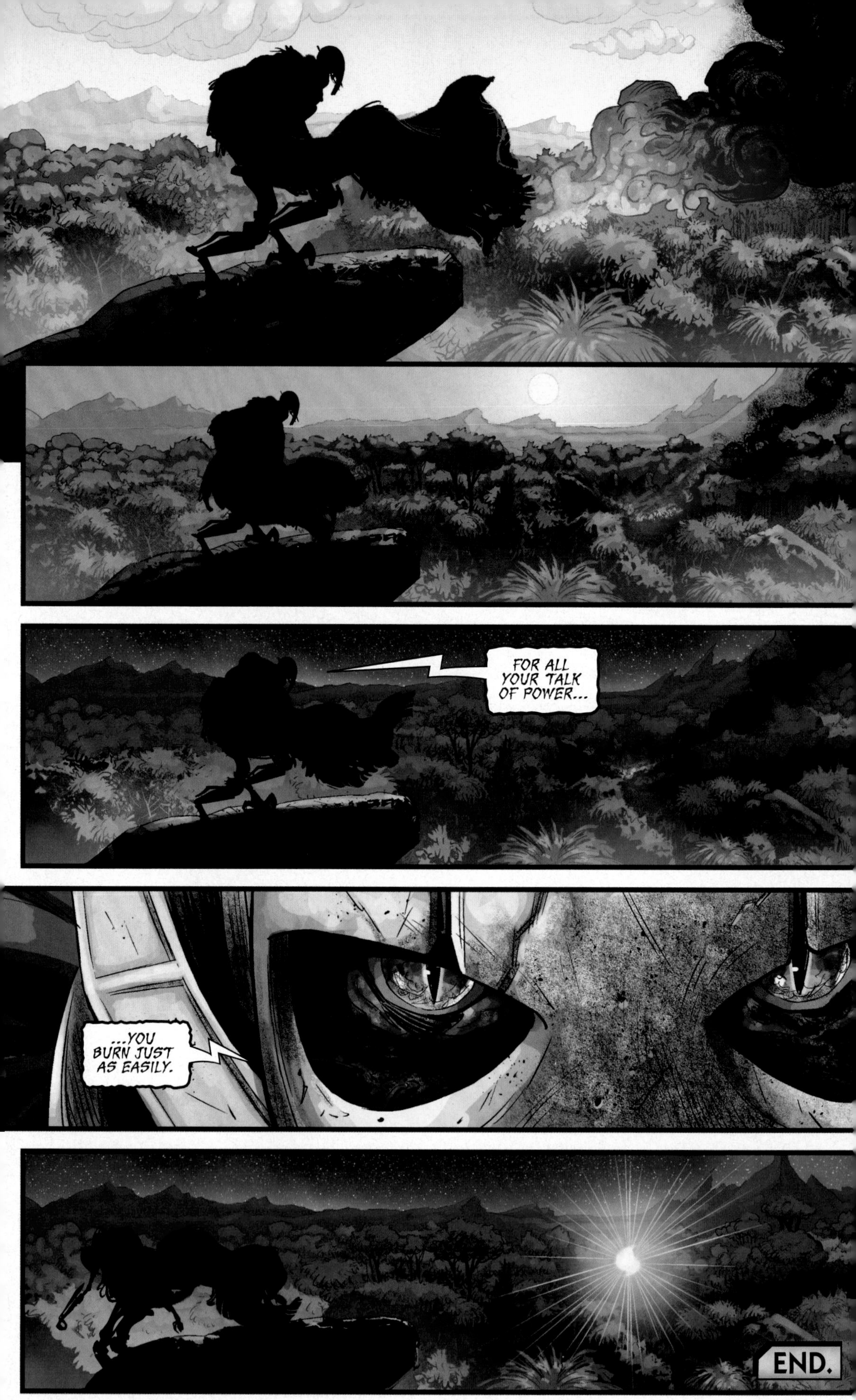
FOR ALL YOUR TALK OF POWER...
...YOU BURN JUST AS EASILY.
END.

AGE OF REPUBLIC
General Grievous: The Infamous Droid General
By Bryan Young

General Grievous didn't get a whole lot of screen time during the prequel trilogy of the *Star Wars* saga. He was introduced in the opening crawl of *Revenge of the Sith* and we were left to wonder where this mysterious droid general came from. Ultimately it didn't matter that he was a Kaleesh warlord-turned perfect warrior and Jedi killing machine. All we needed to know was that he was a villain and going about his dark work. And if he was daring enough to kidnap Chancellor Palpatine on Coruscant, he was a dangerous enough challenge for our heroes with no more information needed.

The behind-the-scenes facts of the character are almost as fascinating and fun as the character himself. For instance, did you know that his wheezing hacks and coughs came straight from George Lucas? During recording sessions, Lucas had a hacking case of bronchitis and the sound editors incorporated those into the performance of the droid general.

THE VOICE

As *Revenge of the Sith* developed, George Lucas had problems filling the role of General Grievous. Lucas knew what he was looking for, but as he went through audition tapes, he still couldn't find *exactly* what he wanted.

In the meantime, Cartoon Network was hard at work on the second season of Genndy Tartakovsky's 2D animated iteration of *Star Wars: Clone Wars.* These animated shorts introduced the world to the lethality of General Grievous and someone had to bring life to the role, even though the part still remained uncast for *Revenge of the Sith.*

Enter veteran voice actor John DiMaggio. You'd recognize him as the voice of Bender on *Futurama* or Jake on *Adventure Time.* He came in and gave the character his unique spin, not knowing what the final version would sound like.

DiMaggio's Grievous was a little tinnier than what ended up in the film, and even he was replaced in the third season by the animation and video game voice actor Richard McGonagle.

In an interview with *LRM Online*, Matthew Wood, sound editor at Skywalker Sound and the final voice of General Grievous, recalls what Lucas was searching for. "George said he wanted something very vampiric, kind of Bela Lugosi–like, and that's kind of where that went." Wood had dabbled in voice acting and had just been on vacation in Eastern Europe and thought he could do exactly what Lucas was looking for. He put in an audition tape blindly and was shocked when he was informed that he had gotten the part.

The rest was history.

THE CLONE WARS

Wood didn't just voice Grievous for *Revenge of the Sith.* The droid general became an important component of *The Clone Wars.*

If one wants to know about Grievous and what motivates him, one needs to look no further than the first season episode "Lair of Grievous." Grievous has built a secret monument to himself, a cold and dark lair dedicated to keeping himself as upgraded and lethal as possible. Another episode that highlights the best of Grievous is "Shadow Warrior," when the general faces off against the Gungan Grand Army and comes up short. In every iteration, Wood brings a delicious lilt to the character's voice.

Henry Gilroy, a writer and producer of *The Clone Wars*, reminds us in an interview with *TheForce.Net* that Grievous, although he's lost so much of his body, is not a tragic character. "He's a cold-blooded mass murderer, a classic old-school villain—and different from Vader—in that he doesn't have any redeeming characteristics. What kind of vain egomaniac has statues of himself in his house? Maybe one who is trying to convince himself he did the right thing."

Sources: TheForce.Net and LRMOnline.

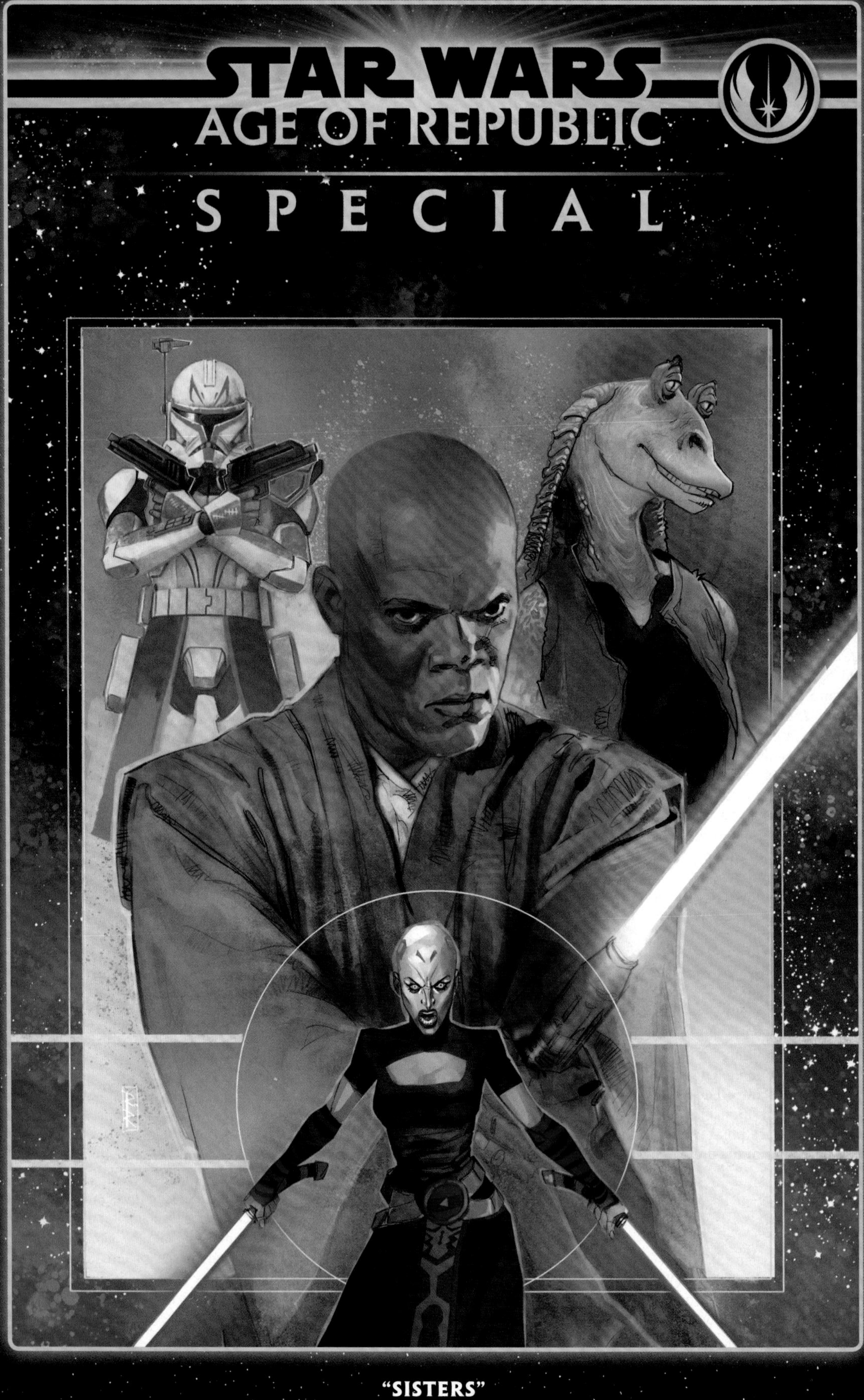
STAR WARS
AGE OF REPUBLIC
SPECIAL

"SISTERS"

After narrowly surviving Count Dooku's betrayal and the destruction of her people by the Separatists, the fearsome Asajj Ventress is forging a new path. She may no longer be a dark apprentice but she's as deadly and determined as ever. . . .

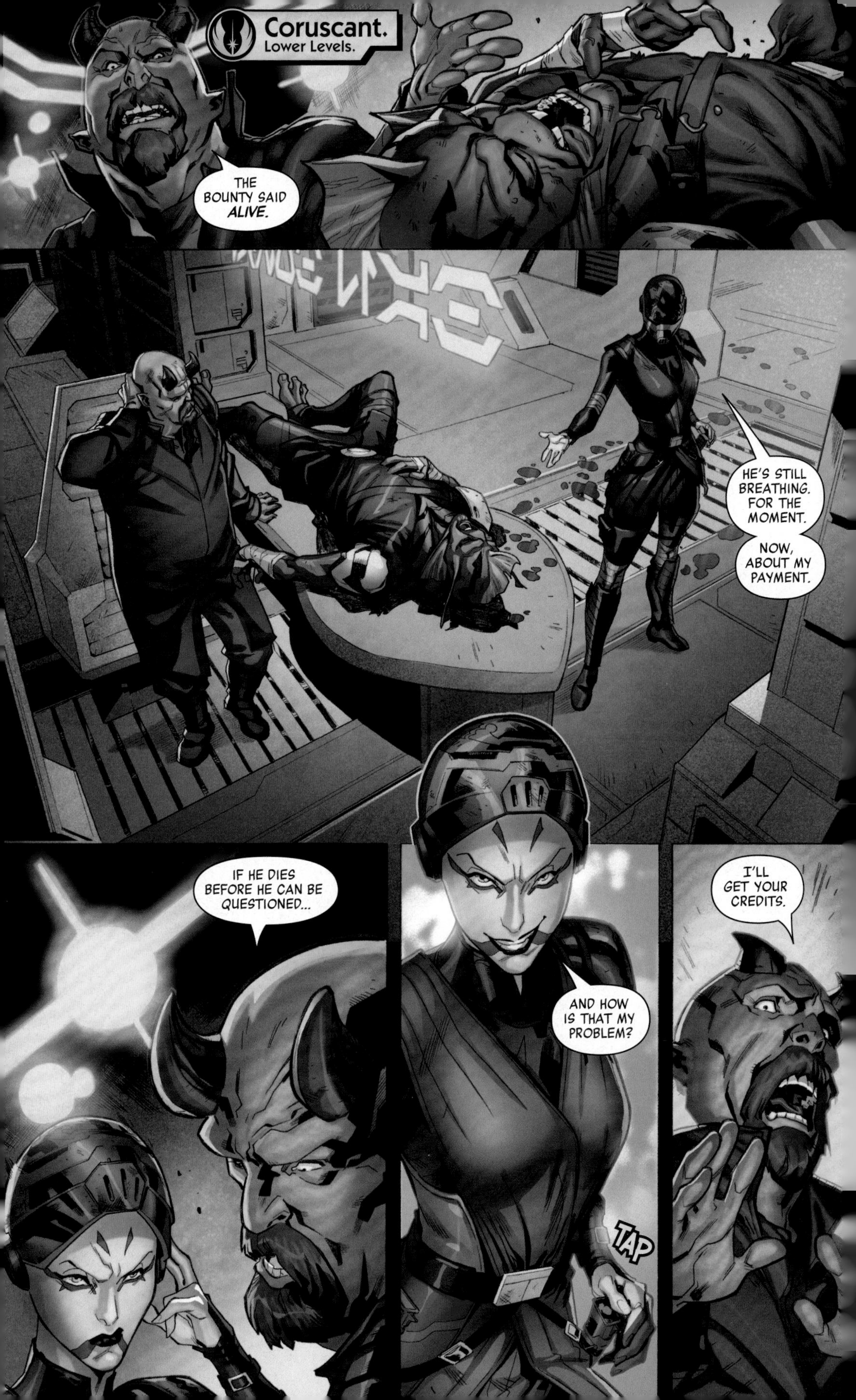
Coruscant.
Lower Levels.
THE BOUNTY SAID ALIVE.
HE'S STILL BREATHING. FOR THE MOMENT.
NOW, ABOUT MY PAYMENT.
IF HE DIES BEFORE HE CAN BE QUESTIONED...
AND HOW IS THAT MY PROBLEM?
TAP
I'LL GET YOUR CREDITS.

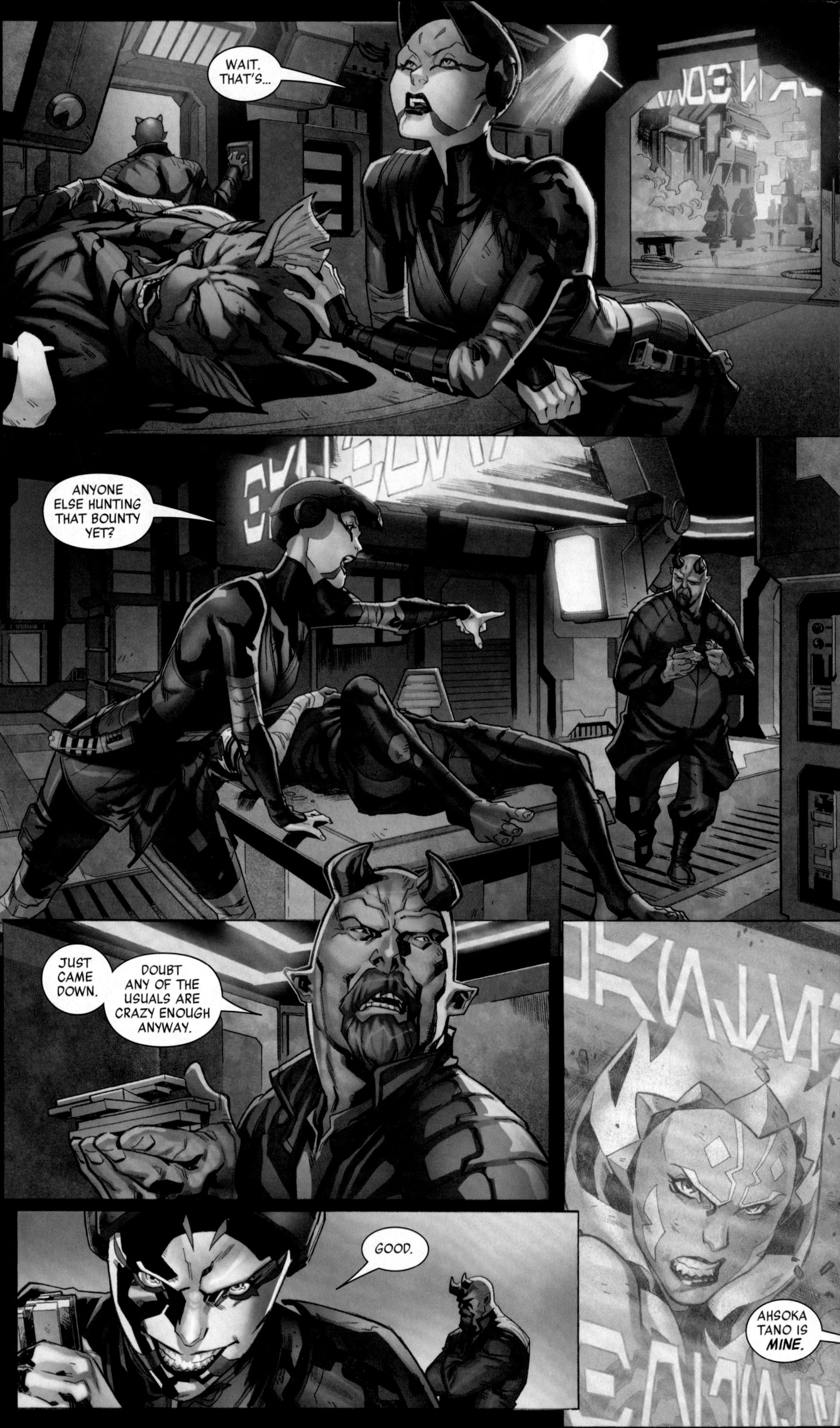
WAIT. THAT'S...
ANYONE ELSE HUNTING THAT BOUNTY YET?
JUST CAME DOWN.
DOUBT ANY OF THE USUALS ARE CRAZY ENOUGH ANYWAY.
GOOD.
AHSOKA TANO IS **MINE.**

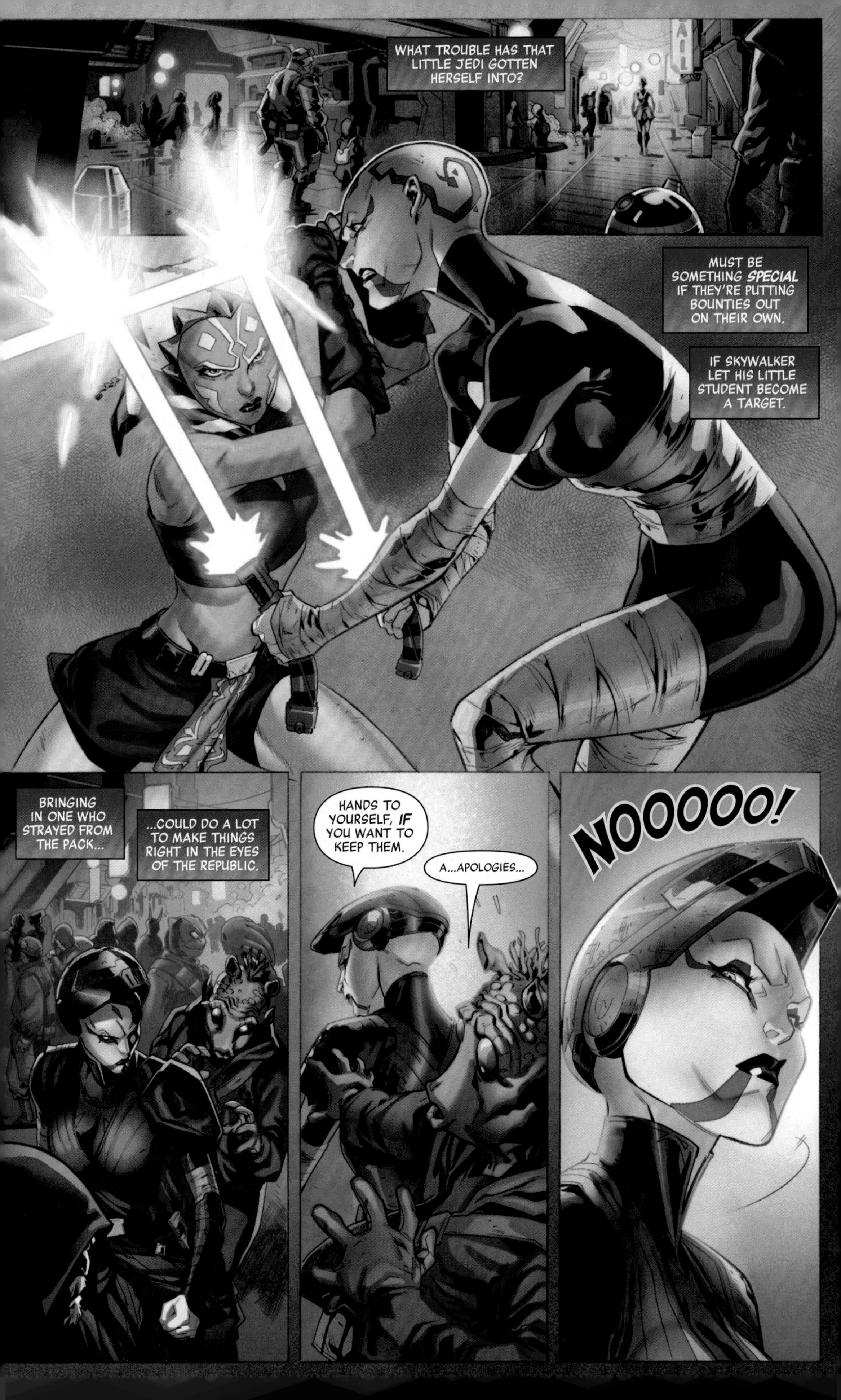
WHAT TROUBLE HAS THAT LITTLE JEDI GOTTEN HERSELF INTO?
MUST BE SOMETHING SPECIAL IF THEY'RE PUTTING BOUNTIES OUT ON THEIR OWN.
IF SKYWALKER LET HIS LITTLE STUDENT BECOME A TARGET.
BRINGING IN ONE WHO STRAYED FROM THE PACK...
...COULD DO A LOT TO MAKE THINGS RIGHT IN THE EYES OF THE REPUBLIC.
HANDS TO YOURSELF, IF YOU WANT TO KEEP THEM.
A...APOLOGIES...
NOOOOO!

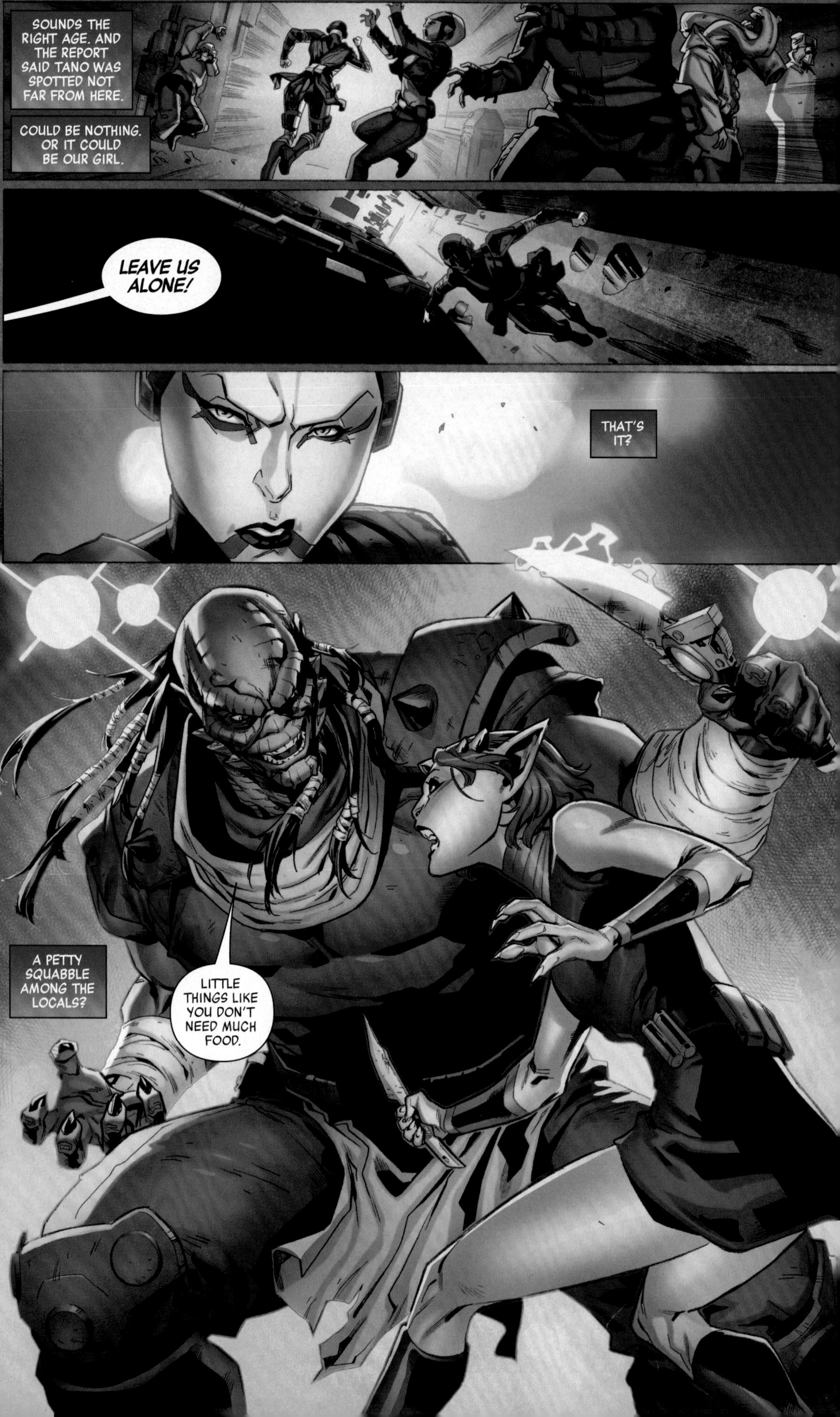

SOUNDS THE RIGHT AGE. AND THE REPORT SAID TANO WAS SPOTTED NOT FAR FROM HERE.
COULD BE NOTHING. OR IT COULD BE OUR GIRL.
LEAVE US ALONE!
THAT'S IT?
A PETTY SQUABBLE AMONG THE LOCALS?
LITTLE THINGS LIKE YOU DON'T NEED MUCH FOOD.

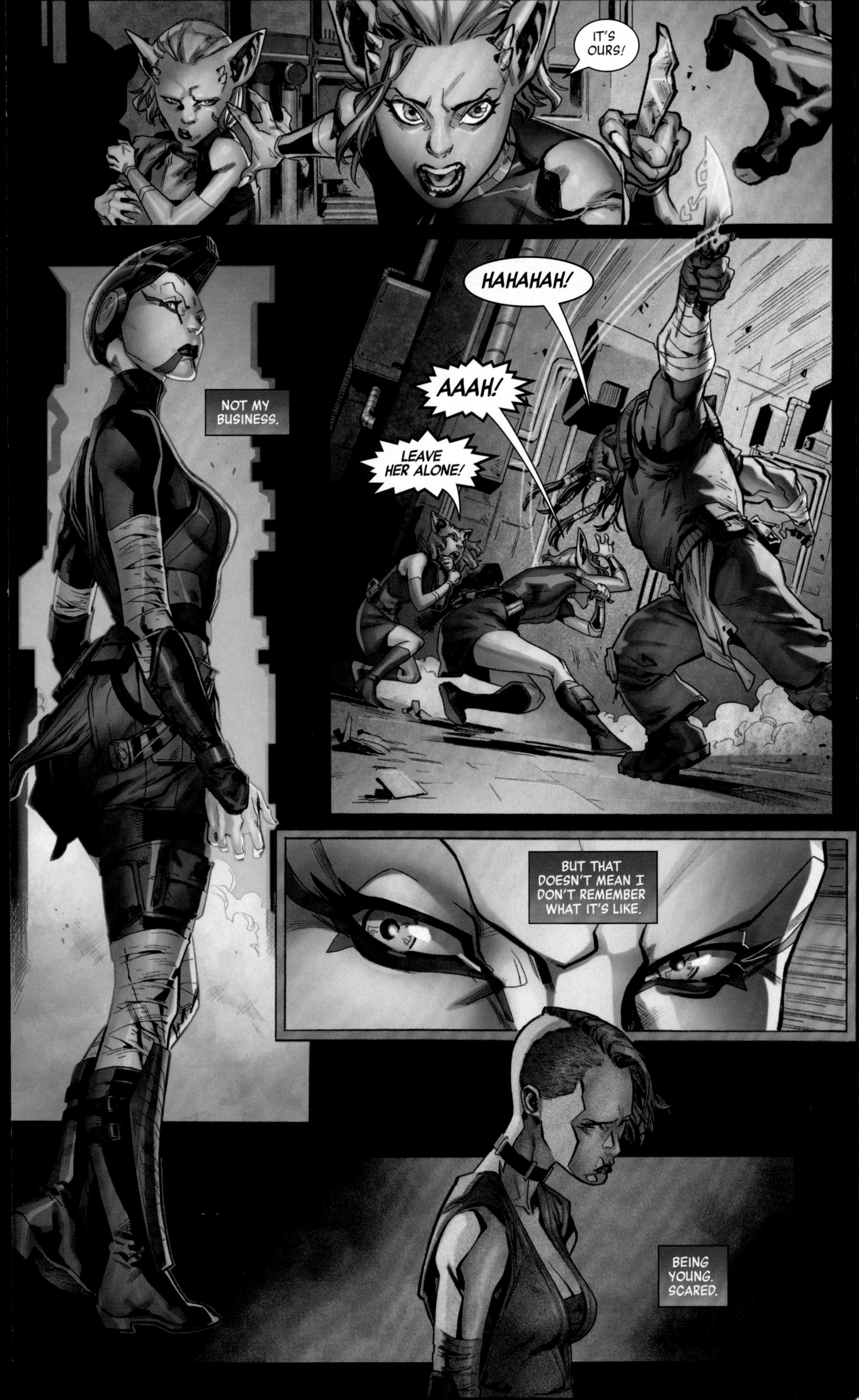
IT'S OURS!
NOT MY BUSINESS.
HAHAHAH!
AAAH!
LEAVE HER ALONE!
BUT THAT DOESN'T MEAN I DON'T REMEMBER WHAT IT'S LIKE.
BEING YOUNG. SCARED.

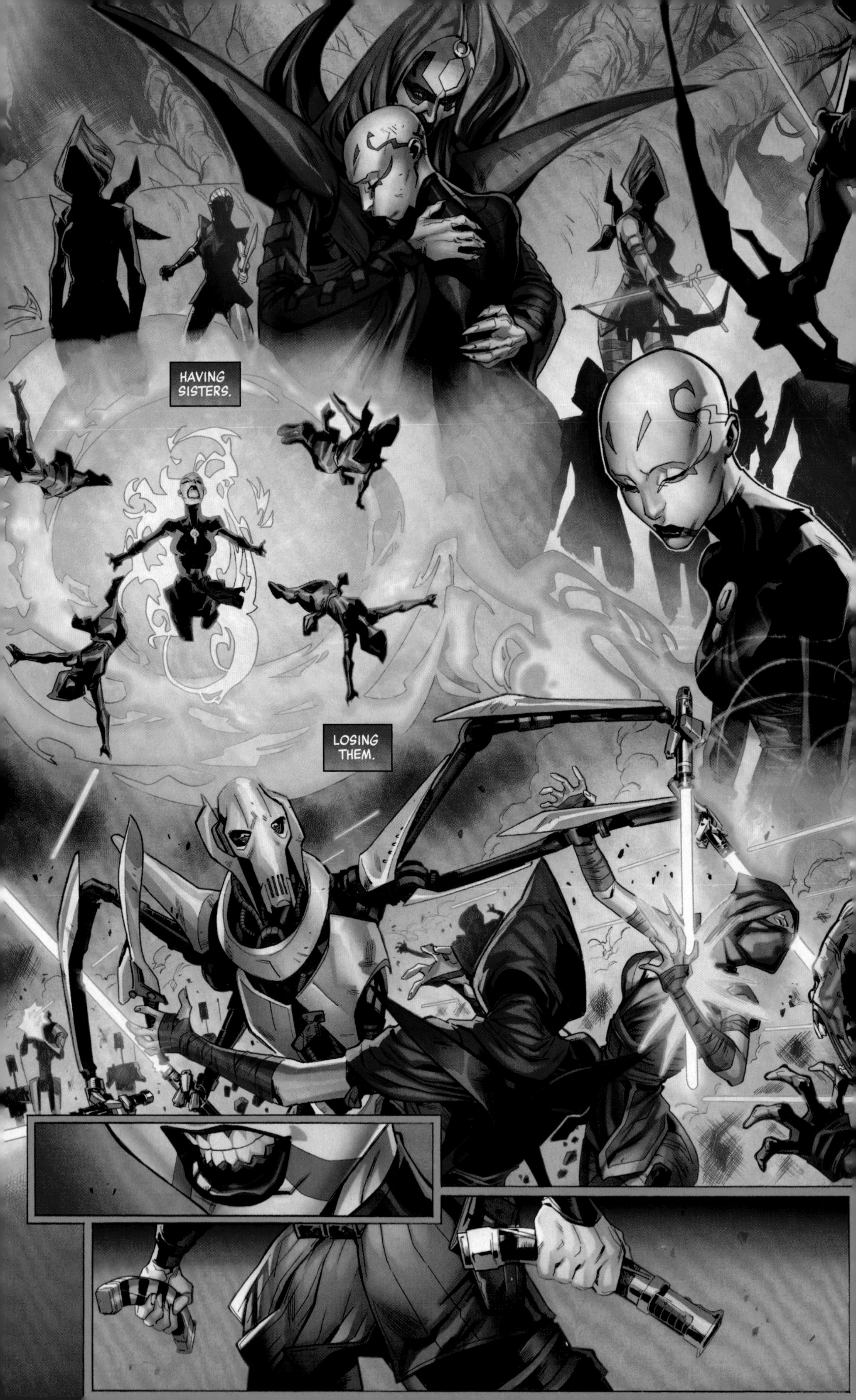
HAVING SISTERS.
LOSING THEM.

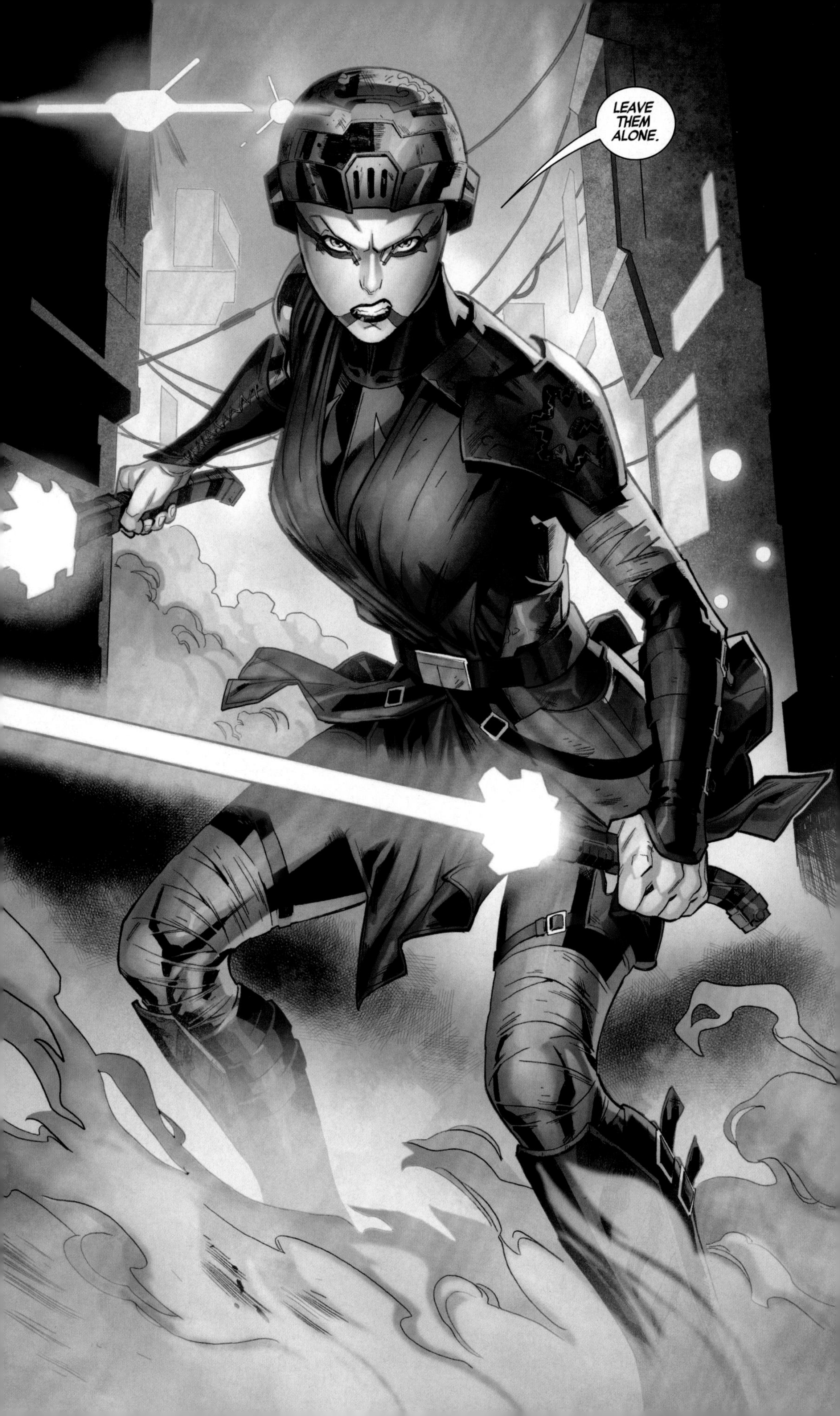
LEAVE THEM ALONE.

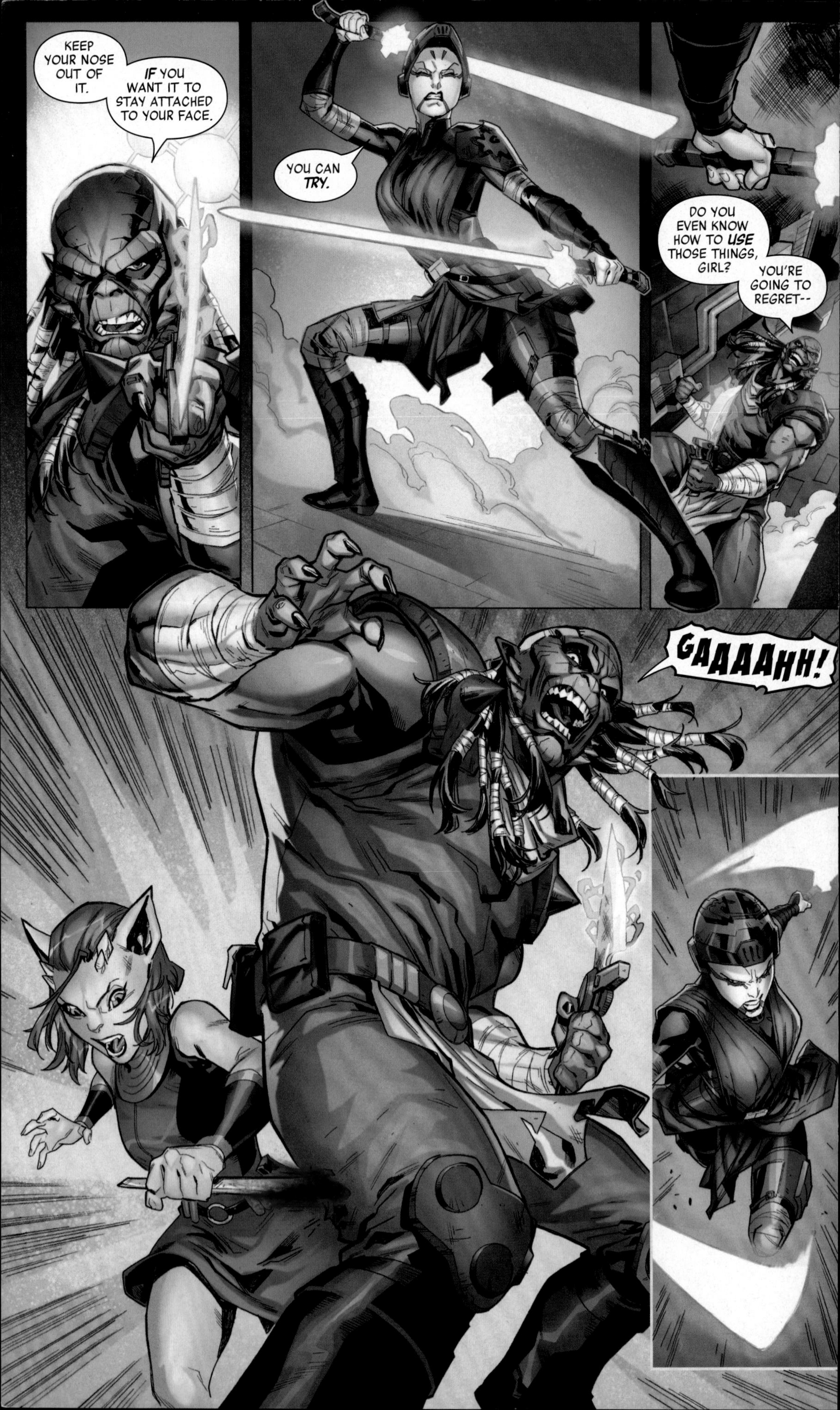
KEEP YOUR NOSE OUT OF IT.
IF YOU WANT IT TO STAY ATTACHED TO YOUR FACE.
YOU CAN TRY.
DO YOU EVEN KNOW HOW TO USE THOSE THINGS, GIRL?
YOU'RE GOING TO REGRET--
GAAAAHH!

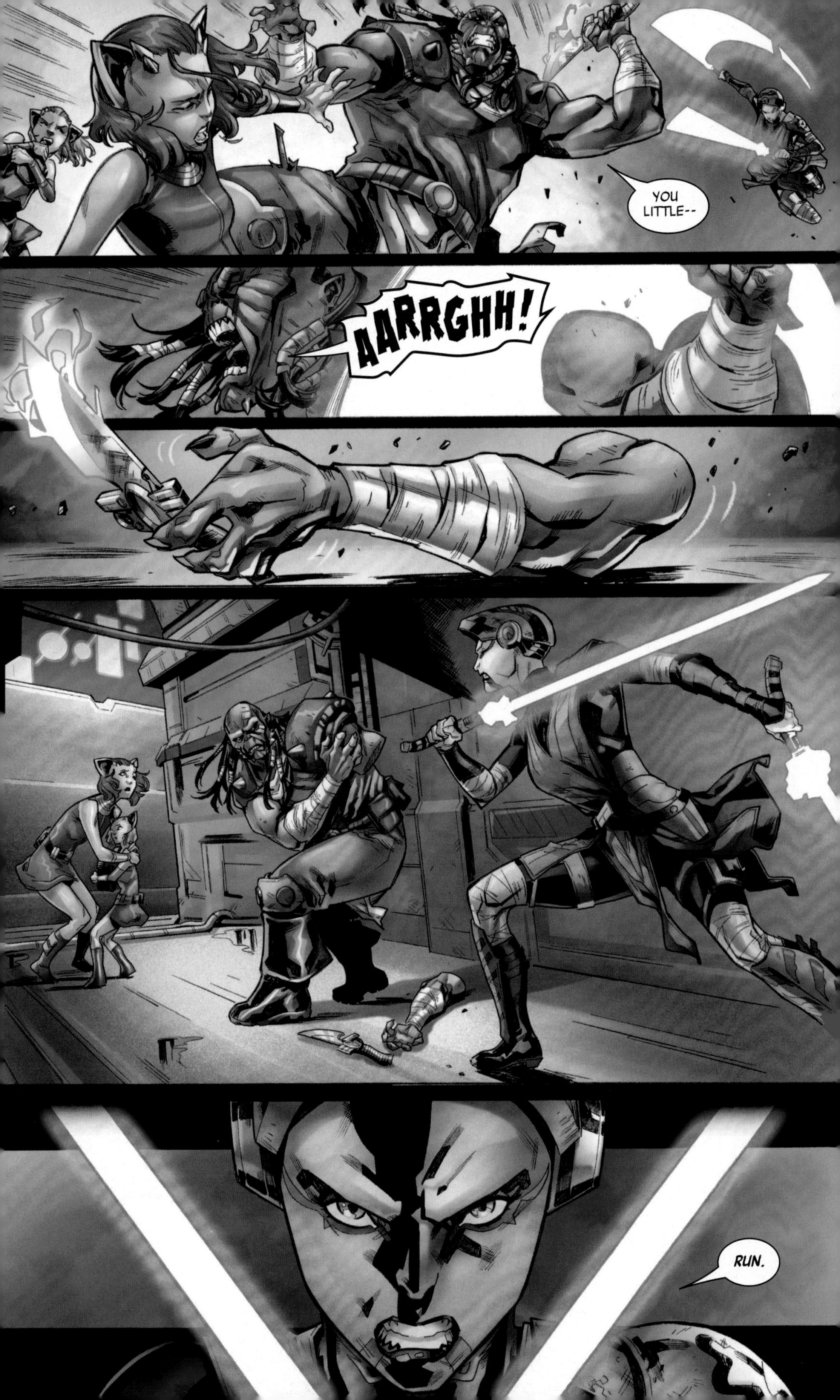
YOU LITTLE--
AARRGHH!
RUN.

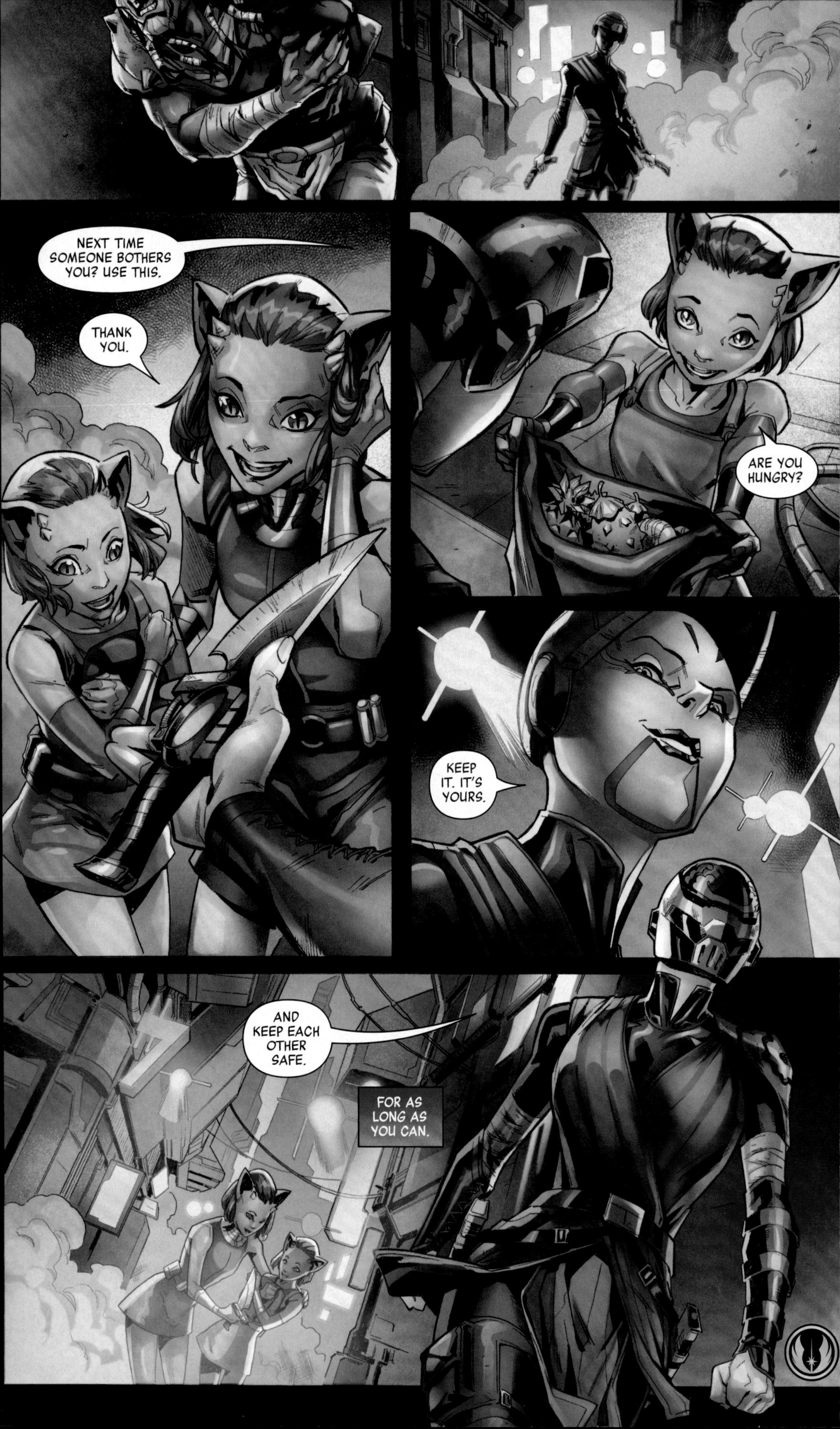
NEXT TIME SOMEONE BOTHERS YOU? USE THIS.
THANK YOU.
ARE YOU HUNGRY?
KEEP IT. IT'S YOURS.
AND KEEP EACH OTHER SAFE.
FOR AS LONG AS YOU CAN.

Concept art by Ryan Church

A GROWING GALAXY
The Star Wars Saga Just Wouldn't Be the Same Without These Stellar Supporting Characters
By Glenn Greenberg

A long time ago—specifically from 1977 to 1983—the *Star Wars* Galaxy was a much smaller place. If you asked fans back then to pick a favorite, you would likely hear the same names repeatedly: Luke Skywalker. Han Solo. Princess Leia. R2-D2. Yoda. Or, from those fans with darker tastes, Darth Vader or the bounty hunter Boba Fett.

But as George Lucas extended the saga, both on the big screen—via the Prequel Trilogy of *The Phantom Menace, Attack of the Clones* and *Revenge of the Sith*—and on the small screen through the animated series *The Clone Wars*, many new characters were introduced. And suddenly, you were likely to hear a completely different bunch of names cited as favorites. Today, many fans would find it impossible to imagine the *Star Wars* Galaxy without these key supporting players.

Asajj Ventress

Although originally conceived as an unused concept for Palpatine's apprentice in *Attack of the Clones*, Asajj Ventress eventually appeared in other media including 2008's *The Clone Wars* TV show. A native of Dathomir—homeland of the

magic-wielding witches known as the Nightsisters and the birthplace of the Sith Lord Darth Maul—Ventress was trained in the ways of the Force by the Jedi Knight Ky Narec. But when Narec was killed, Ventress' rage put her on a direct path to the dark side—and to the Sith Lord Count Dooku, who took her on as his apprentice.

Armed with twin red-bladed lightsabers, Ventress was a formidable combatant and had numerous encounters with Jedi Knights Obi-Wan Kenobi and Anakin Skywalker. But Dooku eventually betrayed her and left her for dead, under orders from his master, Darth Sidious—secretly Chancellor Palpatine, who perceived Ventress as a threat to him and his dark rule.

With few options left to her, Ventress eventually became a bounty hunter. Over time, it became apparent that goodness, compassion and a sense of honor had not been extinguished from her fully.

"We thought of all the characters developed for *The Clone Wars*, Ventress had become one of the most interesting," the show's supervising director, Dave Filoni, told a crowd at

San Diego Comic-Con in 2014. Indeed, she became the subject of a 2015 novel, *Dark Disciple*, which wrapped up her story in dramatic fashion. The book was based on unproduced scripts that the show's creative team had written with George Lucas. "We had these great ideas for Asajj Ventress," Filoni said, expressing his happiness about those ideas coming to fruition. "To me," he said, "the whole thing is just getting the story told."

Concept art by Dermot Power

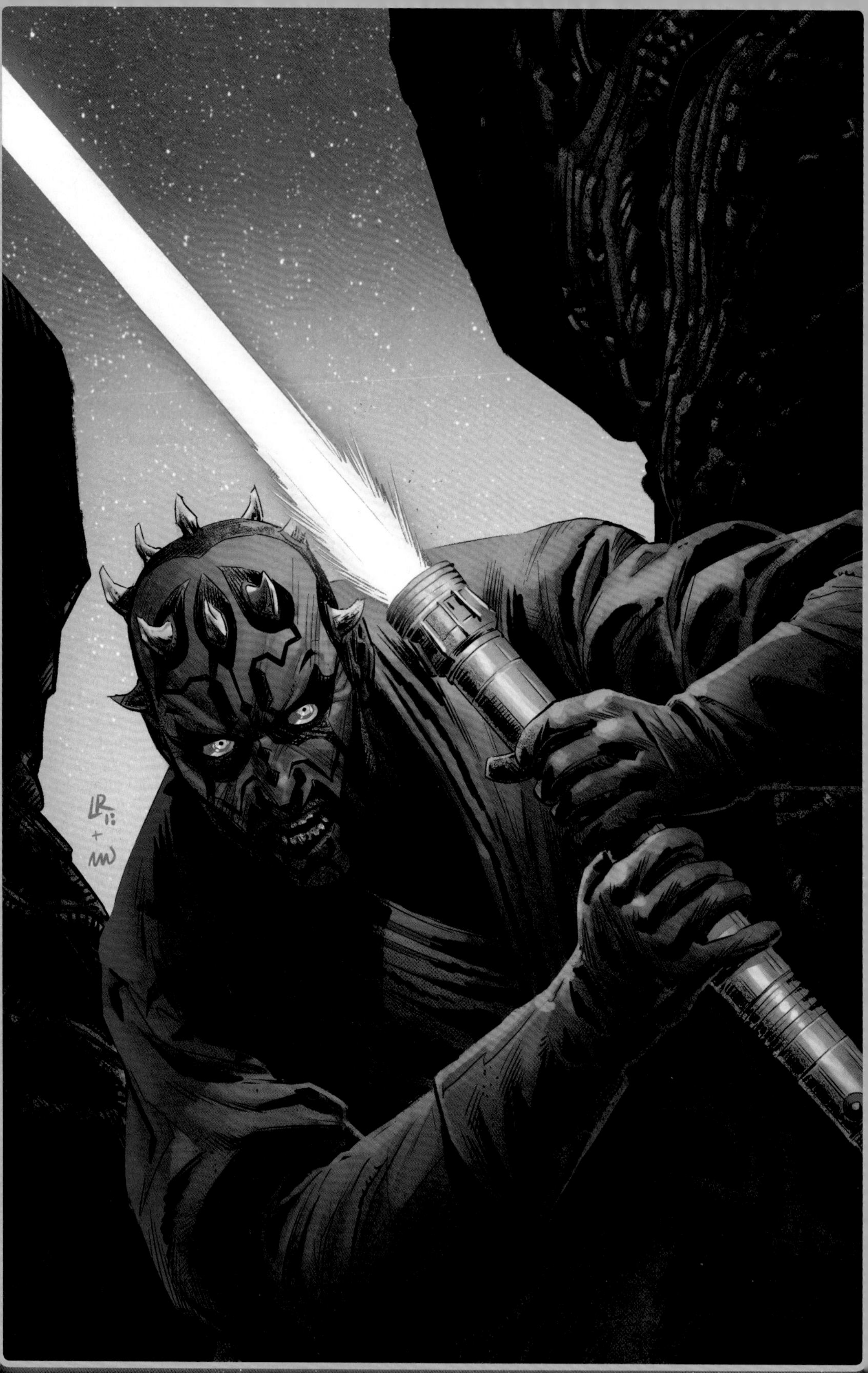

STAR WARS: *AGE OF THE REPUBLIC – DARTH MAUL* **Variant by**
LUKE ROSS & NOLAN WOODARD

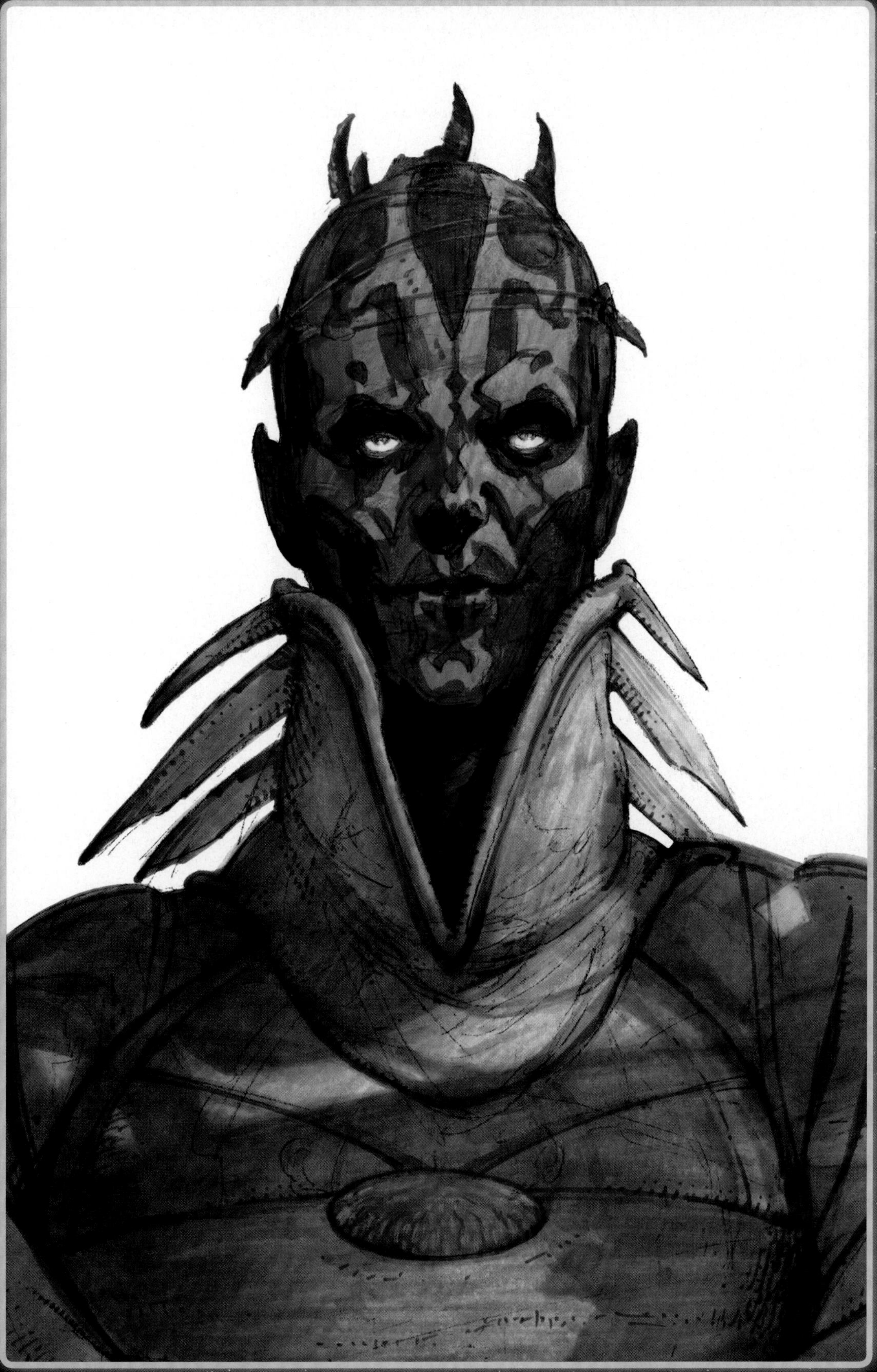

STAR WARS: AGE OF THE REPUBLIC – DARTH MAUL **Concept Design Variant by**
IAIN McCAIG

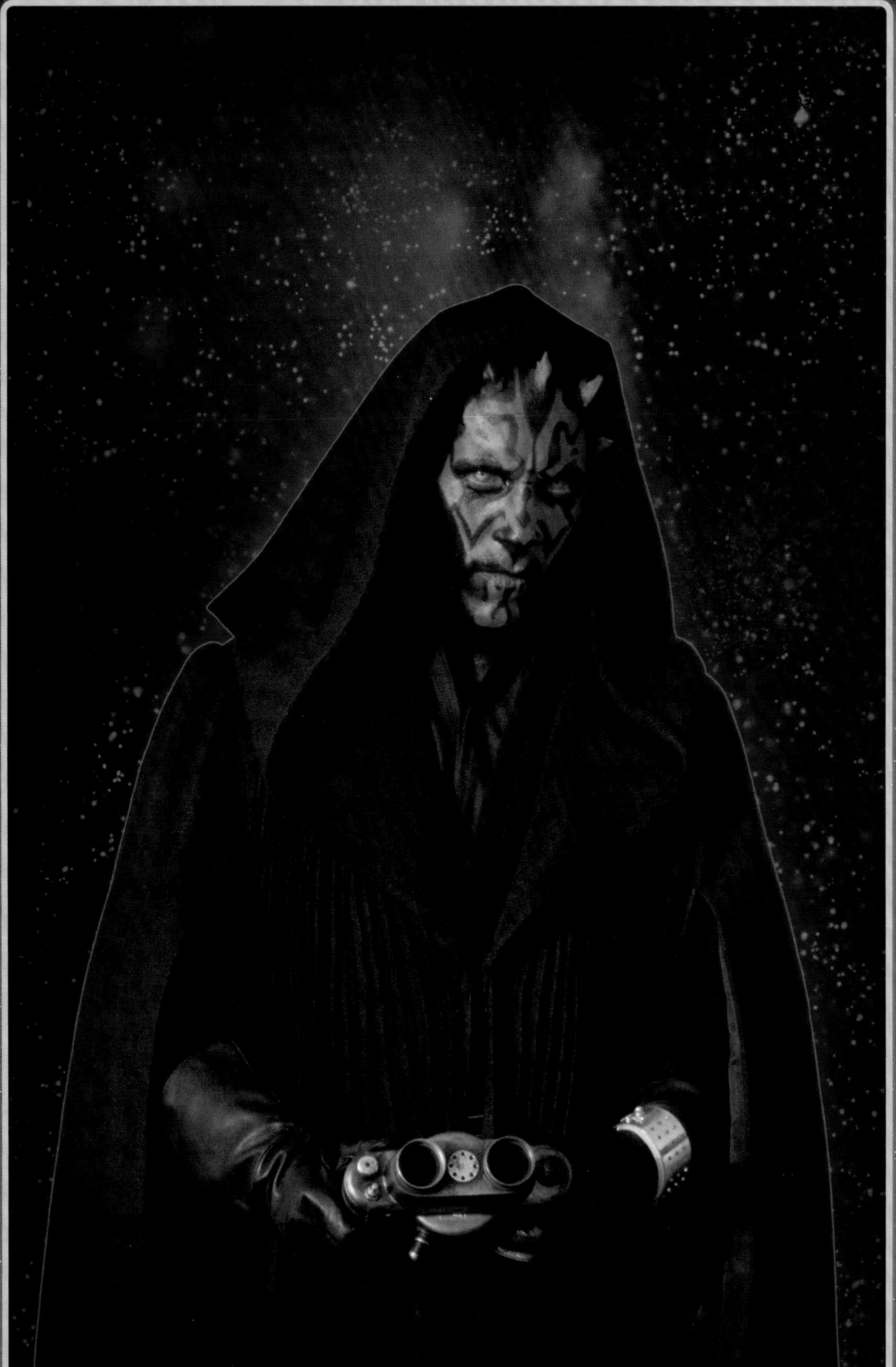

STAR WARS: AGE OF THE REPUBLIC – DARTH MAUL **Movie Variant**

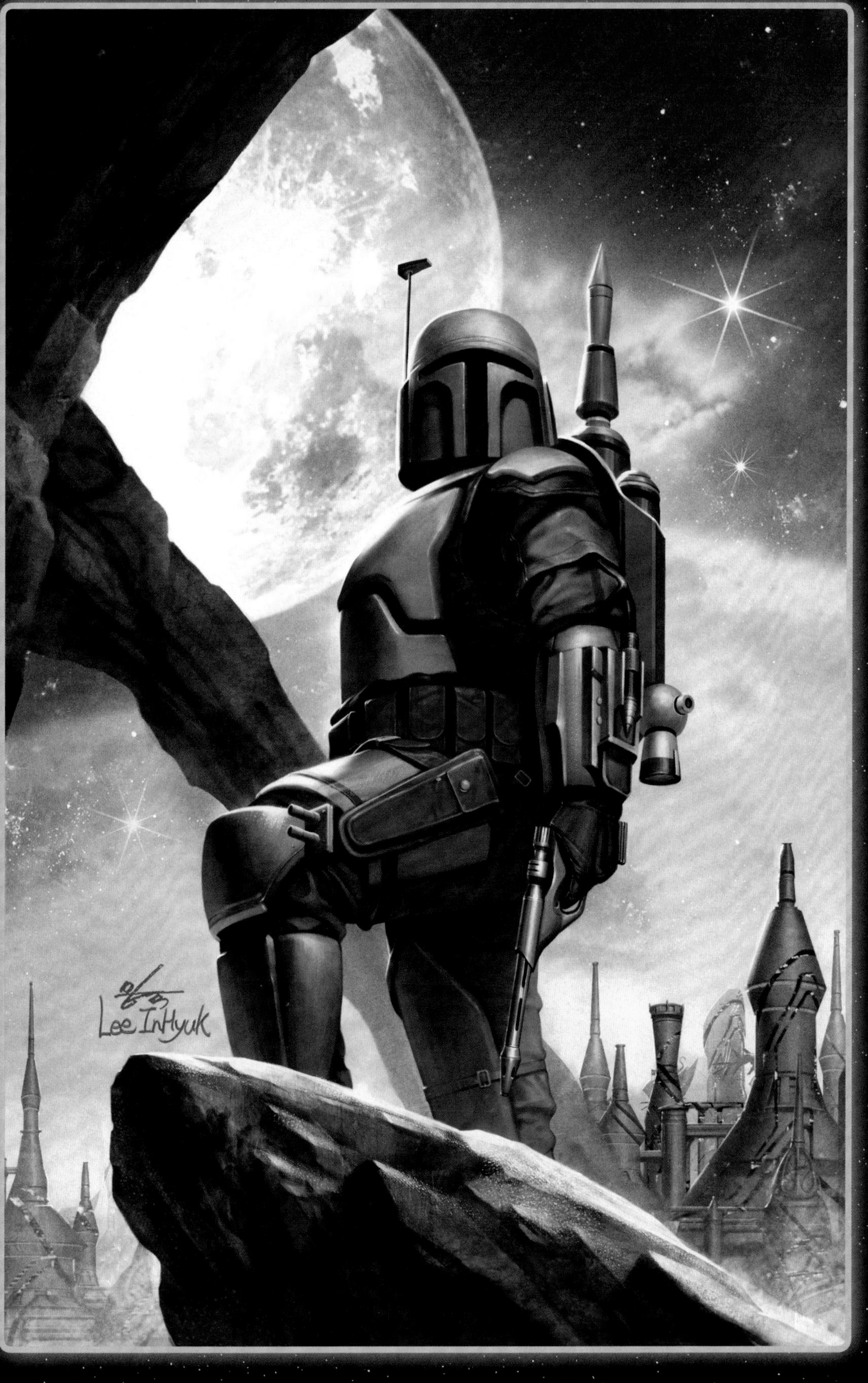
Lee InHyuk

***STAR WARS: AGE OF THE REPUBLIC – JANGO FETT* Variant by**
INHYUK LEE

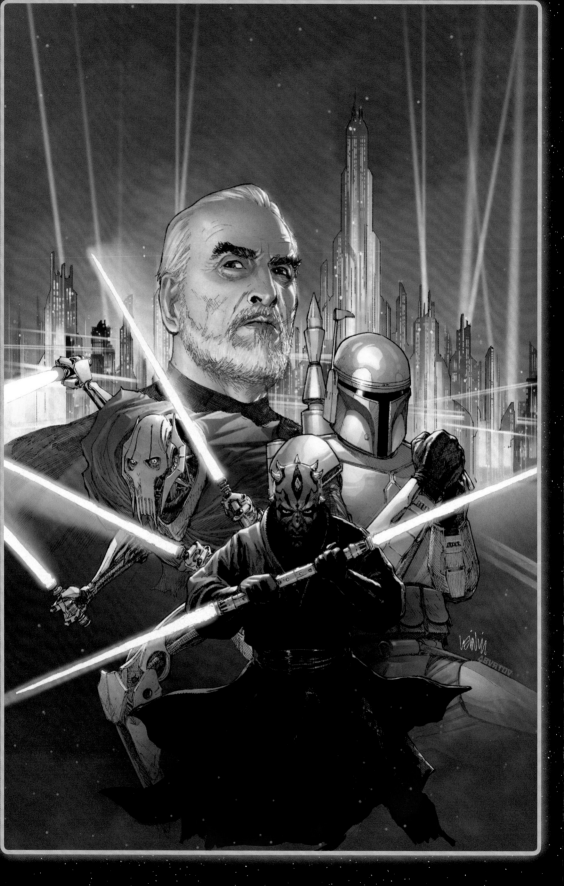

STAR WARS: AGE OF THE REPUBLIC – JANGO FETT Variant by
LEINIL FRANCIS YU & JESUS ABURTOV

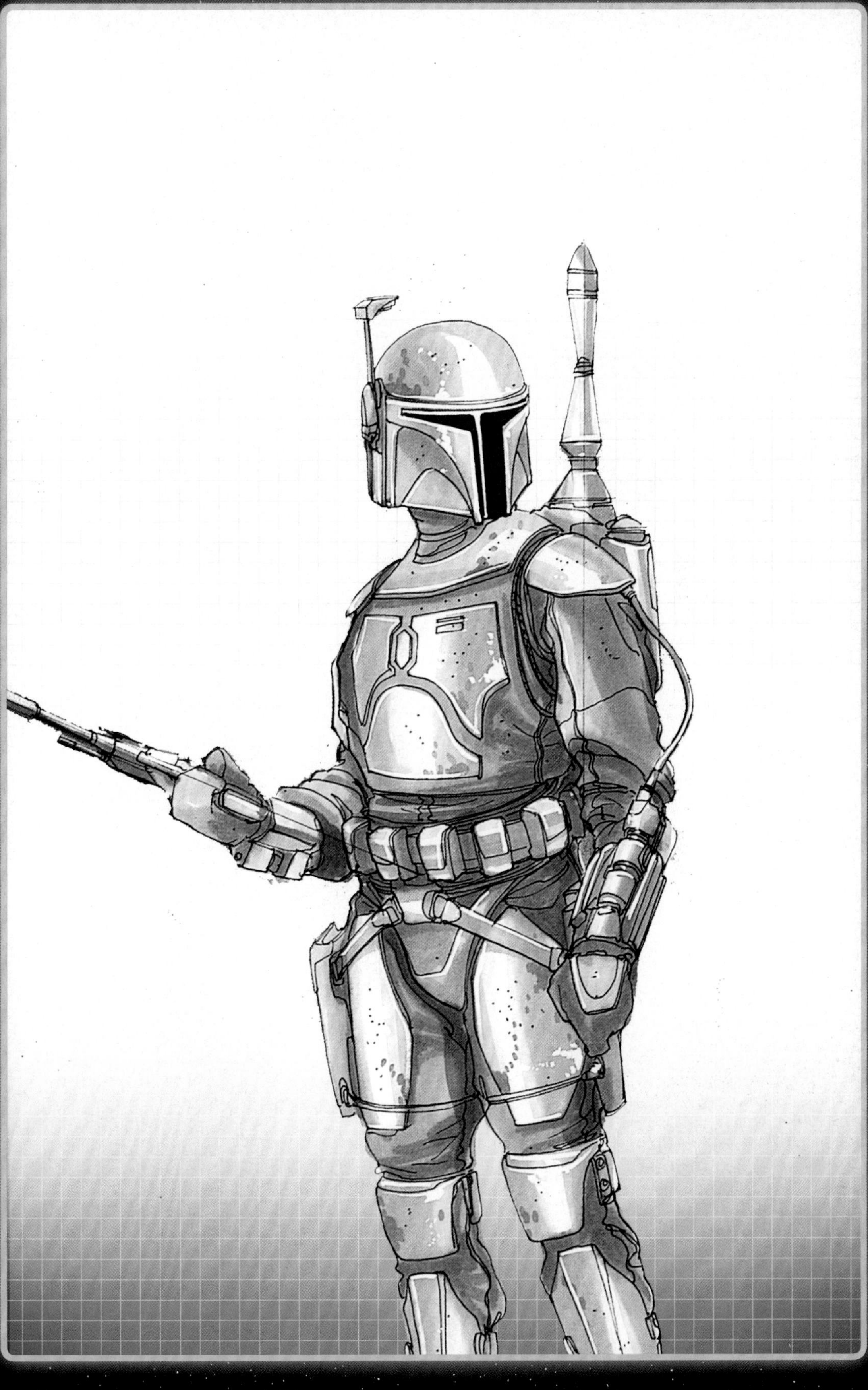

STAR WARS: AGE OF THE REPUBLIC – JANGO FETT **Concept Design Variant by**
DOUG CHIANG

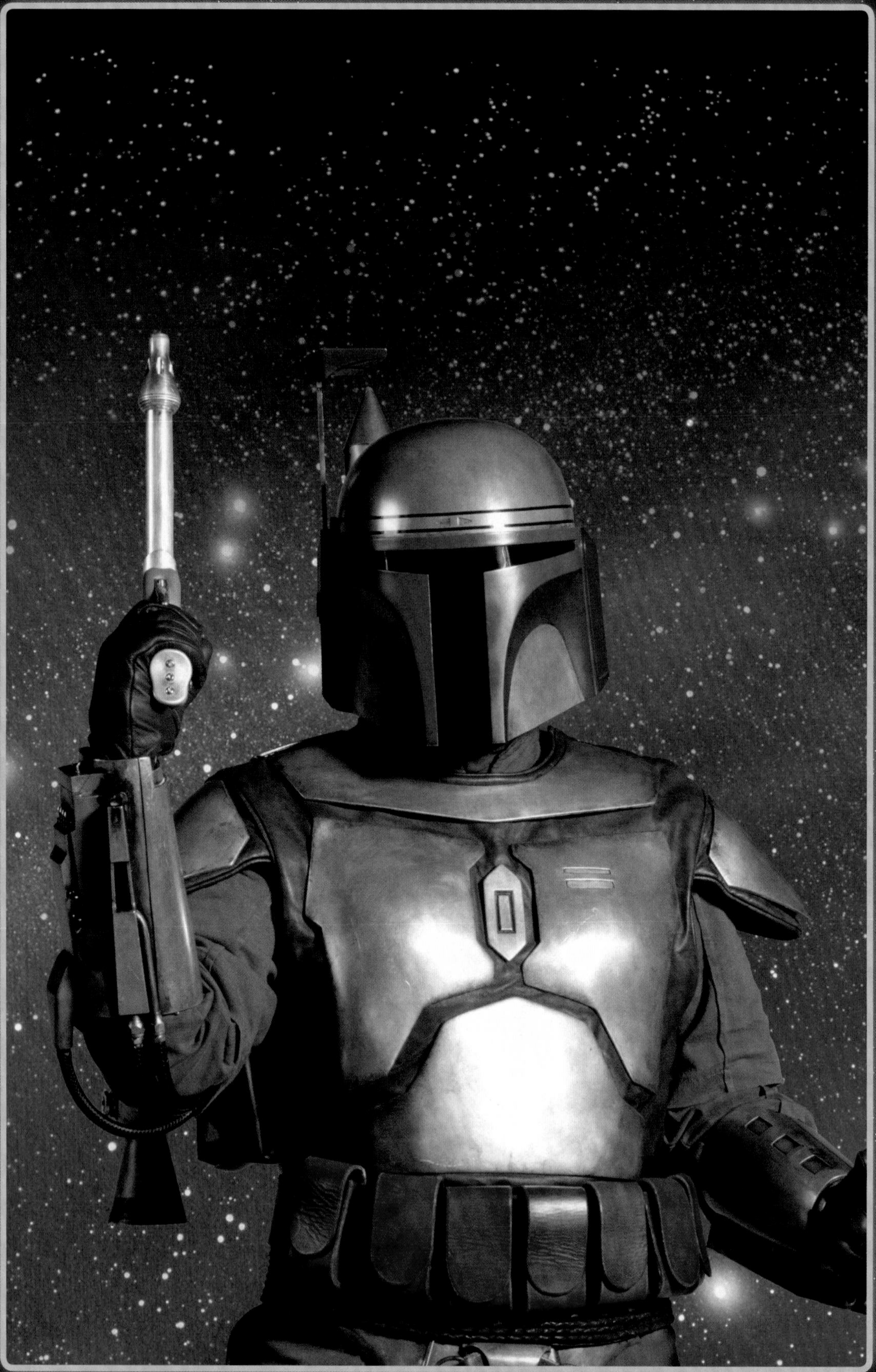

***STAR WARS: AGE OF THE REPUBLIC – JANGO FETT* Movie Variant**

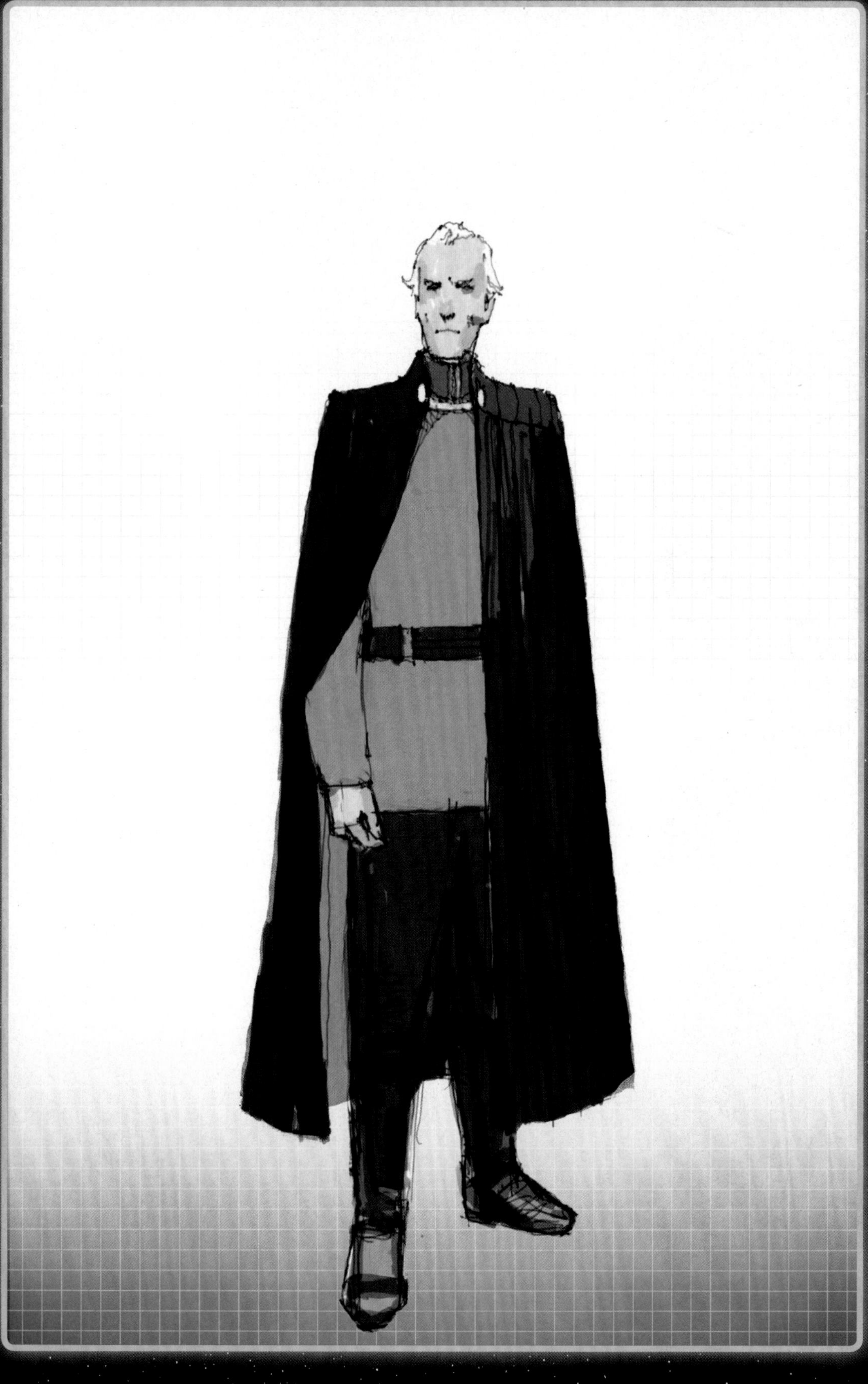

***STAR WARS: AGE OF THE REPUBLIC – COUNT DOOKU* Concept Design Variant by**
DERMOT POWER

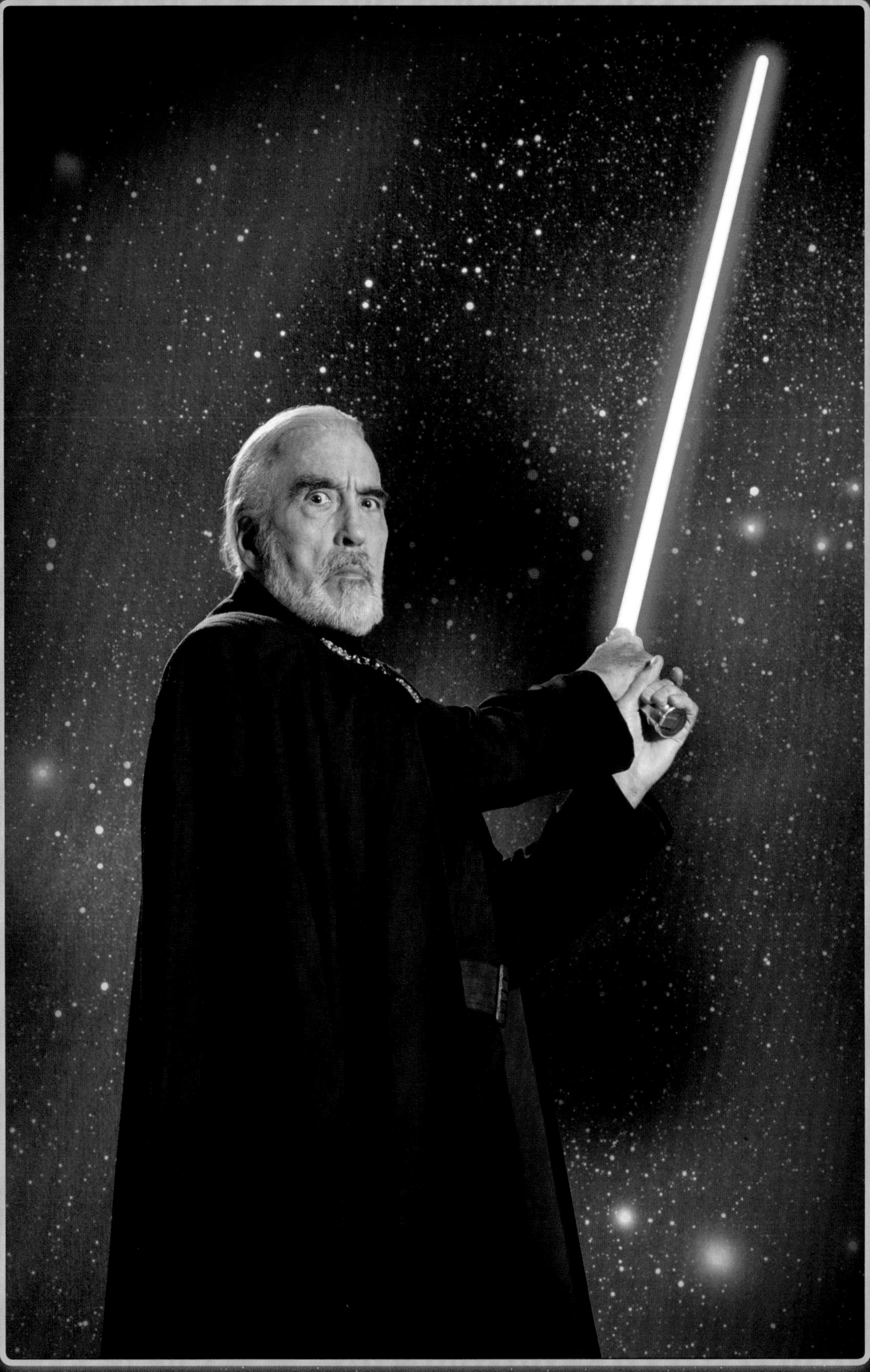

STAR WARS: AGE OF THE REPUBLIC – COUNT DOOKU Movie Variant

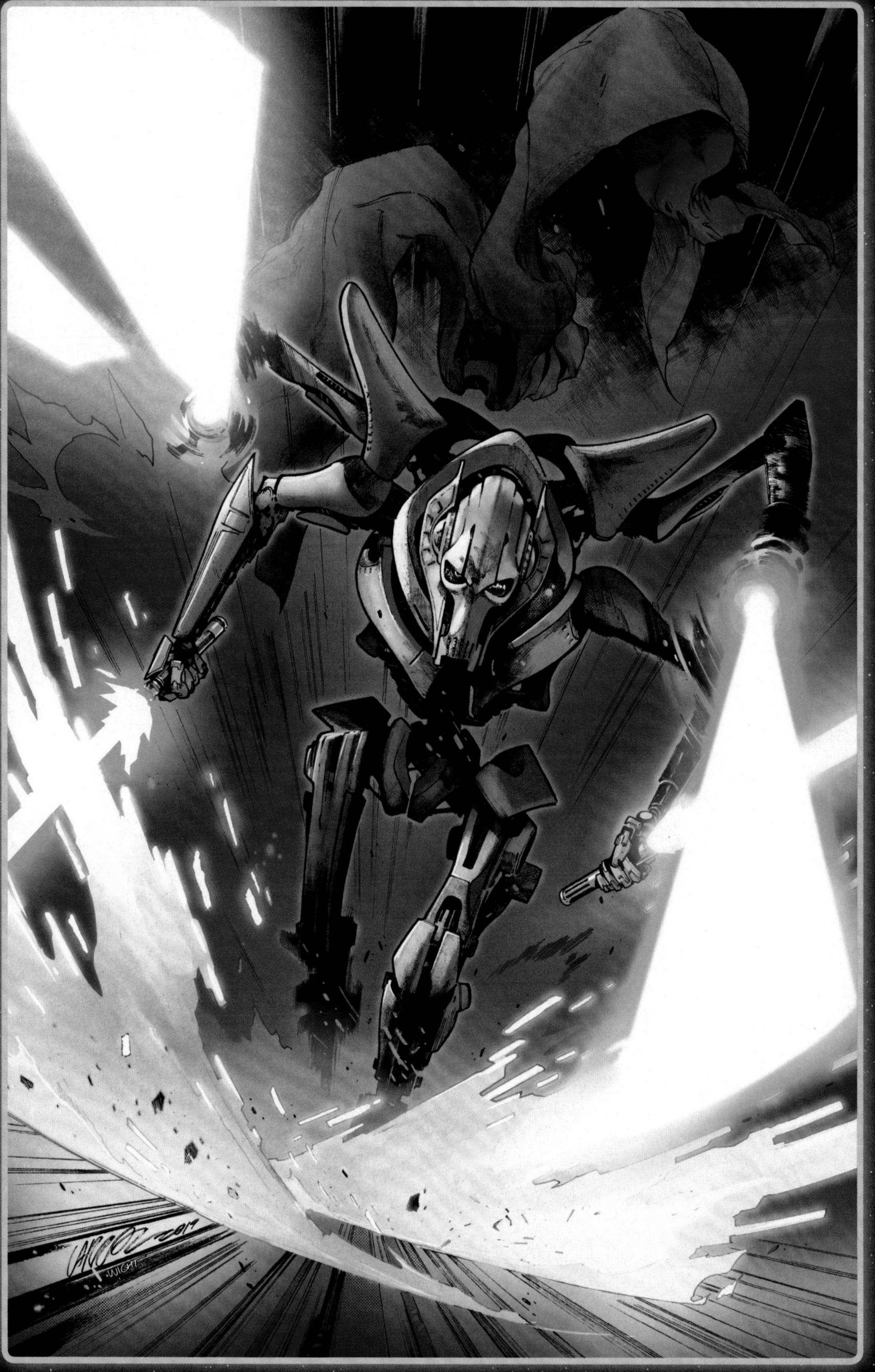

STAR WARS: AGE OF THE REPUBLIC – GENERAL GRIEVOUS
***Star Wars* Greatest Moments Variant by**
PEPE LARRAZ & GURU-eFX

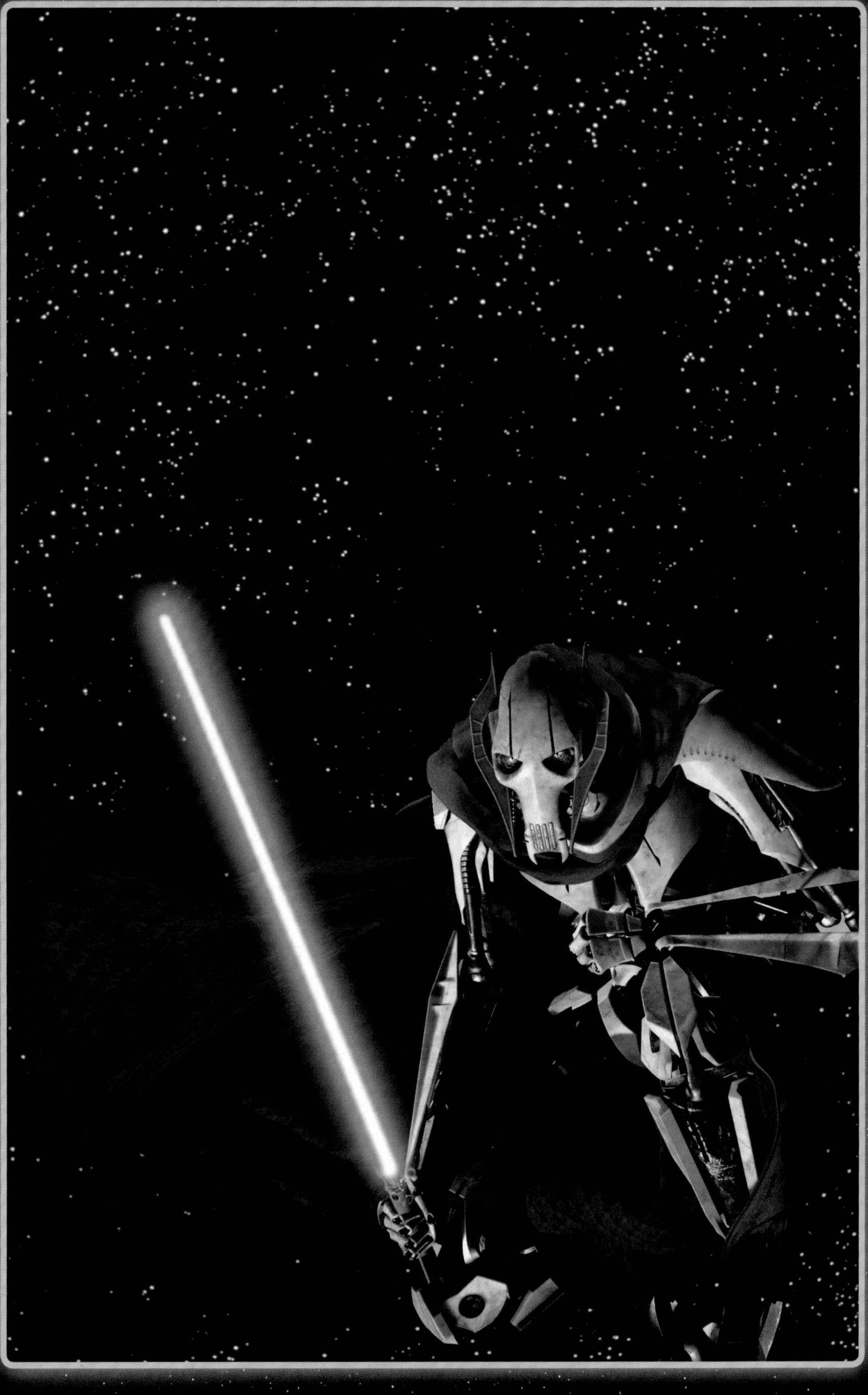

STAR WARS: AGE OF THE REPUBLIC – GENERAL GRIEVOUS **Movie Variant**

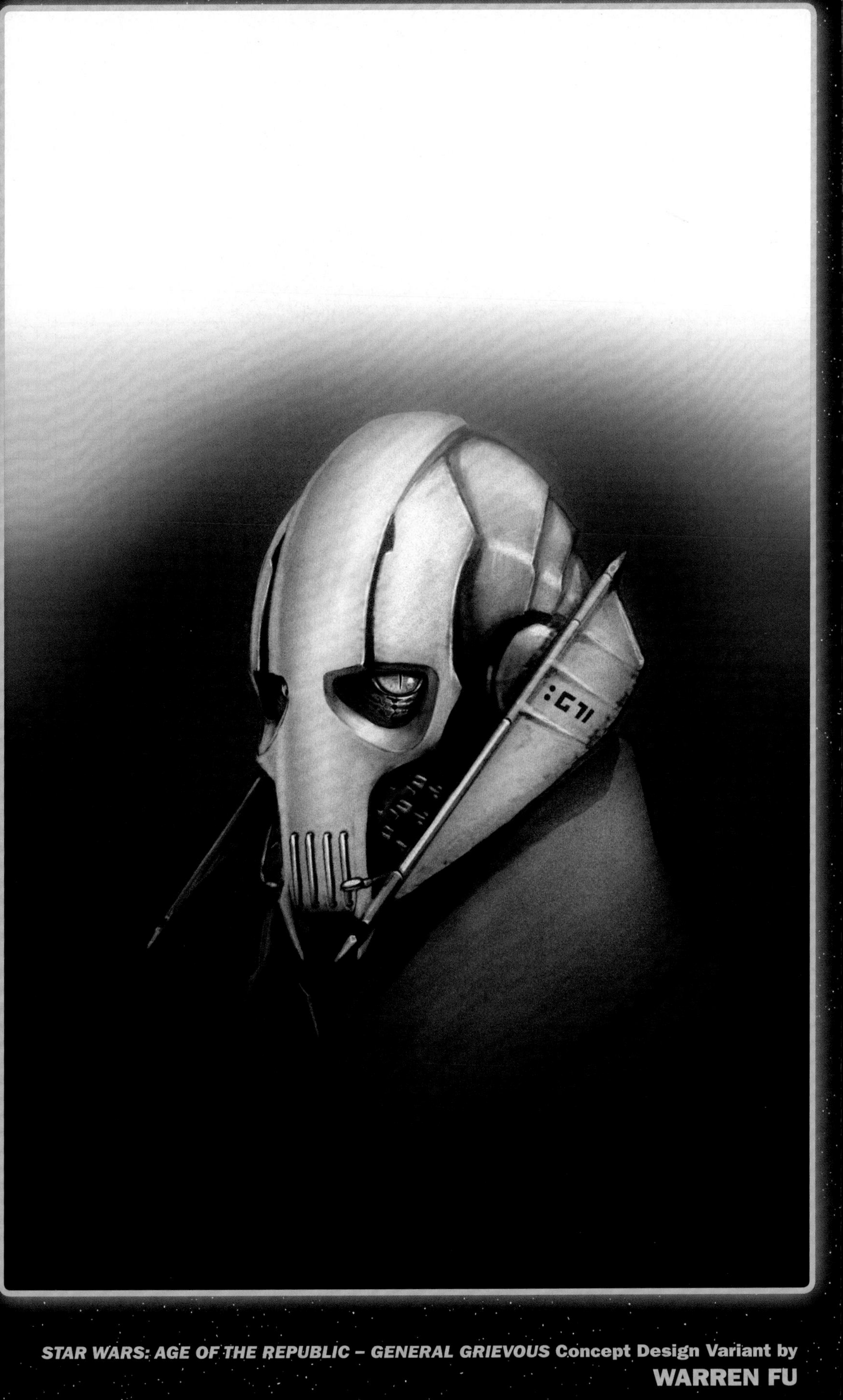

STAR WARS: AGE OF THE REPUBLIC – GENERAL GRIEVOUS **Concept Design Variant by**

WARREN FU

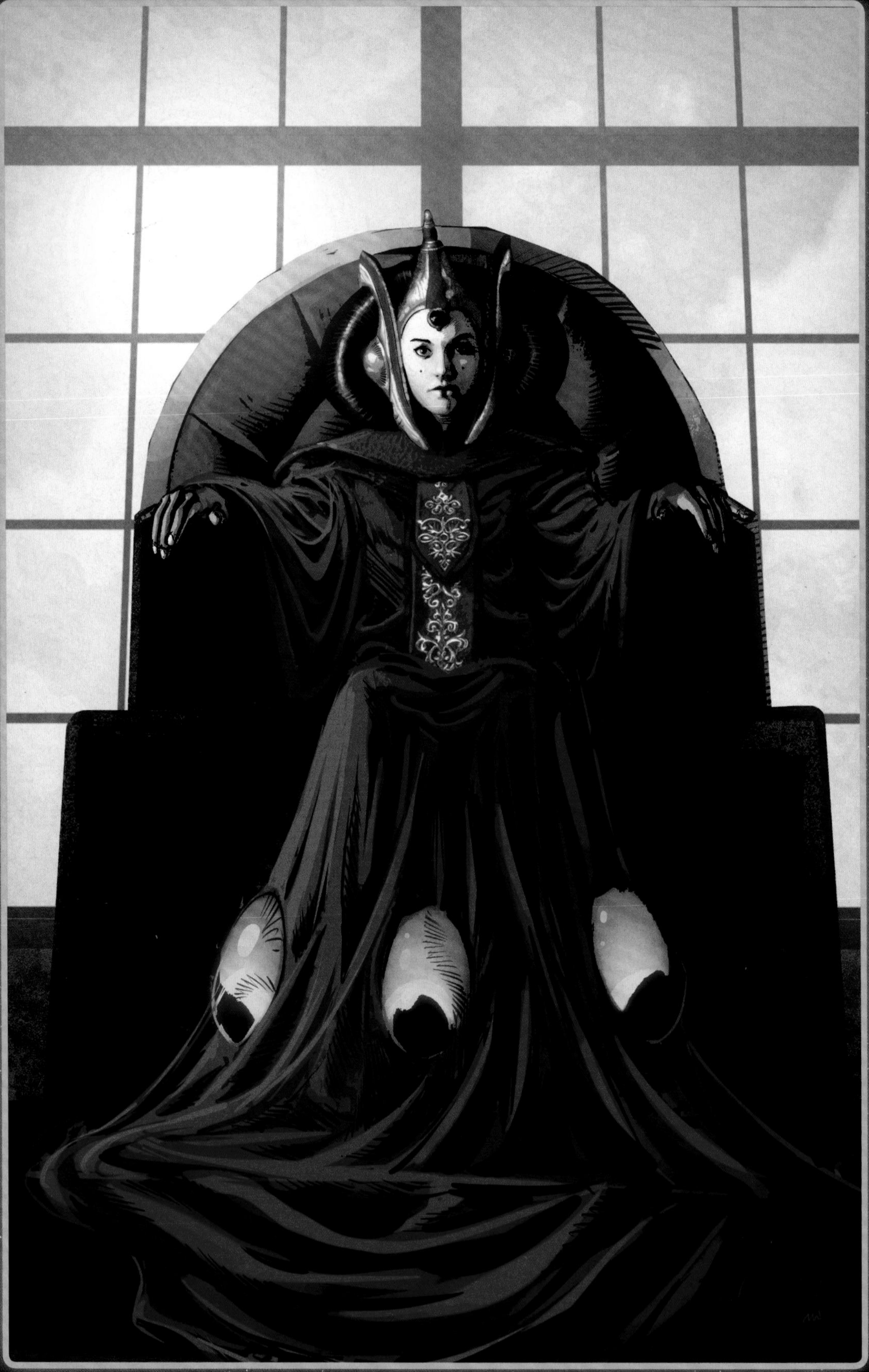

STAR WARS: AGE OF THE REPUBLIC SPECIAL Star Wars **Greatest Moments Variant by**
MIKE DEODATO JR. & NOLAN WOODARD

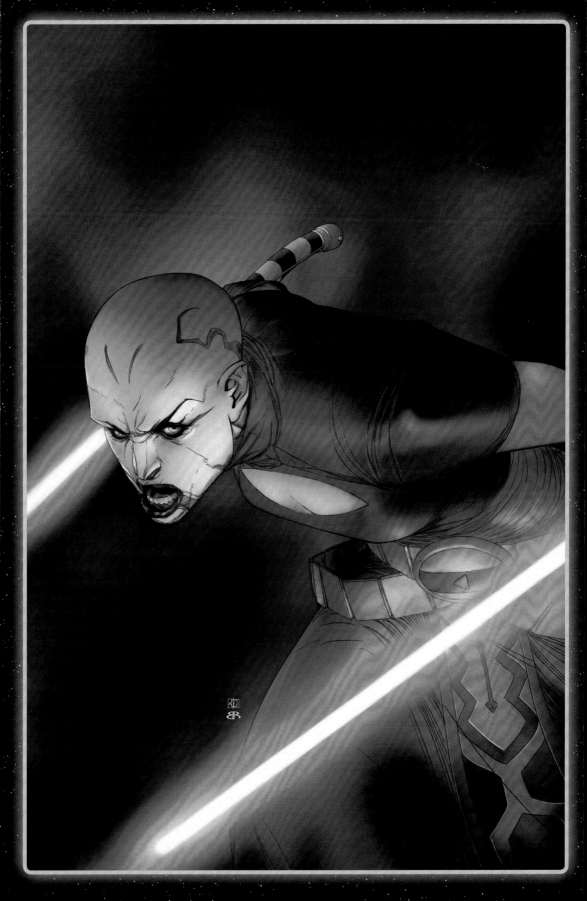

STAR WARS: AGE OF THE REPUBLIC SPECIAL Variant by
KHOI PHAM & **BRIAN REBER**

SPECIAL BONUS PREVIEW...

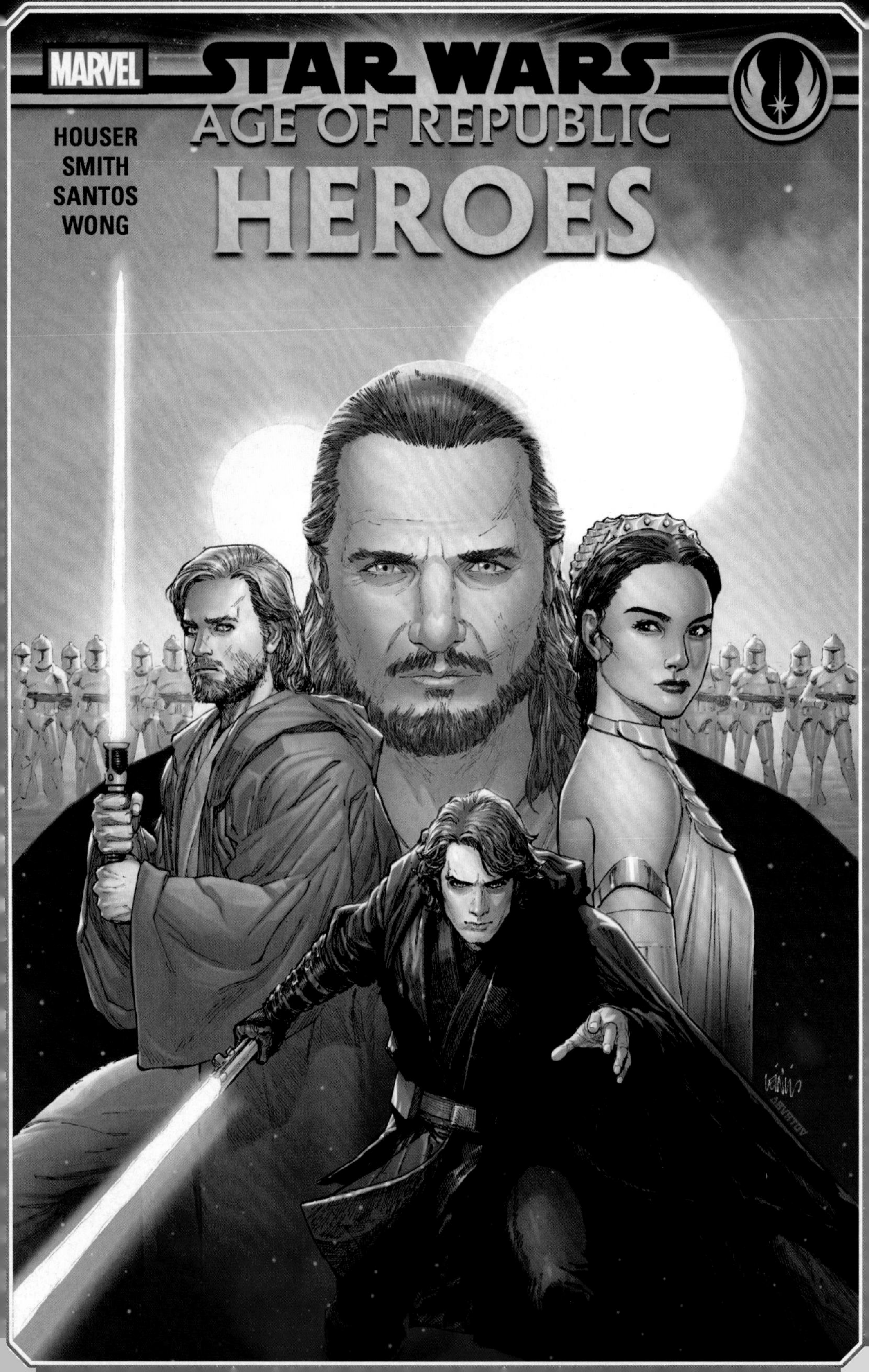
MARVEL
STAR WARS
AGE OF REPUBLIC
HEROES
HOUSER
SMITH
SANTOS
WONG

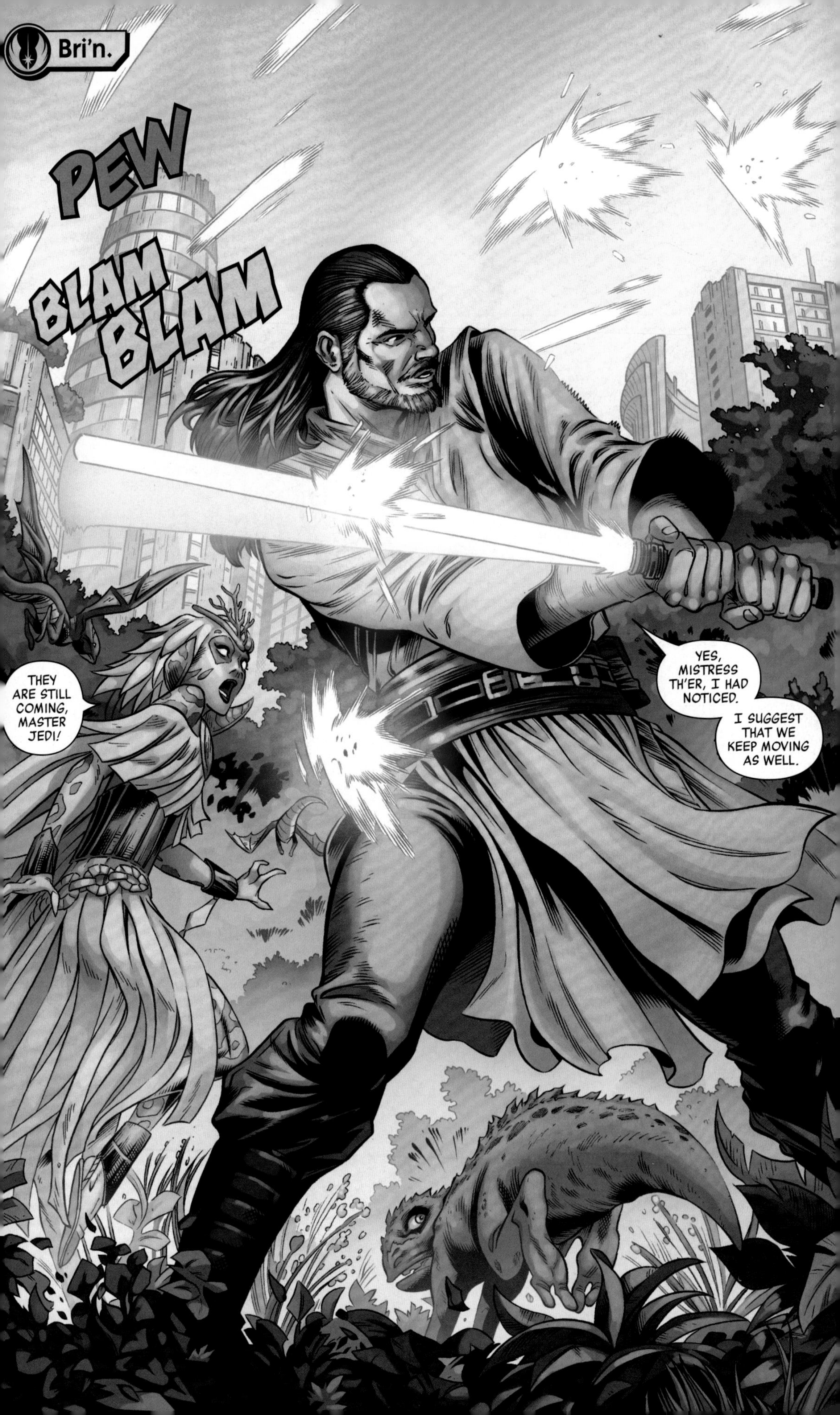

Bri'n.
PEW
BLAM BLAM
THEY ARE STILL COMING, MASTER JEDI!
YES, MISTRESS TH'ER, I HAD NOTICED.
I SUGGEST THAT WE KEEP MOVING AS WELL.

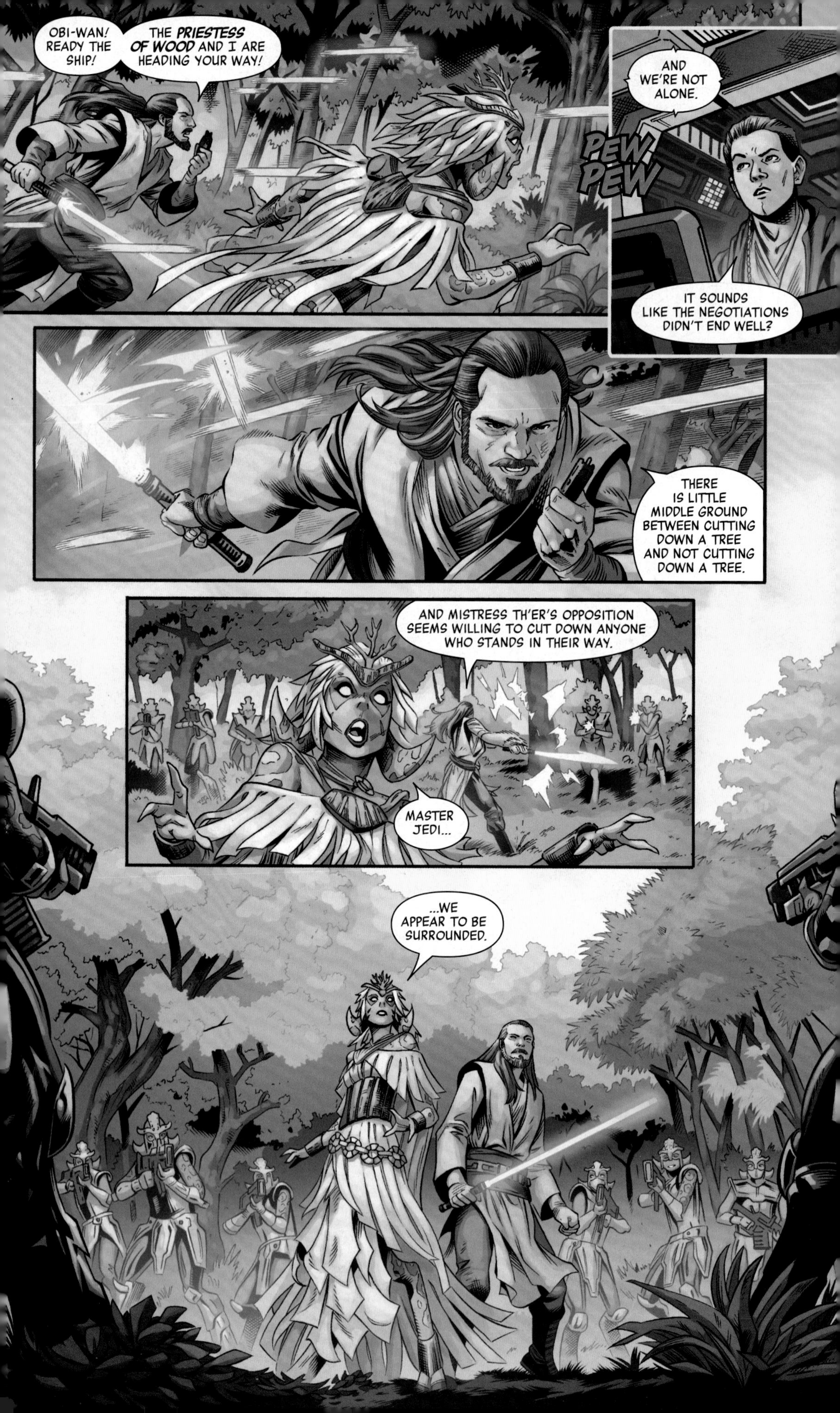
OBI-WAN! READY THE SHIP!
THE PRIESTESS OF WOOD AND I ARE HEADING YOUR WAY!
AND WE'RE NOT ALONE.
PEW PEW
IT SOUNDS LIKE THE NEGOTIATIONS DIDN'T END WELL?
THERE IS LITTLE MIDDLE GROUND BETWEEN CUTTING DOWN A TREE AND NOT CUTTING DOWN A TREE.
AND MISTRESS TH'ER'S OPPOSITION SEEMS WILLING TO CUT DOWN ANYONE WHO STANDS IN THEIR WAY.
MASTER JEDI...
...WE APPEAR TO BE SURROUNDED.

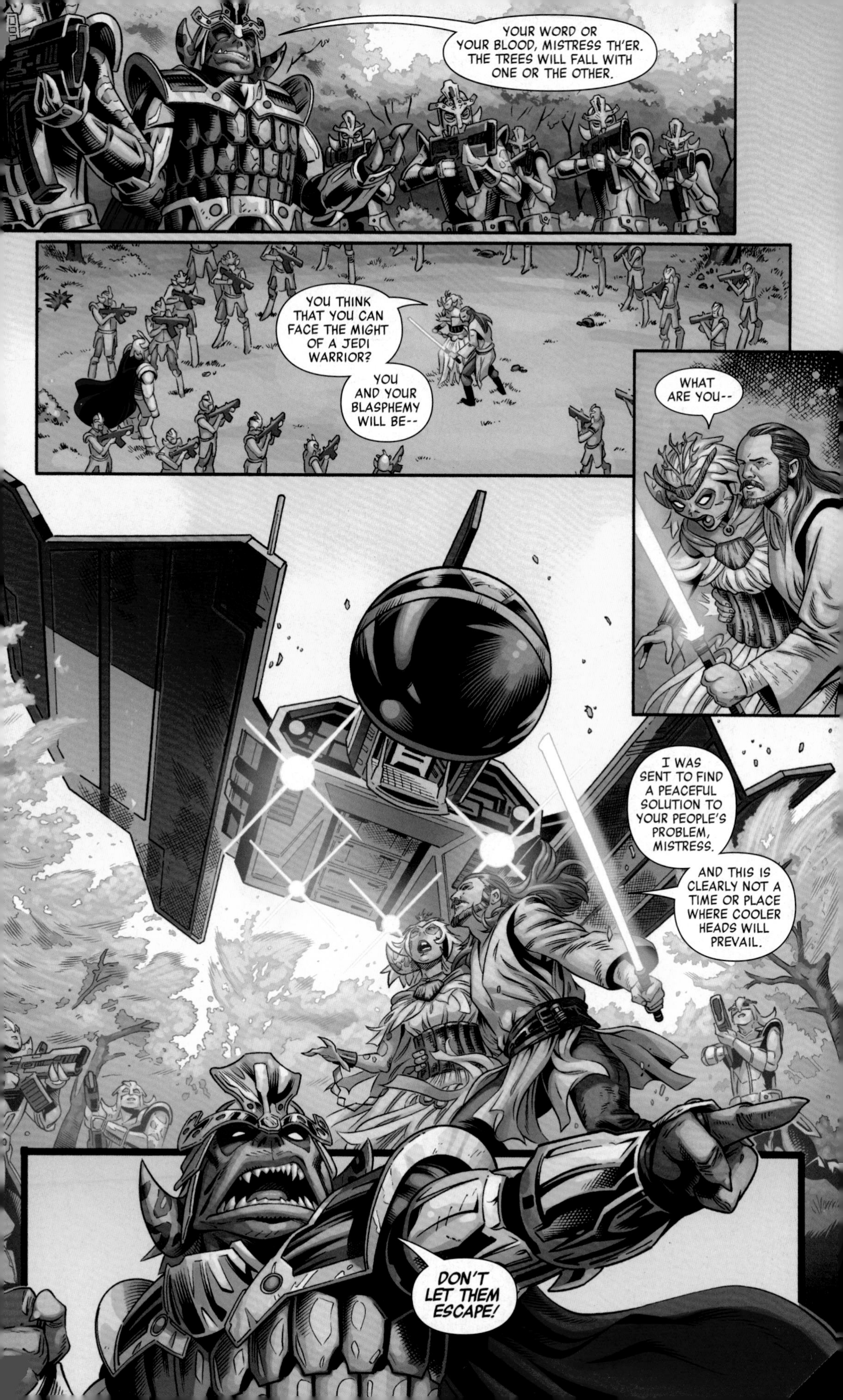
YOUR WORD OR YOUR BLOOD, MISTRESS TH'ER. THE TREES WILL FALL WITH ONE OR THE OTHER.
YOU THINK THAT YOU CAN FACE THE MIGHT OF A JEDI WARRIOR?
YOU AND YOUR BLASPHEMY WILL BE--
WHAT ARE YOU--
I WAS SENT TO FIND A PEACEFUL SOLUTION TO YOUR PEOPLE'S PROBLEM, MISTRESS.
AND THIS IS CLEARLY NOT A TIME OR PLACE WHERE COOLER HEADS WILL PREVAIL.
DON'T LET THEM ESCAPE!

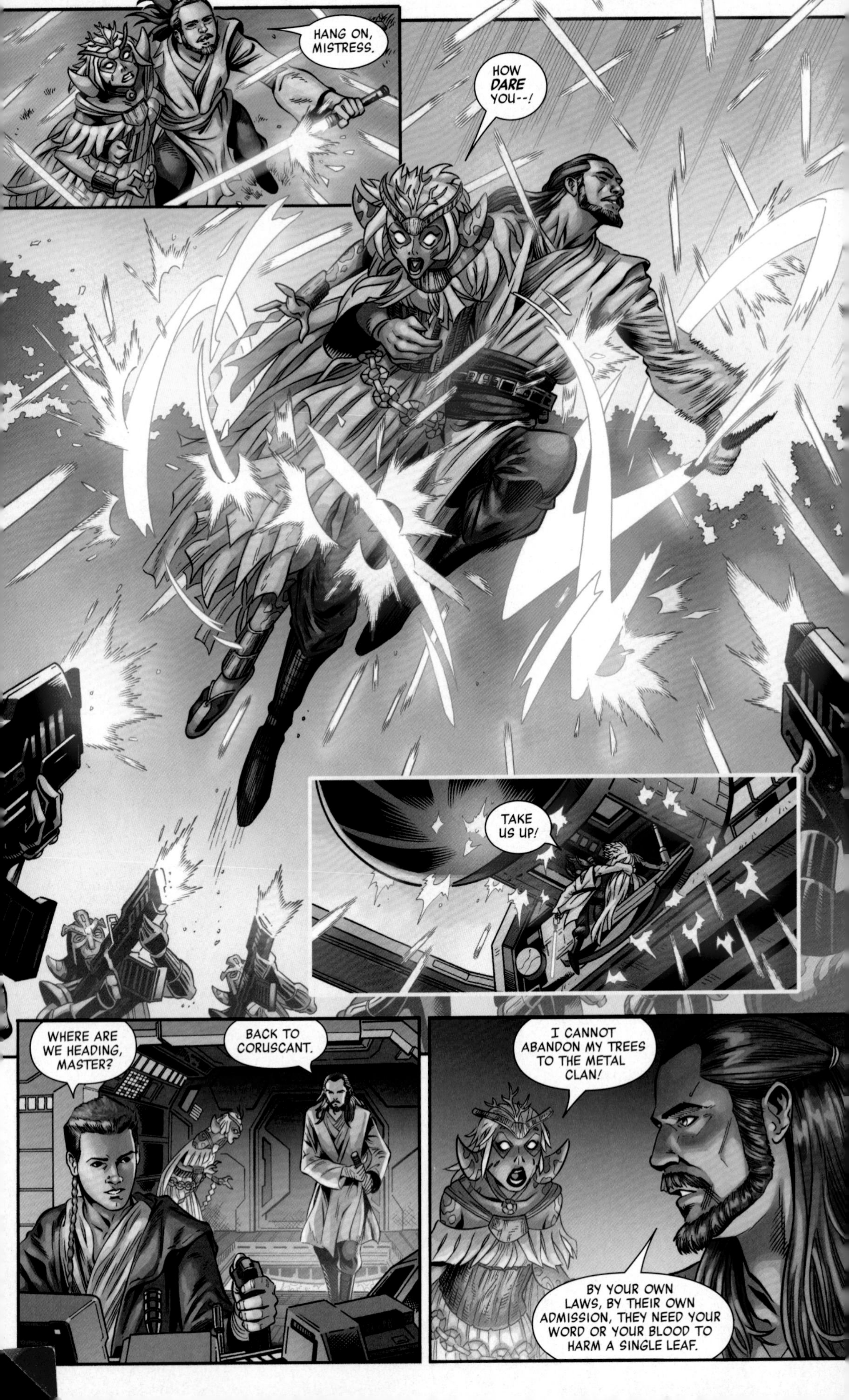
HANG ON, MISTRESS.
HOW DARE YOU--!
TAKE US UP!
WHERE ARE WE HEADING, MASTER?
BACK TO CORUSCANT.
I CANNOT ABANDON MY TREES TO THE METAL CLAN!
BY YOUR OWN LAWS, BY THEIR OWN ADMISSION, THEY NEED YOUR WORD OR YOUR BLOOD TO HARM A SINGLE LEAF.

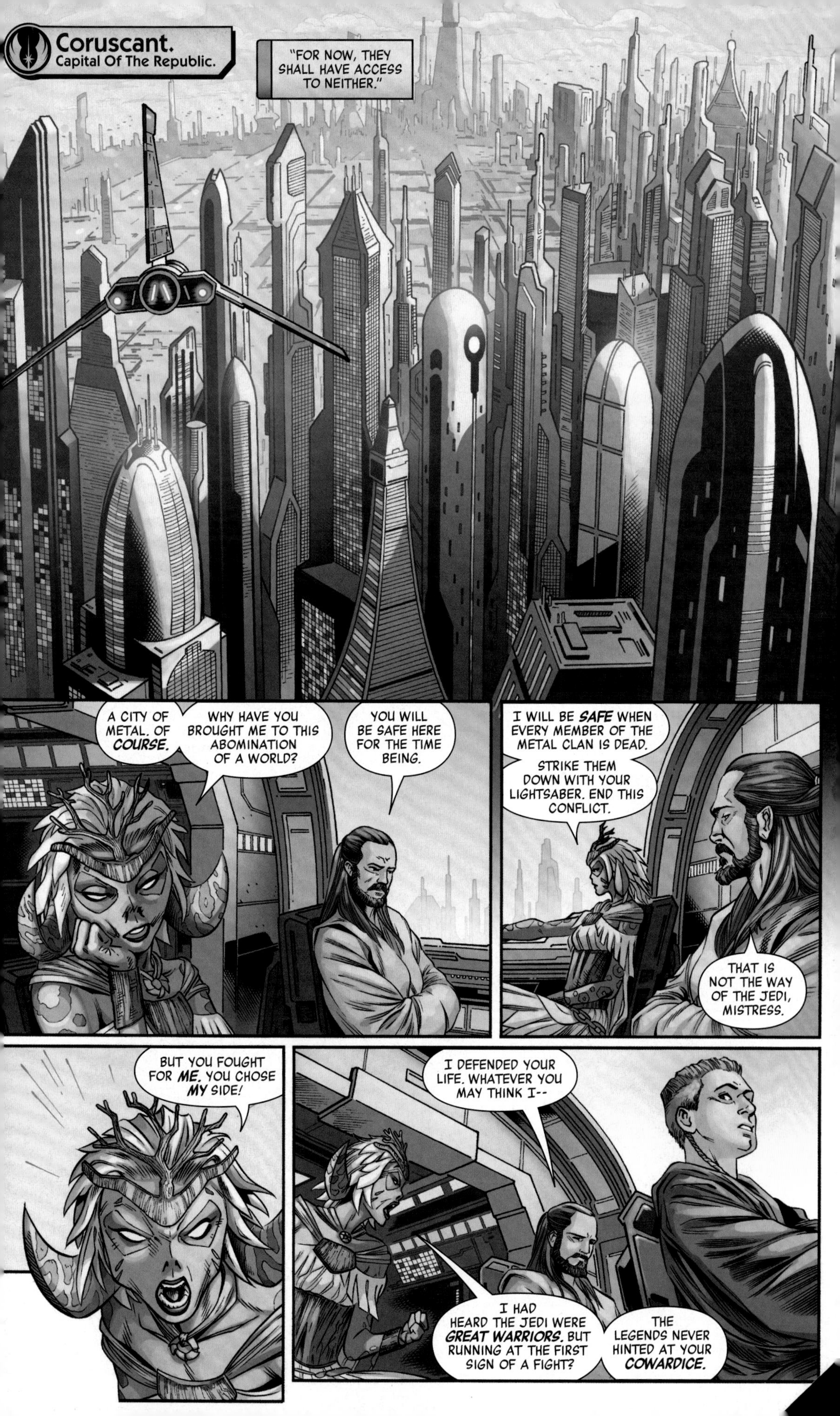
Coruscant.
Capital Of The Republic.
"FOR NOW, THEY SHALL HAVE ACCESS TO NEITHER."
A CITY OF METAL. OF COURSE.
WHY HAVE YOU BROUGHT ME TO THIS ABOMINATION OF A WORLD?
YOU WILL BE SAFE HERE FOR THE TIME BEING.
I WILL BE SAFE WHEN EVERY MEMBER OF THE METAL CLAN IS DEAD.
STRIKE THEM DOWN WITH YOUR LIGHTSABER. END THIS CONFLICT.
THAT IS NOT THE WAY OF THE JEDI, MISTRESS.
BUT YOU FOUGHT FOR ME. YOU CHOSE MY SIDE!
I DEFENDED YOUR LIFE. WHATEVER YOU MAY THINK I--
I HAD HEARD THE JEDI WERE GREAT WARRIORS. BUT RUNNING AT THE FIRST SIGN OF A FIGHT?
THE LEGENDS NEVER HINTED AT YOUR COWARDICE.

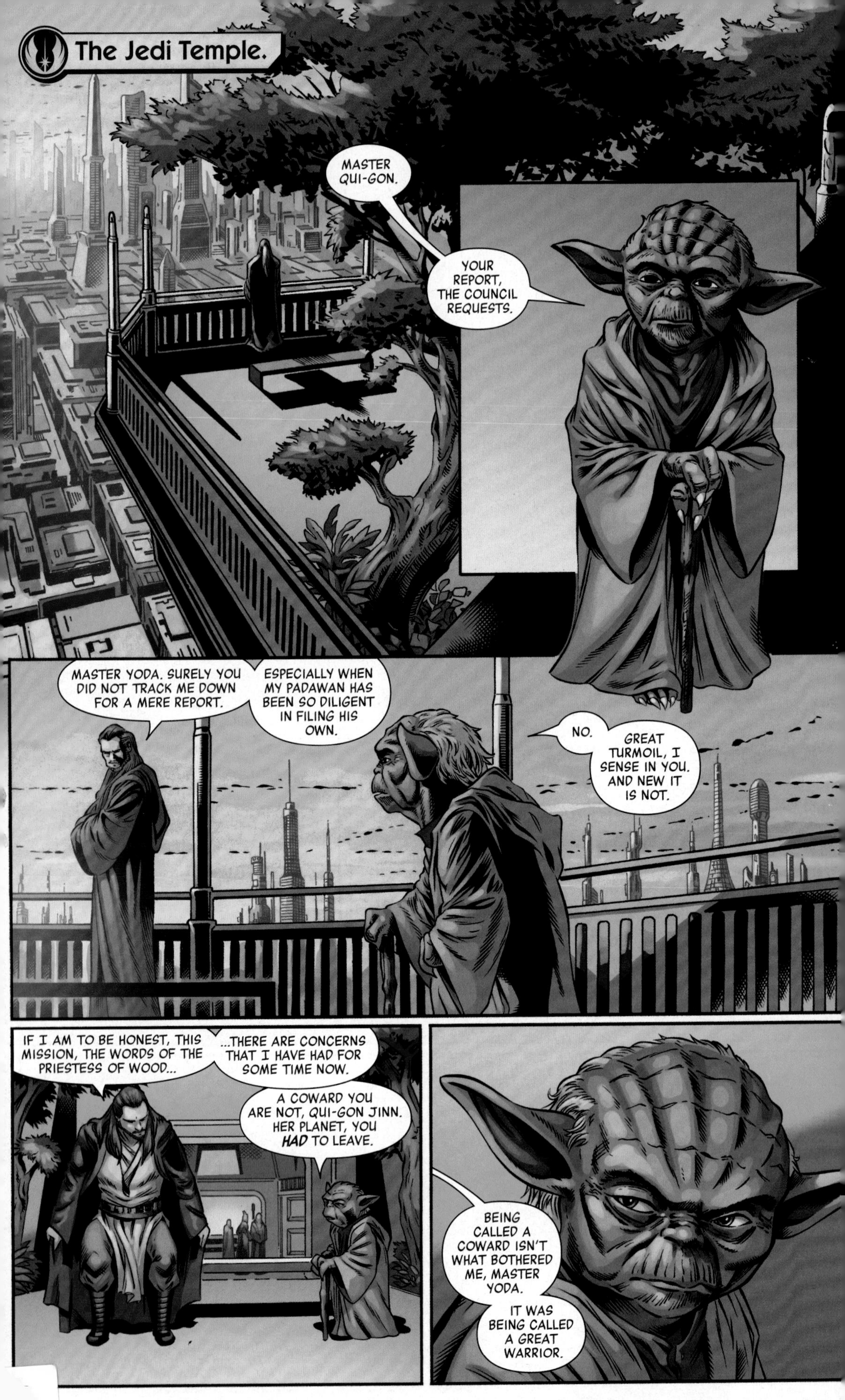

The Jedi Temple.
MASTER QUI-GON.
YOUR REPORT, THE COUNCIL REQUESTS.
MASTER YODA. SURELY YOU DID NOT TRACK ME DOWN FOR A MERE REPORT.
ESPECIALLY WHEN MY PADAWAN HAS BEEN SO DILIGENT IN FILING HIS OWN.
NO.
GREAT TURMOIL, I SENSE IN YOU. AND NEW IT IS NOT.
IF I AM TO BE HONEST, THIS MISSION, THE WORDS OF THE PRIESTESS OF WOOD...
...THERE ARE CONCERNS THAT I HAVE HAD FOR SOME TIME NOW.
A COWARD YOU ARE NOT, QUI-GON JINN. HER PLANET, YOU ***HAD*** TO LEAVE.
BEING CALLED A COWARD ISN'T WHAT BOTHERED ME, MASTER YODA.
IT WAS BEING CALLED A GREAT WARRIOR.

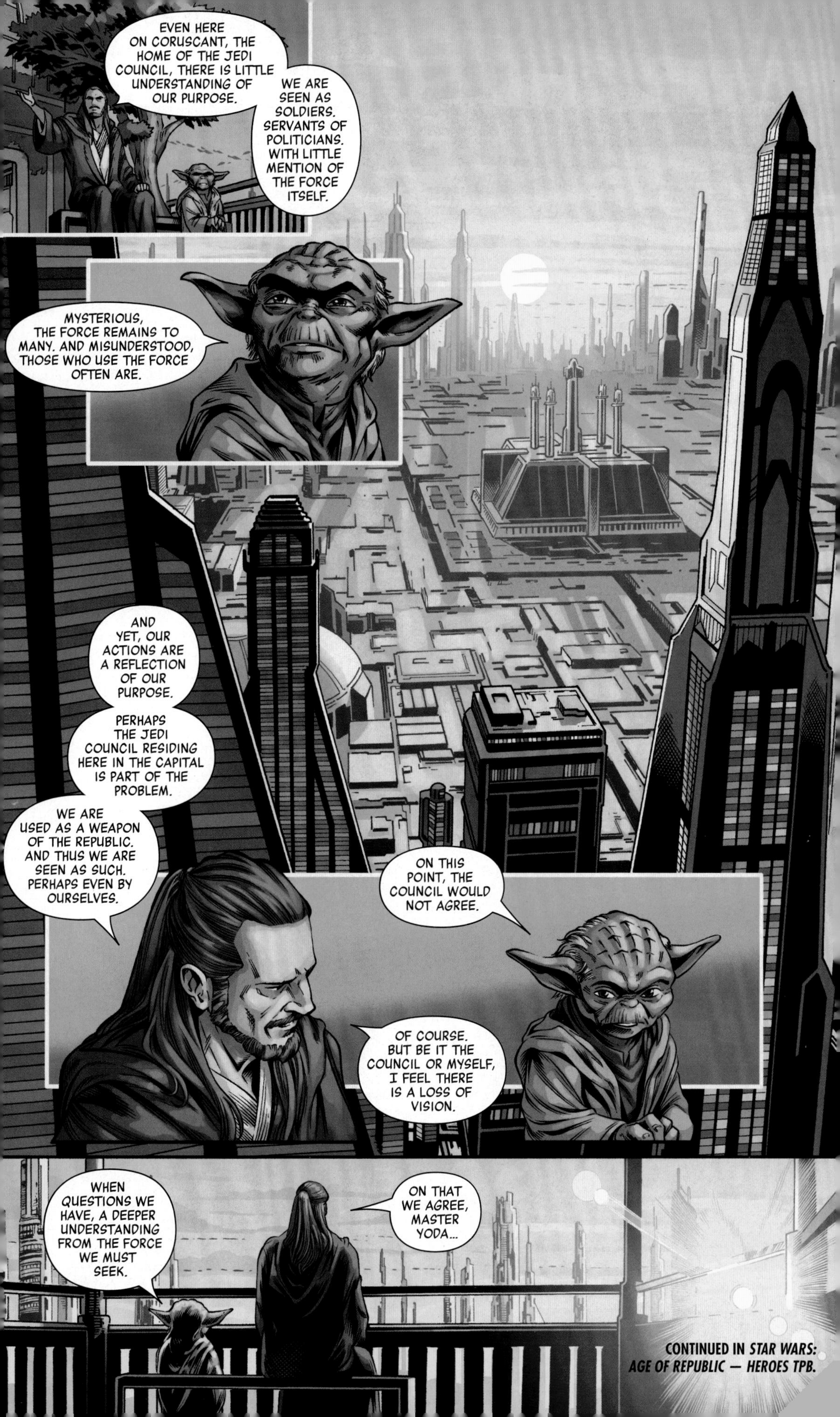
EVEN HERE ON CORUSCANT, THE HOME OF THE JEDI COUNCIL, THERE IS LITTLE UNDERSTANDING OF OUR PURPOSE.
WE ARE SEEN AS SOLDIERS. SERVANTS OF POLITICIANS. WITH LITTLE MENTION OF THE FORCE ITSELF.
MYSTERIOUS, THE FORCE REMAINS TO MANY. AND MISUNDERSTOOD, THOSE WHO USE THE FORCE OFTEN ARE.
AND YET, OUR ACTIONS ARE A REFLECTION OF OUR PURPOSE.
PERHAPS THE JEDI COUNCIL RESIDING HERE IN THE CAPITAL IS PART OF THE PROBLEM.
WE ARE USED AS A WEAPON OF THE REPUBLIC. AND THUS WE ARE SEEN AS SUCH. PERHAPS EVEN BY OURSELVES.
ON THIS POINT, THE COUNCIL WOULD NOT AGREE.
OF COURSE. BUT BE IT THE COUNCIL OR MYSELF, I FEEL THERE IS A LOSS OF VISION.
WHEN QUESTIONS WE HAVE, A DEEPER UNDERSTANDING FROM THE FORCE WE MUST SEEK.
ON THAT WE AGREE, MASTER YODA...

CONTINUED IN *STAR WARS: AGE OF REPUBLIC — HEROES TPB.*

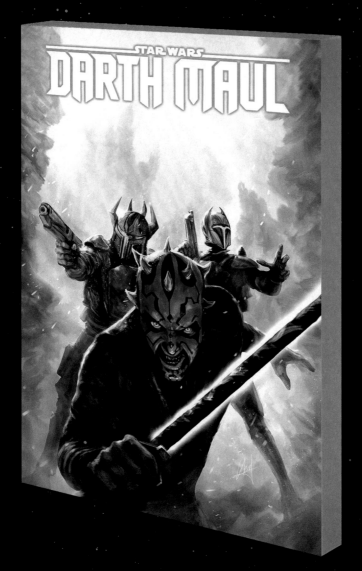